Neighbor
vs.
Neighbor

Legal Rights of Neighbors in Dispute

FIRST EDITION

Mark Warda
Attorney at Law

Sphinx Publishing
Sphinx International, Inc.
Post Office Box 25
Clearwater, FL 34617

This publication is designed to provide accurate and authoritative information in regard to the subject matter covered. It is sold with the understanding that the publisher is not engaged in rendering legal, accounting or other professional services. If legal advice or other expert assistance is required, the service of a competent professional person should be sought.

> —From a Declaration of Principles jointly adopted by a Committee of the American Bar Association and a Committee of Publishers.

First Edition, July, 1991

ISBN 0-913825-41-7
Library of Congress Catalog Number: 91-61607

Manufactured in the United States of America by Graphic Arts Resources, Inc., 13740 McCormick Dr., Tampa, FL 33626

Cover photo by R. Llewellyn/SuperStock

Published by Sphinx Publishing, a division of Sphinx International, Inc., Post Office Box 25, Clearwater, Florida 34617-0025. This publication is available through bookstores or by mail fron the publisher for $12.95 plus Florida sales tax if applicable, plus $2.00 shipping. Call (800) 226-5291 to order by credit card.

Table of Contents

Acknowledgments

Special thanks are due to Annette Melnicove of the Brevard County Law Library for providing the idea for this book. Mary Lynn Sneed at Stetson University School of Law provided invaluable help in researching and summarizing many of the cases.

This book could not have been finished without the help and support of everyone at Sphinx Publishing (in alphabetical order): Whitney Creech, Wendy Delph, Richard Frank and Maria Moraca.

Last but not least I'd like to thank my parents, James and Jennie Warda and my grandmother, Anna Skrebnevski, for always providing needed encouragement.

Introduction

Ever since the first cavemen shared a cave, people have had disagreements with their neighbors. Often the disagreements can be worked out calmly, but sometimes they seem irreconcilable. Since we can no longer solve these problems by hurling our neighbors over a cliff, we must resort to the legal system to settle our differences.

Not surprisingly, the same problems have come up again and again over the centuries and many of the legal principles regarding neighbor law are well settled. In researching nuisances and trespass, two of the most common areas of neighbor law, it is not unusual to find very similar problems in cases a hundred years old. Dig a little deeper and you will find a similar case from two hundred or three hundred years ago. As for trespass cases, many can be found seven hundred years old and older!

This book is written in the hope that if people can learn their legal rights and responsibilities, they can avoid spending their money and a court's time fighting over them. Considering the cost of legal advice these days, this book can save you hundreds or thousands of dollars if it helps you settle your differences yourself.

However, it must be kept in mind that each case has a unique set of facts and each state has its own set of laws and court opinions. Every rule of law has exceptions and seemingly small differences in your case can make a big difference in the result as compared to an example in this book. The question is, is it worth your time and money to fight over the minute points if you know the main body of the law is against you.

Courts seem to have fun with silly neighbor dispute cases. In ruling on a tree case a court might talk about the "root" of the issue, and then go on to analyze the state of "tree law" across the entire country. In a cat case a state supreme court justice might mention some good books on the history of cats. A surprising number of the cases have been appealed as high as the supreme courts of the various states.

One of the more amusing cases of a neighbors' dispute started with a scuffle between neighbors in Pottawattanie County, Iowa in 1898 and ended up in the Iowa Supreme Court. This case now and forever more stands for the legal proposition that putting one's arm over a fence constitutes trespass. The gory details are in Chapter 45.

Not every case in this book involved people who were actually neighbors. In some instances the best case to illustrate a legal principle involved persons who were not neighbors. In other instances there just are no available cases on the topic. However the cases chosen for this book are used to illustrate the same legal principles which would apply to neighbors.

Many of the chapters in this book can be the subject of entire books in their own right. It is therefore impossible to cover every aspect of each area of neighbor law in a book like this. The intent of this book is to give you the basic principles in each area of neighbor law. For further information on any subject of particular interest the last chapter of this book explains legal research. In most instances there is much more detailed information readily available.

This book is also a history book. The stories in this book are all actual cases with the true names of the parties and the addresses of the places where they occured. If you live in a city mentioned you might be able to find the building involved in a suit still standing. However, if it was a victim of a particularly awful nuisance, it may have been abandoned or demolished. If you do locate a building mentioned in this book, see Chapter 67.

If you are reading this book to learn about your rights in a particular situation you can probably find it listed in the table of contents or the index. If you are interested in neighbor law in general, the beginning is the best place to start. If you are just looking for good stories, they start in Chapter 7.

Besides being a law book, a history book and a book about settling neighbor disputes, it is a book about life. Many of the people in this book are dead, and some have been so for hundreds of years. The stories in this book are some of the emotional moments in their lives. Yet today, what does it matter if their building was two inches over the line or if the crowd at the local ballgame occassionally cheered too loud? Maybe they would have been happier if they went for more walks on the beach, laid in the grass and watched the clouds go by or spent time with someone they cared about.

General Principles of Neighbor Law

Before going into the specific laws regarding problems between neighbors one must understand which types of laws control the different types of situations confronted by neighbors. There are five types of rules which govern neighbor relations. These are constitutional rights, specific laws, zoning laws, property restrictions, and common law principles.

Chapter 1 Constitutional Rights

Constitutional rights can become an issue in neighbor relations in a few different ways. The most obvious is where a government agency is your neighbor. In such a case, most actions between you and the governmental entity would involve your constitutional rights.

Another way that a neighbor dispute could involve constitutional rights is when there is a state statute or local ordinance which controls some activity which becomes a problem between neighbors. In such a case an important question would be whether the law complies with the state and federal constitutions. If not, it is unenforceable.

Some constitutional rights which might be invoked in a neighborhood dispute are freedom of speech, freedom of association, equal protection and the right to just compensation for property taken by the government. However, it is important to understand the meaning behind these rights. All of them have some limits.

Constitutional rights are not absolute. The Supreme Court has ruled that when the government has a compelling interest and that interest cannot be achieved by a less restrictive means, the right may be limited.

Freedom of speech is usually understood to mean that we as Americans can say anything at any time. But the limits to this freedom are numerous. We cannot yell "fire" in a crowded theater because that could cause a riot which would injure people. We cannot say false things about people. That would be slander and we would have to pay for any damages caused by our false statements.

Speech which is advertising has further limitations. Courts have ruled that "commercial speech" is subject to more limits than other types of speech. Thus most laws which control advertising have been found to be constitutional.

Equal protection requires that citizens in equal positions be treated equally. For example, courts will not enforce property restrictions which limit ownership based upon race. But, again, this right is not absolute. The courts have held that zoning laws are valid, even though they may give property owners who are next door to each other different rights in the use of their property. This is because the courts look at the objectives behind the laws and how the groups are classified. If the objectives and classifications are legitimate then the laws are valid.

There is a right to **due process**. Actually there are two types of due process, substantive and procedural. Substantive due process concerns the power of the state to regulate the life of citizens. Procedural due process concerns what steps the government must take before it can deprive a person of "life, liberty, or property."

Substantive due process, like most areas of constitutional rights, has changed and evolved over the years. In the economic area the Supreme Court has expanded the power of the government to control our lives. In the area of liberty, the court has limited the power of the government. Undoubtedly the changes will continue as the composition of the court changes.

Procedural due process concerns what process is due to a person before the government can take his life, liberty or property. The process depends upon what is being taken from the person. Where a person's life is being taken in a death penalty case the person is entitled to the most carefully reviewed procedures. Where some value is taken from a person's land by the building of a jail next door, a less strict procedure is required.

The right to **just compensation** was our country's answer to the habit of the king taking what he wanted when he wanted it. Since kings had been thought to have divine rights, they were considered to have the ultimate ownership of everything and were allowed to take what they needed from people.* Seeing how unfair this was, Americans evolved the principle that the government must pay a fair price whenever it took something from a person.

One of the first questions which then came up was how to define a "taking." When a government airport created so much noise that it ruined a neighbor"s poultry business, this was held to be a "taking" of his property. Also, when a governmental body ruled that a person could no longer use his property for the purpose he intended, that too was a "taking" of the value of his property. Both of these types of takings required the government to pay the citizen compensation.

---

* Under the custom of Prima Nox, the overlord was allowed the privilege of having the "first night" with the bride whenever one of his serfs got married.

These constitutional rights apply to actions by both the federal government and state governments. They do not apply to actions by individuals. For example, a government action which lowers the value of your property can give you the constitutional right to just compensation, but a similar action by a private party would not. (It might give you the right to compensation under another legal theory such as negligence. If you do not use the right theory when filing a law suit you can lose.) Constitutional rights can be asserted either in a court action against you, or in a court action by you against the government or a neighbor aided by the government.

In addition to the federal constitution, each state has it own constitution and many of these include additional rights not included in the federal constitution. For example the constitution of the state of Washington contains a provision allowing a landowner to obtain damages if his land is damaged by excavations on the neighboring property. In some cases the rights can be asserted against either the government or private parties.

When researching a neighbor dispute you might want to read over your state constitution to see if it has anything which looks like it may be related to your problem. But keep in mind that rights in a constitution are not always easy to understand. One seemingly simple sentence may have been interpreted in a hundred court opinions to include an elaborate scheme of rights.

If you find anything related to your problem in your state constitution, you should check with a local law library to see if they have an "annotated" copy of the constitution. This is a copy of the constitution along with information on all of the court cases which have ever discussed the meaning of the different clauses of the constitution.

Chapter 2 Specific Laws

Specific laws are what we will call the statutes and ordinances[*] which forbid or require certain behavior. These would be laws which forbid burning leaves, disturbing the peace, keeping dangerous animals and so forth. The specific laws may be either criminal laws or civil laws. When there is a specific criminal law against behavior which is annoying you, it will most likely be very easy to stop the behavior—just report the offending party to the proper authorities. If the law is civil it will probably say that you have the right to bring a private law suit in the matter. This will not be as easy, but pointing out to the offending party that he or she is violating the law may be of some help.

To find out if there are any laws about the problem which is annoying you, you should check both your state statutes and local ordinances. Every state has a set of statutes. These may be just a couple volumes or over a hundred. They are usually available at your public library. Both cities and counties have codes of ordinances and these may also be available at the library. If not, check your county courthouse law library or the city, town, village or county clerk's office.

Statutes and ordinances are usually composed of the hundreds or thousands of laws which were passed since the state was admitted to the union. They are not always well organized or indexed. Sometimes the title of a law does not accurately describe what is in the contents. Often the index is incomplete or inaccurate. This means you will have to comb the laws carefully if you want to be sure not to miss one that may apply.

In some cases there may other obscure laws which affect your situation. For example, when a shipbuilder got spray paint on some cars parked on neighboring property, research by the car owner's lawyers revealed that the shipbuilder was violating admiralty law.[1]

But not all annoying behavior is against a specific law. If you cannot find anything in these laws you should check the other types of laws and rules.

---

[*] Statutes are laws passed by the state government and ordinances are laws passed by a subdivision of the state such as a city or county.
[1] Numbered footnotes are located after the last chapter of this book beginningon page 215.

Chapter 3 Zoning Laws

Zoning laws are laws defining what can be done on property in certain designated areas. A typical zoning ordinance will divide a city into separate districts such as residential, office, commercial, industrial and agricultural. Some ordinances will have subclassifications such as R-1, R-2, R-3 for residential in which different types of residential uses are allowed in each district. One district may allow only single-family homes on at least three-acre lots and another may allow up to 20 units per acre.

Zoning laws not only define what use may be made of a piece of property, they also may define how that property may be used within that classification. For example, a zoning law may define how many stories a home may be, how big a garage may be and even what constitutes a single family.

Examples: Two students rent a house in a single family district. Do they violate the single-family rule? What if they are engaged to be married, sleeping in one bed? What if they are brother and sister sleeping in separate rooms? What if they are two unrelated men? Sleeping in the same bed?

Next door to the two students live a couple, their four children (one of which has her own baby) and two of the couple's parents. Are they a single family? If so, does it make sense for the law to allow nine people in one house, but to forbid two students in the house next door? What if this is a family of bikers and the students are scholars?

As you can see, zoning laws (like most laws) can present some difficult questions. The answers to the questions above can only be answered by looking at the exact wording of the zoning law, any other state or local laws on the matter, how they are interpreted by the courts and how the courts interpret the state and federal constitutions.

In the above examples some courts have held that distinctions between married and unmarried couples violates the equal protection clauses of the constitution as discussed earlier.

To find out if your neighbors' behavior violates a zoning ordinance, you can check with the local zoning department. This may be part of the county or city or it may be that both governments have zoning ordinances which overlap. If you discuss the matter with someone at the zoning department, he or she may be able to take action to eliminate the problem. If the person you talk to says that the activity is not illegal or that nothing can be done, don't take them at their word. Government employees are not known for their ambition or accuracy. You may want to ask someone else in the department or to research the matter yourself.

In some areas private parties have a right to enforce zoning laws. This right may be given by state statute, local ordinance or by court decisions. Two types of court actions may be brought to enforce zoning laws. One is an action for an injunction against the violator and the other is a request for a **writ of mandamus** against the zoning department. A writ of mandamus is a court order requiring a public official to perform some duty. Requests for both an injunction and a writ of mandamus may sometimes be included in the same suit.

But not all areas of the country have zoning laws and those that do do not cover all types of problems with neighbors. So if these don't help you you should next check for restrictive covenants.

Chapter 4 Restrictive Covenants

Restrictive Covenants are sets of rules governing the use of property which are voluntarily put on the property by the owners. These may be basic restrictions which say that only single-family homes may be built on the lots, or they may be elaborate rules which even control what color the homes may be painted and what color the drapes may be. Restrictive covenants may be in the form of deed restrictions, a condominium declaration, or other similar legal document.

You may wonder why a person would put a restriction on his own property stating what color he may paint his house or what he can build on the land. These restrictions are usually put on the property by developers who turn raw land into subdivisions. The restrictions make the lots more valuable because they insure that the character of the neighborhood will remain the same. While restricting the use of one piece of land would make it less valuable compared to a piece next to it which is unrestricted, controlling the uses in a subdivision protects the owners from things which would devalue their properties.

Example: Consider a large executive home in an area where only single-family homes can be built and where lots must be at least 5 acres. Next consider how the value would be affected if someone could put several mobile homes or a used car business on the lot next door.

There are hundreds of types of restrictions placed on property. Most of them require single-family homes. Some say that no clothes lines may be set up in the front yard, that boats may not be stored on the property, that the building must be a certain size and must be set back a certain distance from the street. Years ago it was common to put restrictions on property that it could "not be sold to anyone not of the Caucasian race" or similar language. However, these restrictions have been held null and void by the United States Supreme Court.[2]

Occasionally an article will appear in the newspaper which will describe someone at war with his neighbors because he wants to do something in violation of the restrictions. Often it will seem like an innocent thing the person wants to do, like paint his house a color forbidden in the restrictions, or put up a basketball hoop for his kids. The person will be outraged that a court is telling him what to do with his property and he will scream that this is no longer a free country.

However, in cases based upon property restrictions the court is not enforcing the government's will against people. It is enforcing restrictions voluntarily placed on property by its original owner. Every person buying a piece of property should know what they are buying and what restrictions have been placed on it. By accepting title to a piece of property a person agrees to abide by the restrictions. Therefore he cannot complain when they are enforced against him.

Unfortunately, few people understand restrictions and fewer read them before buying property. The picket fence is so cute and the kitchen so clean that they sign the contract without a thought that they might not be able to keep their boat or their truck on the property, or raise dogs in the yard. Real estate agents aren't eager to disclose restrictions since this may kill the deal. Title companies usually do not have the restrictions ready to show the buyer until the day of closing. And considering the costs, many people, in some areas at least, do not choose to have an attorney represent them in the purchase of their home.

A real estate contract should not be signed until the buyer has read all of the restrictions (and zoning laws) affecting the property, or without a clause making the sale contingent upon buyer determining that the restrictions do not affect his use of the property.

To find out if there are restrictions on your property or your neighbor's property you can check the papers you received when purchasing your property and the county recorder's office at your county courthouse.

If you received either a title insurance policy or an abstract of title when you purchased your property, it should list the restrictions which apply to your property. Usually they are put on the property around the time that the land was subdivided into lots.

Sometimes there are two or more sets of restrictions placed on property. Also, keep in mind that although two pieces of property are next to each other, they may be in different subdivisions and therefore subject to different restrictions. Be sure to check both your property and your neighbor's. If you and your troublesome neighbor are in different subdivisions you may not be able to do anything to enforce the restrictions on his property. One of his other neighbors would have to do it.

If your property is not in a platted subdivision it may not have any restrictions on it. If it does have restrictions, they would usually be contained in the deed. If they have once been put in a deed, they should have been repeated in every deed of the same property executed in the future.

You can usually tell whether your property is subdivided by checking the legal description on your deed. If your property is described as a certain lot by number, it is in a subdivision. If it is described by a long description such as "Starting at the northwest corner... run East 55 feet...etc.," then it is probably land which has never been subdivided.

If you cannot find out what restrictions affect your property or your neighbor's you can check with the county recorder's office, a title company or an attorney. Some county recorder's offices keep a separate listing of restrictions which is easy to use, but others have complicated systems which are difficult to use. Some county clerks are eager to help and others can only say "It's not my job, I cannot give legal advice." If you cannot find the information at the courthouse, check with a title company or attorney who specializes in real estate law. If you do not know whom to go to you might check with a friend who is in the real estate business. He or she would probably know who can provide the service at a reasonable price. With something like this it pays to compare prices. One attorney or title company might be able to provide the information for $25 or less while another might charge several hundred dollars for the same information.

If it is found that an annoyance in the neighborhood violates restrictions on the property there is a remedy. The bad news is that it may involve an expensive court action. The good news is that several of the neighbors may join together and split the cost. In some cases a letter from an attorney is enough to solve the problem. If the offending party is clearly in the wrong he will be told so by his own attorney and when he realizes the potential cost of continuing the violation, he will be likely to stop.

However, if the issue is fuzzy, such as if the wording is not clear enough to cover the activity, or if other violations have been allowed in the past, then the party may decide to ignore the restriction. In such case the remedy is a court action for an **injunction**. This is an action where you ask a judge to enjoin the activity, meaning to order that it be stopped. If it is not stopped the person can be fined or jailed. Such a suit is usually expensive and in most cases it is impossible without the services of an attorney. Sometimes the restrictions will say that the violator will have to pay the attorney's fees of the persons enforcing the restrictions. However, there may also be a chance that he will win and the persons attempting to enforce the restrictions will have to pay his attorney's fees.

Chapter 5 Common Law Principles

If there are no laws or restrictions forbidding the annoying activity, then **common law** principles may offer some relief. The common law is the law which has been created over the centuries by judges. This law is made up of the thousands of decisions made by judges using "common law principles" of right and wrong on matters which were not covered by statutes.

When things like fireworks, trains and airplanes were first invented there were no laws about how they should be used. When people started getting hurt and killed by them, the judges had to start making rules governing responsibility and liability for such injuries.

Example: When someone was first brought into court for throwing fireworks into a crowd, he could argue that there was no law against throwing fireworks into crowds (since they were just invented). But the court could rule that throwing fireworks into a crowd was just like throwing a spear into a crowd so the liability would be the same if anyone was hurt.

The common law is composed mostly of **civil law**, that is, law regarding relations between citizens. In most areas of this country we do not have common law crimes because our courts have held that crimes must be very specifically spelled out in the statutes so that everyone may know ahead of time what is a crime. (Part of the process that is due.)

Wrongful acts which are not crimes are called **torts**. When a person commits a tort against another person he may be held liable in a civil court action for damages, or he may be ordered by the court to stop the activity.

It has been well noted that in this country at this time the civil court system is out of reach of a large percentage of Americans. The process is so slow and the lawyers' fees are so high that most people cannot afford a lengthy lawsuit. Therefore a civil suit is probably not the best way to handle a neighbor dispute unless it is small enough to be filed in small claims court.

Most American common law is based upon English common law. When each state[*] joined the United States it adopted the common law as it had existed in England. This way it did not have to create a new body of law. Everyone knew that the principles of law under which they had conducted themselves in the past were still in effect. Then, as new cases came before the courts, new decisions were added to the common law. In some matters the law may have remained the same as in England and in others it may have been different.

Since each state has its own legal system the common law in each state is not the same. In most areas the law may be similar, but in some matters the states take divergent views. This is sometimes because of the nature of the population. For example, Montana may take a more individualistic approach than New York. In some matters half of the states may follow one line of reasoning while the other half follows another.

Over the years, as the population shifts, political parties change and judges are replaced, a state may change its position. Occasionally one state will take a totally new approach to a problem and other states will jump on the bandwagon, claiming it is the "progressive" approach or the "modern" view.

For this reason, and others, it would not be possible to tell you exactly what the law is at this moment in your state on a particular problem. What this book can do is give you the basic principles of law, some examples of how they have been applied in the past, and some guidance on how to find specific cases and laws in your area. In many types of cases the law is well settled and this book contains cases from as far back as 1593.

The most common area of law which may be involved in neighbor disputes is nuisance. Such things as dogs barking, obnoxious smells and noise would come under the category of nuisance. Other areas of law which might come up in a neighbor dispute are trespass, easements, fences and adjacent landowner law.

Because nuisance law applies to so many areas of neighbor disputes it is explained in detail in this chapter. The other areas of law will be discussed under each topic in the next section of this book.

---

* The lone exception to this is Louisiana, in which the legal system is based upon the French system and the Napoleonic Code.

Chapter 6 Nuisance Law

History and definition

When a person does something which is so annoying to his neighbors that it is illegal, it is called a **nuisance**. A nuisance is a tort, which is a wrongful act or injury. Torts include such things as assault and battery, libel and slander, negligence and wrongful death.

There is no precise definition for the word nuisance. In fact the most famous author on the subject of torts has written, "There is perhaps no more impenetrable jungle in the entire law than that which surrounds the word 'nuisance.' It has meant all things to all men, and has been applied indiscriminately to everything from an alarming advertising to a cockroach baked in a pie."[3] So don't be surprised if this discussion seems a little confusing. It is also confusing to lawyers, judges and law professors.

To give you some idea as to what will be considered a legal nuisance we can start with a few definitions. Blackstone, one of the earliest writers on English common law, described a nuisance as "Any thing that unlawfully worketh hurt, inconvenience, or damage."[4] American courts have expressed the opinion that it is hard to define exactly what falls into the category of nuisances. The Wyoming Supreme Court said "There seems to be no definition of nuisance which is broad enough to include all those things that are nuisances, and so limited as to exclude those things to which the law gives another name."[5] An Illinois court held that a nuisance includes everything that endangers life or health, gives offense to the senses, violates the laws of decency, or obstructs reasonable and comfortable use of property.[6]

The United States Supreme Court at one point described a nuisance as "a right thing in the wrong place, —like a pig in the parlor instead of the barnyard."[7]

Public or Private Nuisances

Nuisances can be classified as being either public or private, and this classification affects the legal rights of the parties concerned with the nuisance. A **public nuisance** is one which is a nuisance to the community at large. Some examples of public nuisances are someone blocking a road, polluting a river used by the community, practicing medicine without a license, shooting off fireworks in the streets or running a brothel. A **private nuisance** is one which interferes with a specific person's use or enjoyment of his or her property.

If a nuisance is judged to be a private nuisance then the persons who are injured by it are entitled to take legal action to receive compensation for their damages and to stop the nuisance from continuing. A private nuisance is a situation where there is interference with someone's use and enjoyment of their land. Because the notion of nuisance is based upon interests in land, persons who do not have an interest in the land, such as employee or guests do not have a right to take court action for nuisances.[8]

If a nuisance is judged to be a public nuisance, then in most cases only some governmental authority can take action to remedy it. The logic behind this is that it would be too burdensome to people and businesses if every member of the public would be able to file a suit against them.

One exception to this rule is that if some member of the public suffers some particular injury from the nuisance, then that person may seek compensation for his injury. This was first recognized in 1536 so it is a well-founded principle.[9] In such cases it is said that there is both a public nuisance and a private nuisance. However, determining when the private injury is enough to allow a person to sue has been a difficult question with which many courts have wrestled.

Another exception to this general rule is that in some states such as Florida,[10] Michigan[11] and Wisconsin,[12] specific laws have been passed which allow individual citizens to take legal action in the public interest to stop a public nuisance. Other states may follow this trend.

Part II   Specific Problems of Neighbor Law

Chapter 7 Aircraft/Airports

The original concept of property ownership included the notion that ownership of land included the space from the center of the earth up into endless space. A famous statement by Lord Coke, "cujus est solum ejus est usque ad coelum,"[13] (he who owns the soil owns upward to heaven), was quoted often in the days before the invention of the airplane. And even putting one's arm across a fence has been held to be a trespass.*

However, new technology has required a change in the principles of law. If flying over private property were to be considered trespass today, then the airlines would all be out of business. This fast change in the notion of property rights in response to the invention of flight is a good example of how flexible our system of law is.

In the United States the right of airplanes to fly over private property is controlled by federal laws and regulations. The laws are contained in the United States Code, Title 49. This law gives any U. S. citizen a "right of freedom of transit through the navigable air space of the United States."[14] The navigable air space is defined to include different altitudes depending upon the location.[15] Airplanes flying at these levels cannot be guilty of trespass.

Under the Second Restatement of the Law of Torts, §159(2), published by the American Law Institute, only an entry in the immediate reaches of the airspace which substantially interferes with use and enjoyment of the property is a trespass.

Even though flying over a person's property is not trespass, the noise, vibrations and dangers associated with airplane flights and airports can be a nuisance. If any of these factors are bothersome to a large part of the community then it may be considered a public nuisance and may be stopped by government action. If only one or a few property owners are bothered, then it may be a private nuisance.

War stories: Frederick L. Swetland had owned a 135-acre estate worth $115,000 (in 1930 dollars) in Richmond Heights, Ohio for 25 years when a subsidiary of the Curtiss-Wright Corp. purchased land next door for an airport and flying school.

---

* For more on this interesting incident see Chapter 46

They built a hanger for 20 planes and planned three more. They also planned parking for 460 automobiles. Mr. Swetland filed suit in federal court and the court did an analysis of the law of rights to the sky from the year 1200 to the present. The court noted that aviation was a growing field which was encouraged by the government and that it had contributed millions of dollars to the economy of Ohio. It concluded that the airport was not necessarily a nuisance but that certain activities, such as creating too much dust or flying lower than 500 feet could be stopped.[16]

When Stewart Ruhl obtained a permit to build an airport in New Jersey, John J. Oechsle and other neighbors filed suit to stop the construction. The court ruled that since an airport was a lawful business it would not stop the construction, but that if it became a nuisance the neighbors might be able to be compensated.[17]

If a court decides that the flights of airplanes are a legal nuisance, then there are two primary remedies. The court can order the flights to be stopped or limited or it can order payment to the injured neighbor for the damages suffered due to the flights.

War stories: Charles J. Dodge, in Macomb County, Michigan, started using part of his land for an airstrip. His neighbor, Peter Gruber, complained that the planes scared his cattle and that the noise was a nuisance. When Mr. Dodge expanded the use of the airstrip, began giving flying lessons and started allowing others to use the airstrip, Mr. Gruber filed suit. The court ruled that the flights had become a nuisance and it ordered Dodge to only use the airstrip for his personal use. Years later when Mr. Gruber died and Mr. Dodge obtained state and federal approval for expanded use of his airstrip the court refused to dissolve the injunction because it would still constitute a nuisance to Mr. Gruber's widow.[18]

In 1948 neighboring property owners brought suit against the Valley Forge Airport located near the village of Audubon in Pennsylvania. They claimed the airplanes made such loud noises as to disturb their sleep, conversations and general enjoyment of their property. The court noted that airports are not automatically nuisances, but that they can be nuisances if they are in an unsuitable location or if operated so as to interfere unreasonably with the comfort of the adjoining property owner. The court held that this airport was in a rural area and was operated reasonably except for night flying. It balanced the property owners' rights against the nation's need for expanding the then-experimental stages of aviation. The court refused to stop the flights completely, but enjoined the airport from operating after 10 p.m.[19]

Neighboring residents around Morristown, New Jersey were so upset about the proposed expansion of the Morristown airport that they convinced four of the surrounding municipalities to file a suit against it asking for an injunction against the expansion. The Superior Court did a thorough study of the history of noise from the blacksmith pounding on the anvil to the shrill whine of the jet engine. It noted that Benjamin Franklin moved away from the busy part of Philadelphia because "the din of the Market increases upon me; and that, with frequent interruptions, has, I find, made me say some things twice over." But the court concluded that in accepting the blessings of civilization, citizens must accept some noise. It refused to block the expansion, but it limited operations to certain hours and required the use of noise suppression devices. Fourteen months later the Business Aircraft Assn. attempted to reopen the case, but the courts ruled that it was too late to do so.[20]

Where monetary damages are awarded, these may be for actual losses to the neighbor, such as broken windows, or they may be compensation for the diminished value of the property.

War stories: In 1957 the Keene, New Hampshire Airport took part of Doris Ferguson's land through eminent domain in order to expand its airport. Later it used the property near her home for a jet warm-up area. This caused noise and dust and broken windows in her home. She was awarded $9,500 in damages.[21]

In 1967, when Thomas J. Morris refused to cooperate in his neighbor Jacob Ciborowski's efforts to build an airport on the latter's property in Rye, New Hampshire, by selling or clearing his land, Mr. Ciborowski went onto Mr. Morris' land and cut down trees and cleared the land himself. A jury later awarded Mr. Morris $16,000 for the trees and

$10,000 for the diminished value of his land due to over-flights of planes.[22]

If a person is awarded damages for the diminished value of his property because of flights at a neighboring airport, then future owners of that piece of property cannot claim damages. The theory is that when the first owner is paid for the diminished value of his property, he can now sell it for that much less and come out even. Sometimes future owners do not pay less for the property and expect to be paid by the airport again.

Some courts have not been sympathetic to neighbors who live near airports. It may be because of the perceived value of air travel, or the fact that the people knew there was an airport nearby when they bought their property, but the neighbors don't always win in their suits.

Also, people whose lawyers use the wrong theories when they file their suit usually lose their case.

War stories: When jet flights began at the Rochester-Monroe County Airport the noise level on adjacent properties rose dramatically. James Cunliffe, James Dabbert, Francis Lambert and their wives filed suit against the airport but their suit was dismissed because the court found that the noise was not serious enough to amount to a taking of their property.[23]

In 1952 the city of Atlanta constructed a new runway at their airport which ended about 500 yards from the property of R. W. Chronister. The planes on the runway continually flew just 50 to 100 feet directly over Mr. Chronister's home. When Mr. Chronister brought a suit it was dismissed, but when he appealed the court ruled that while the Federal Government has the right to regulate airspace, it does not have the right to invade property rights. It concluded that Mr. Chronister did have a claim against the airport.[24]

In the early 1960s, property owners in the Loma Portal area of San Diego County, California filed suit against several commercial airlines to force them to stop flying over their property. The California Supreme Court ruled that the property owners did not have the right to stop the flights, but that if they had sued the airport they may have been entitled to damages for the taking of rights in their property. [25]

In the 1960's the government decided to conduct sonic
boom tests over Oklahoma City to find out if they would
upset the public and/or damage buildings. Some of the
residents of Oklahoma City did get upset and filed suit in
federal district court to stop the flights. In ruling against
the people the court said that the citizens did not establish
any actual damages and that if they did, they could sue for
a monetary award. Therefore, there was no need to stop
the flights.[26]

Edward Luedtke and other property owners around General Mitchell Field near Milwaukee, Wisconsin filed suit in
federal court against the airport and several airlines claiming that the flights were a nuisance, a violation of federal
rules and regulations and a taking of their property. The
court held that the property owners must first complain to
the FAA about the violation of federal regulation and if the
airport did comply there could be no nuisance since the
federal rules preempt nuisance law. It held that the taking
claim could not be made against the airlines, only the
airport. It noted that an inverse condemnation claim had
already been filed in a state court and that it would retain
jurisdiction until the state court action is decided.[27]

Where the flights are made by agents of the United States government and actual harm is caused to private parties, the United States
Supreme Court has recognized a type of remedy other than nuisance.
This is based upon the Fifth Amendment to the United States Constitution which states that no property may be taken from citizens without
just compensation.

The theory is that when a government action causes a person a
financial loss, that action is a "taking" of property and must be compensated.

War stories: The United States was conducting low altitude flights over
the land of Mr. Causby. These flights frightened his
chickens, lowering their production, forcing him to go out
of business. The United States Supreme Court ruled that
this amounted to a taking of his property and that under
the constitution he must be compensated.[28]

Mr. and Mrs. Bernhart Thornburg lived 1500 feet from the
end of a runway at Portland International Airport. Their
home was directly under some flight paths and nearby

others and because of the noise from the jets using the
runways their property was unusable. They sued and the
court ruled that since the flights were more than 500 feet
over their property and sometimes not directly over their
property, they were not entitled to compensation. They
were not happy with this ruling and appealed to the
Oregon Supreme Court. The court ruled that noise could
be serious enough to amount to a taking of their property,
even if the flights were not directly over their property.[29]

Around the same time some people had a similar problem in
Kansas but federal courts are less sympathetic to people who are
harmed by flights which are not directly over their property.

War story: When Topeka Army Air Field was deactivated after World
War II some nearby land was platted into a residential
subdivision and homes were built of it and sold. A few
years later the base was reopened as Forbes Air Force Base
and expanded for the use of jet planes. Although the planes
usually did not fly over the homes in the subdivision, their
flights caused windows and dishes to rattle, smoke to blow
into the homes and noise which interfered with the residents' enjoyment of their homes. They sued the United
States government saying that the value of their homes had
been taken by the government and should be compensated. The federal courts ruled against them.[30]

In recent years homeowners have still been having better luck in
state courts.

War stories: Over 700 neighbors of the Santa Monica Airport brought
suit against the City of Santa Monica because of the noise
and lowered value of their property caused by the airport.
They claimed that the value of their property had been
"taken" by the government in inverse condemnation and
that the airport was a nuisance. The city claimed that a state
statute did not allow a city to be liable for a nuisance. The
court ruled that the low level noise and decrease in property values did not amount to inverse condemnation, but
that the property owners could present their claim for a
nuisance. It held that the statute forbid injunctions, not
monetary damages.[31]

In 1982 Kenneth L. Baker and other residents near the
Burbank-Glendale-Pasadena Airport brought a suit against

it for inverse condemnation for monetary damages for the
lost value of their property. Their suit was dismissed, but
the Supreme Court of California said that they could sue
the airport. It noted that they could not interfere with the
commercial flight patterns and schedules, but that they
could sue for inverse condemnation. The airport appealed
to the U. S. Supreme Court, but it did not take the case.[32]

Los Angeles International Airport is the third largest commercial aviation facility in America. In the late 1960's the
nearby residents found that the noise from the jets on the
north runways was so loud that they could not conduct
normal conversations, hear their televisions or talk on the
phone and that their children could not study. When they
sued, 41 of them were awarded a total of $86,000 in dam-
ages, but the airport did not have to pay their $200,000
attorney's fee because they sued under a nuisance theory,
not an inverse condemnation theory.[33]

One solution used by some neighbors of airports is to build tall
structures on their property which prohibit low-altitude take-offs and
landings. This can force the airport owner to point the runways in
another direction. However, some courts have ruled that if there is no
legitimate purpose for the structure and it is just to harass the airport
owner, it may be a nuisance.

War stories: Winifield Wells had operated a small private airport in
Panama City for four years when A.W. Simpson bought
the land north of the airport with the intention of opening
a drive-in theater on it. Wells sought to enjoin Simpson
from doing this on the grounds the theater would constitute a nuisance and hazard to the planes and people on
them. The trial court held for Simpson. The Florida
Supreme Court affirmed, holding that Wells had not shown
that the theater would add measurably to the already
existing hazards of lights, poles and electrical wires. Wells
also had not shown that traffic problems created by ingress
and egress of patrons of the theater would constitute a
public nuisance.[34]

Charles Jarnigan owned a farm next to a small airport. He
placed six 30 foot poles on his land in line with the runway.
The airport paid him $60.00 to remove them for a year
which he did, but then notified the airport that unless they

paid him for another year he would replace the poles. Jarnigan sought an injunction from low-flying planes. He claimed he was trying to protect his farm and family and that he wanted an injunction from anything that violated his rights in living in his home and cultivating his field. The court noted that due to the changing direction of winds, the planes sometimes had to take off and land over Jarnigan's land. In doing so, they could fly as low as 20 or 30 feet over the fence which is the common dividing line between the two properties. Based upon Jarnigan's son's testimony that the flying of planes had not interfered with the use of the land for farming purposes, the court's belief that Jarnigan was trying to extort money by erecting the poles, and the fact that the airport was operated in the daytime only, in a reasonable manner, the court denied the injunctive relief sought by Jarnigan.[35]

Large airports cannot be built without careful scrutiny of zoning laws and proper permits, but in some cases zoning laws may be useful in abating a nuisance caused by private aircraft.

War story: When Dean Kamen built a helipad on his property in Bedford, New Hampshire, so that he could commute to work by helicopter, none of his neighbors objected except one, Robert S. Treisman. The zoning board granted his permit to build the helipad, saying that nothing in the zoning ordinance prohibited it. And the local court threw out Mr. Triesman's suit, noting that there were no laws against helipads. But Mr. Treisman appealed to the Supreme Court of New Hampshire and the case came before Justice Souter, later to become a Supreme Court Justice. Justice Souter ruled that since the zoning ordinance was worded to permit no uses other than those specified, and that since helipad uses were not specified in the law, such use was improper. He also held that the use of a helipad could not be accepted as a normal accessory use to a residence without a specific finding and ruling on that point.[36]

Chapter 8 Alienation of Affections

The best thing to do when a spouse runs off with a neighbor is move on and find someone else. There are better and worse people than your spouse in the world, and you can easily find someone better.

But in some states there is an option which, though it won't bring your spouse back, might make you feel better. It is a court action for "alienation of affections." This is an old type of action which has not been used much in recent years. But it is still available in some areas. In the Second Restatement of the Law of Torts published by the American Law Institute, it is still recognized as a legitimate court action.

The following sections of the Restatement apply to these types of actions:

§683 **Alienation of Spouse's Affections.** One who purposely alienates one spouse's affections from the other spouse is subject to liability for the harm thus caused to any of the other spouse's legally protected marital interests.

Legally protected marital interests are defined to include affections, companionship, sexual relations, services in the home and support.

§684 **Causing One Spouse to Separate From or Refuse to Return to the Other Spouse.** (1) One who abducts a spouse or by similar intentional action compels a spouse to be asunder from the other spouse is subject to liability to the other spouse for the harm thus caused to any of the latter's legally protected marital interests. (2) One who for the purpose of disrupting the marital relationship induces one spouse to separate from the other spouse or not to return after being separated, is subject to the liability stated in Subsection (1).

§685 **Criminal Conversation With a Spouse.** One who has sexual intercourse with one spouse is subject to liability to the other spouse for the harm thus caused to any of the other spouse's legally protected marital interests.

§686 **Privilege of Parent or Other Person.** One who alienates the affections of one spouse or causes that spouse to separate from or not to return to the other spouse is not liable to the aggrieved spouse if the actor (a) is a parent or near relative or is otherwise in a relation with the alienated spouse that justifies the giving of advice in personal matters, or is one who acts reasonably in response to a request from that spouse for advice, and (b) acts not for the purpose of appropriating the affections of the alienated spouse but primarily to advance what is reasonably believed to be the welfare of the alienated spouse, and (c) makes no fraudulent statements and employs no means in themselves wrongful.

In some states suits of this type have been abolished by statute. (Arizona, California, Colorado, Connecticut, Delaware, District of Columbia, Georgia, Indiana, Maine, Maryland, Michigan, Minnesota, Montana, Nevada, Oregon, Virginia, West Virginia, Wisconsin, Wyoming) These laws are known as "Anti-Heart Balm" statutes. In Iowa and Washington the courts have abolished these types of suits.

In other states they have stopped allowing monetary damages in alienation of affections actions, but still allow injunctions. (Alabama, Florida, New Jersey, New York, Ohio, Vermont)

Louisiana never recognized the action, Oklahoma only permits it if the spouse was a minor or incompetent and Pennsylvania only permits it if the person sued is a blood relative.

In North Carolina the Court of Appeals tried to abolish it, but the North Carolina Supreme Court said that the court "acted under a misapprehension of its authority to overrule decisions of the Supreme Court of North Carolina and its responsibility to follow those decisions until otherwise ordered by the Supreme Court."[37]

War stories: When his wife Cherie divorced him for Ronald, Donald was "totally devastated." His job performance declined and he sought counseling at his church. Eventually he sued Ronald for alienation of his wife's affections. He said their marriage was fine until she had met Ronald and he gave her gifts and took her on trips. She said their marriage had already deteriorated. The jury awarded Donald $100,000.[38]

Eighteen months after Lola found out that Ruth had engaged in illicit activities with her husband, Lola sued for alienation of affections. The case was dismissed because the court felt that alienation of affections was part of criminal conversation and the time limit for filing such suits was one year. However, Lola pointed out that Ruth had also engaged in "sexual perversion" with her husband

and because of this the suit was allowed to go forward
under the rule that there is a three-year limit for other types
of alienation of affections cases.[39]

Gerald and Lila were married in 1966. Shortly thereafter
Gerald started abusing Lila. Lila sought a divorce in 1976
and had several people, including Gerald, corroborate the
abuse she described. Since 1970 they had been socially
seeing Sidney and his wife. One month after Lila filed for
divorce, she and Sidney began seeing each other. Gerald
found out about the relationship and threatened Sidney
with a shotgun. Then Gerald and Lila attempted a reconciliation. Gerald signed a release saying he would not
claim criminal conversation or alienation of affection if
Sidney would not press charges from the shotgun incident.
The reconciliation failed, and Sidney and Lila were married in 1977. Gerald sued for alienation of affection and
criminal conversation. The trial judge held the release
valid, and instructed the jury to consider only the period
following the date agreed in the release when considering
damages and liability. The jury found no alienation of
affection, but awarded Gerald $5,000 compensatory and
$75,000 punitive damages for criminal conversation. The
judge ordered a reduction of punitive damages or a new
trial on issue of damages. The Supreme Court of Rhode
Island held that Gerald was entitled to judgment in the sum
of $5,000.[40]

For a marriage that lasted less than 16 months Brett and
Brenda had a tumultuous time. There were allegations of
beatings, excessive drinking, adultery and death threats.
After their divorce, Brett filed suit against Jeff, with whom
Brenda had moved in, claiming alienation of affections.
Jeff gave his attorney $7000 to settle the case but by the time
a settlement of $5000 was reached the attorney had ex-
pended all but $1300 on his own fees. Jeff dismissed the
attorney and through some confusion ended up in court
without an attorney. Brett was awarded $84,600 including
$25,000 in punitive damages. Jeff appealed and the court
held that while alienation of affections suits were still legal,
the husband must prove that the other person's actions
were the controlling cause of the alienation and that they
outweighed all of the other actions by the husband which
might have caused the wife to become alienated.[41]

Patsy and Milton, according to Patsy, had a happy and harmonious marriage until he moved himself out of their home on June 15, 1980. Patsy claimed that until he moved out, nothing in Milton's actions led her to believe he was unhappy. In July 1980 Milton showed Patsy a picture of Constance and told her that sex with Connie was exciting and he wanted to marry her. Patsy and Milton's divorce was final in October. Milton and Constance married one month later. Patsy sued Constance for alienation of affections. The judge ruled for Constance without holding a trial. The appeals court reversed and said Patsy was entitled to a trial It said that there was a genuine issue of fact as to whether Milton's involvement with Constance existed before he left Patsy. The reason this issue existed was due to the actions of Greg, Milton and Patsy's son. He had followed his father to Constance's home when Milton said he would be at a motel and visited Milton's apartment three times between 11 p. m. and 2 a. m. and found no one home. The court held this raised an inference that Milton was involved with Constance before leaving Patsy.[42]

In 1979 Nanette consulted her pastor Alan for marital counseling. Alan counseled her for three weeks. Their relationship continued after the counseling ended, and eventually became sexual. The church discovered the affair, and Alan ended the relationship along with resigning as pastor. When Nanette's husband found out about the affair, he sued the pastor for negligent impairment of consortium and outrage. The lower court dismissed the case because Washington had abolished alienation of affections actions. The Washington Supreme Court held that a conceivable malpractice action for negligent care which also injured the other spouse through loss of consortium could be made. However, since here the alleged tort was based upon an extramarital relationship with the "impaired" spouse, and the "impaired" spouse refused to assert a claim, the action became one for alienation of affection. Since this action had been abolished, the court upheld the lower court's dismissal of the action.[43]

It is not usual, but in some cases it may be possible to sue for alienation of a child's affections. The position of the Restatement is as follows:

§699 Alienation of Affections of Minor or Adult Child.
One who, without more, alienates from its parent the
affections of a child, whether a minor or of full age, is not
liable to the child's parent.

**§700 Causing Minor Child to Leave or not to Return
Home.** One who, with knowledge that the parent does not
consent, abducts or otherwise compels or induces a minor
child to leave a parent legally entitled to its custody or not
to return to the parent after it has been left him, is subject
to liability to the parent.

§701 Sexual Intercourse with Minor Female Child. One
other than her husband who, without her parent's consent,
has sexual intercourse with a minor female child is subject
to liability to (a) the parent who is entitled to the child's
services for any resulting loss of services or ability to
render services, and to (b) the parent who is under a legal
duty to furnish medical treatment for expenses reasonably
incurred or likely to be incurred for medical treatment
during the child's minority.

No court is known to have recognized the right of a child to sue for
alienation of a parent's affection.

War story: After 18 years of marriage and five children, James was
allegedly lured away from his family by Jane, a wealthy
widow with a finer home, sexual charms, and other in-
ducements. His wife, Marian filed suit against Jane on
behalf of herself and her children. The jury ruled against
Marian in her action and the courts dismissed the suit by
the children, noting that children have never had a right to
sue for alienation of a parent's affections.[44]

Chapter 9   Amusements

An amusement area is a nice place to visit, but you wouldn't want to live next door to one, especially if it stayed open late at night. If an amusement area violates zoning laws it can be put out of business easily. However, if it is in the proper zone and still causes problems to nearby property owners, it will have to be declared a nuisance before it can be stopped or limited in its operations.

Specific problems such as noise and lights are explained in separate chapters of this book, but some amusements which have come before the courts for a variety of other reasons follow:

Baseball: J. W. Dickson, of Fulton County, Georgia filed suit against the Warren Company to stop the baseball games it was holding across from their residence. The Dicksons were in their mid-sixties and had paid their rent four years in advance. In their complaint they alleged that the games kept them up at night and on the Sabbath when they like to rest "as do all good Christian people." In weighing their claims the court held that baseball was a lawful business which would not be a nuisance unless it produced unreasonable noise or was conducted in an indecent, disorderly or improper manner. It held that the correct measure would be whether it disturbed an ordinary person, not whether the Dicksons were unusually sensitive.[45]

In 1947-49 the trustees of the Lake City, South Carolina School District leased an athletic field at Main and Blanding Streets to the Lake City Baseball Club for night games. J. H. Carter and other neighbors filed a suit to stop the ball playing, but the court ruled against them. They appealed to the Supreme Court of South Carolina which held that the lease was illegal and that baseball must stop. It noted that baseball is not necessarily a nuisance, but it may become one such as when it is conducted in a field which is too small. It also noted that the students at Lake City High School were not able to use their field when the professionals were playing.[46]

In 1948 in Whitewater, Kansas, the school athletic field was improved, and flood lights were installed along with a public address system including a loud speaker. Four sisters living nearby sought to have the school district enjoined from allowing any group to use the field who was not directly connected with the grade and high schools athletic programs. They also sought to have the loud speaker, flood lights, trespasses from spectator's parking on their property, and dust from the working of the field stopped. The district court granted temporary injunction. The court held that a softball game is not a nuisance but did allow the injunction with respect to the public address system and also as against working the field so as to cause dust to be blown onto the Neiman's property. The court also enjoined using the flood lights later than 10 p.m.. They denied the other requests for injunction.[47]

Bingo: In 1939 Mr. and Mrs. Edward Zrimsek owned a building at 1118-1126 West North Avenue in Milwaukee, Wisconsin. Mr. Zrimsek operated a tavern on the first floor and there was a large hall on the second floor. The Auxiliary to Sons of Union Veterans and the St. Victoria Society, patriotic and charitable organizations rented the hall and held bingo games there in the afternoons and evenings. The state of Wisconsin sued and got an injunction prohibiting the holding of bingo games since they were considered gambling and a lottery which was prohibited by the state constitution.[48]

Bullfights: On September 4, 1904, Dennis Canty and others began holding bullfights on the property of Beredith Realty Company near the World's Fair Exposition being held in St. Louis, Missouri. They had contracted with Louis Terriers of Socorro, Mexico to supply 20 bulls which had been bred for fighting. On the instigation of the St. Louis Humane Society, the state of Missouri brought an action for an injunction to stop the fights. In the trial court Mr. Canty won and the complaint was dismissed, but the state appealed to the Supreme Court of the State of Missouri, which held that a bullfight "is debasing in its character, debauching to public morals, and brutalizing in its effect on the spectators, is a public nuisance which equity will enjoin, notwithstanding the act may also be a crime."[49]

When Jaime Gonzalez of Cartagena, Columbia, applied to the City of Baltimore for a license to hold a bullfight in which the bull would not be killed or injured he was declined. He explained that the bull would be protected by a leather jacket and be given a rest, but that didn't help his cause. John Ghingher, the City Treasurer, conferred with the mayor and wrote to Sr. Gonzalez that "because bull-fighting has never, to our knowledge, been held in Baltimore City, it is therefore, probably not understood by our citizens, and we must regretfully decline your application." [How nice of them to decide what the citizens would understand and what they should be allowed to see!] Fortunately, Sr. Gonzalez knew you can fight city hall in America and he took the matter to court. Judge Joseph Carter of the Circuit Court of Baltimore ruled for the city, agreeing that the poor citizens of Baltimore were too stupid to understand something foreign, but Sr. Gonzales persisted and on appeal he won. The appeals court ruled that when a person applies for a permit for something which is not illegal, the city fathers do not have the right to deny it.[50]

Gambling: When the Monterey Club, a nonprofit social club in Gardena, California obtained a license to conduct draw poker games and other types of gambling the district attorney went to the court and obtained an injunction against the holding of the games. The club appealed and the California appellate court ruled that in California gambling was not a nuisance per se and that without a law specifically against gambling the court could not order it stopped. It held that the ancient common law rule that gambling was a nuisance was obsolete and superseded by the California statutes.[51]

When the New York Off-Track Betting Corporation opened a betting office at 244-246 West 23rd Street in Manhattan, an orthodox Hebrew synagogue 38 feet away filed a complaint. It said that the office would "disrupt, degrade and impede" the religious services and "disturb the spiritual tranquility" of the congregation. The court ruled that since gambling is no longer condemned "in our permissive society" the business was legal and not a nuisance.[52]

Golf: Anne B. Gleason was riding in the front seat of an automobile with a gentleman friend on Union turnpike in Jamaica, New York when a golf ball driven by a Mr. Knorr struck the windshield of the car and injured her. In awarding her $750 in damages, the court held that the danger presented by a golf ball at high speeds can be either a nuisance or negligence.[53]

Carnival: A merry-go-round in the town of Davis, West Virginia, operated by a Mr. S. T. Davis, run by a steam engine, the whistle of which blew every few minutes, accompanied by a band, and attended by a large, noisy and boisterous crowd until after 10 at night, disturbing some of the people living nearby was ruled to be a nuisance by the West Virginia Supreme Court.[54]

Museum: Back in 1912, before Hugh Hefner started his anatomy magazine, there were few ways people could learn about human bodies other than their own. To help solve this dilemma, enterprising citizens opened "museums of anatomy" where interested parties could research human anatomy for scientific or other reasons. Thinking that the intentions of the patrons of such establishments might not be pure the city of Chicago passed a law against any such establishments "wherein the principal part of the exhibition is illustrative of the human anatomy, or wherein are exhibited any books, pamphlets, circulars, pictures, charts, diagrams, models, casts or other articles, paintings, drawings or designs of any kind of illustrating or describing the genital organs, or containing any other obscene, lewd, indecent or immoral exhibition of any kind" Albert Shaynin managed a museum of anatomy which contained models showing various stages of the diseases of syphilis, gonorrhea, leprosy and gleet. The museum was operated in connection with a medical treatment facility. No women or children were allowed in the museum. Mr. Shaynin was acquitted but the case was appealed to the Illinois Supreme Court which held that the ordinance was valid and that the exhibition of offensive and repulsive models on sexual subjects which may pander to the morbid tastes could be a nuisance.[55]

Zoo: In 1969 William R. Munro obtained a $7,500 judgement against the City of Louisville as damages for depreciation of the value of his property caused by the establishment of the city zoo next door to his residence. The Court of Appeals reversed saying that Munro had failed to show that the Louisville Zoological Gardens constituted a nuisance. Munro proved only that the value of his property had depreciated when the site was selected for the zoo. He did not show that the zoo disturbed physical comfort or was offensive to physical senses. Munro filed suit before the zoo was actually built, which made it very hard for him to show a nuisance. He probably would have had better luck if he had waited until the zoo was built and then sued![56]

Chapter 10 Animals

The problems involved in the keeping of animals by neighbors usually relate to things such as noise, odors, health problems and dangers. General legal principles regarding such things as noise, odors and dangers are included in the chapters under those titles. Information about problems specifically related to animals is included in this chapter.

In many cases there are laws and regulations which protect people from problems like these. Therefore, the second approach to an animal problem with a neighbor (after approaching the owner directly) would be to contact local government agencies. In some areas there may be specific agencies which deal with dog or animal problems. In other areas the problems may be handled by the health, police, agricultural or other department.

If no solution is found through the owner or the government then you may want to rely upon your common law rights and bring a civil suit.

Too many animals

War stories: Mary Boudinot lived in Muskogee County, Oklahoma, and kept some forty cats at her residence. Several neighbors brought suit claiming that the noise and odor arising from keeping the cats created a nuisance. The lower courts granted the injunction forbidding the cats at the residence. The Oklahoma Supreme Court affirmed holding that the noise and odors and annoyance to quite a number of persons showed that the keeping of the cats was a nuisance which could be abated by limiting the number of cats kept upon the premises. The court held that Mary could not keep more than four cats upon her residence.[57]

The city of Topeka once passed an ordinance which limited the number of cats or dogs that a person could keep in a residence to five. William R. Smith, an attorney owned eight cats and lived with them in a large residence. The cats were born in the house and had never been allowed to leave the residence. Mr. Smith filed suit against the Police Judge, William S. Steineauf, and the chief of police to have enjoin the police from enforcing the ordinance. The case was dismissed but Mr. Smith appealed to the Supreme Court of Kansas. The court apparently enjoyed the case.

Justice Burch wrote the opinion and included a bit of the history of cats in it. He suggested some good books on the history of cats including *The Fireside Sphinx*. He ruled that the ordinance was void because it arbitrarily limited the number of cats to five without any determination as to whether or not they were an actual nuisance. He ruled that the ordinance would also be void because it allowed cat hospitals to keep an unlimited number regardless of how much of a nuisance they were.[58]

In 1960 R. J. Belcher operated a veterinary hospital for small animals at the corner of Eastview Avenue and West Fifth Avenue in Columbus Ohio. Residents in the area complained to the city and Dr. Belcher was charged with violating the section of the City Code which stated: "No person shall keep or harbor any animal or fowl... which howls or barks or emits audible sounds to the annoyance of the inhabitants of this city." The trial court found that Dr. Belcher had been operating his hospital for many years in a municipal zone area permitting small animal hospitals. The Supreme Court of Ohio dismissed the charges and ended with the following poem:

"Dogs will howl and cats will yowl
    When placed in congregation
These grating sounds may oft result
    In human aggravation.
Laws passed to curb such pesky noise
    Should fit the situation
And be so phrased in artful ways
    To cause no obfuscation.
In other words, the laws so passed
    Must plainly be effective.
Inaptly framed, they lack the force
    To meet their planned objective."[59]

Breeding Animals

War story: In a suit filed in Webster County, Nebraska, in the 1880s, a Mr. Cook of Red Cloud charged that John Farrell was creating a nuisance by "putting jacks and stallions to mares, in full view of the plaintiff and his family." The Nebraska Supreme Court thought that this was as bad as running a brothel and allowed an injunction against its continuance.[60]

Diseased Animals

In rural areas the keeping of diseased animals can be a problem for all of the surrounding neighbors because the disease can spread. For this reason there are many laws dealing with this problem.

If the animals have just been brought into the state from another state, then the federal laws dealing with inspection and quarantine of animals in interstate commerce would be applicable. Several states also have rules covering the importation of animals.

For animals which have not been transported there are also numerous laws. These include bovine tuberculosis statutes, tick eradication statutes and quarantine statutes. In some areas the government can require owners to have their animals treated for certain diseases or even to be killed if necessary.

For more information about these remedies contact the United States Department of Agriculture or your local state department handling similar matters.

Cruelty to Animals

Under the common law animals had no rights whatsoever, and being cruel to them or even torturing them was not illegal. It would only have been illegal to be cruel to someone else's animal because it was interference with that person's property.

Today most areas have laws against cruelty to animals, and these laws have been upheld as valid exercises of governmental power. Scientific experimentation, however, has usually been held to be an exception to these laws.

Enforcement of animal cruelty laws may be handled by different departments depending on the locale. If you are bothered by a neighbor who is cruelly treating an animal you can probably find out from your local police who to call for such complaints. In some cases it would be the police and in others it may be a special animal control department.

In most areas there are societies for the prevention of cruelty to animals. Two of these groups are the American Society for the Prevention of Cruelty to Animals and the Humane Society. These groups will take a special interest in the problem and probably help you put an end to it.

War stories: In Vanderburgh County, Indiana, representatives of the county Humane Society found five Great Dane dogs in a building owned by Marion Biggerstaff. The dogs were suffering from worn teeth, malnutrition, hook worms, and dehydration. The dogs had been confined for eight weeks,

but after three months of care from the animal shelter, they
had improved dramatically. Biggerstaff was convicted for
cruelty to animals and appealed. The conviction holding
that the evidence supported the inference that Biggerstaff
had intentionally neglected the dogs was affirmed.[61]

James Tweedie was convicted of cruelly killing an animal,
and he appealed. The Supreme Court of Rhode Island
affirmed the conviction stating that when Tweedie put a
cat into a microwave and turned it on causing the death of
the cat, "no idiosyncrasy of a trier of fact is required to
conclude that the killing of the cat in this case was cruel."
Tweedie admitted to putting the cat into the microwave at
his place of employment. Apparantly the only remorse
Tweedie felt was worrying that his actions might cost him
his job. Thankfully, the court affirmed. Perhaps Mr.
Tweedie should have been placed in a microwave.[62]

Near Newberry, California, Mr. Duval was engaged in the
business of raising chickens upon the land of Mr. DeFlon.
DeFlon lived in a small house on the property. The chicken
ranch had no phone, and it was customary for Mr. Rowell,
who ran a grocery a few miles away, to deliver phone
messages to the surrounding farms. Mr. Rowell went to
deliver a message to Mr. DeFlon one day and encountered
two hostile dogs. He decided to remain in the car and to
summon the occupants of the house by honking his horn.
The sound of the horn caused great panic and confusion
among the chickens who were not used to such noises.
When all the feathers settled, 720 of the 9500 chickens on
the ranch had been crushed and smothered. Duval sued to
recover the value of the lost chickens, alleging that Rowell
was trespassing. The trial court found for Rowell. The
appellate court affirmed, stating that Rowell was not a
trespasser but an invitee, the action of honking the horn to
attract attention rather than risk being bitten by the dogs
was reasonable, and Rowell was not negligent in honking
the horn.[63]

Damages by Animals

Under English common law principles, an owner of animals other
than dogs and cats is liable for any damages they do when they trespass
on other people's lands. This is because the owners are considered to

have a duty to keep the animals locked up.

Most states in America have adopted this rule, but several western states have laws that relieve an owner of animals from liability if he at least makes an attempt to fence in his animals. In some states there are laws which require people to fence their property to keep animals out. If they fail to do so, then the owners are not liable for any damage they cause.

When wild animals do damage there is usually nothing which can be done since that is considered an "act of God" or just part of nature. But occasionally one can find someone to sue.

War story: Harvey Latham in Wyoming was growing a crop of barley which was substantial in size. A huge flock of ducks descended upon the area. The testimony was, "Nobody ever see that many ducks in the sky before", "a cloud of ducks", "the sky was black over his field several nights", "just as thick as you could see." They wiped out the part of his grain which he hadn't harvested. Latham sent a damage claim to the Game and Fish Commission for $3,954.25 for duck depredation of his grain crop, but the Commission rejected his claim. The District Court awarded Latham $1,113.75 for the damage to his grain and the commission appealed. The supreme court affirmed holding that there was no evidence of an abuse of discretion by the lower court.[64]

With domestic animals such as dogs and cats, in most cases the owner is not liable for injuries caused by them unless he has reason to know that they have dangerous propensities. This is the so-called "one bite" rule. Once an animal has bitten someone it is known to be dangerous and therefore the owner is liable for any subsequent bites. However, this rule is not strictly followed and even an animal which has never bitten anyone can be known to be dangerous.

War stories: Walter Guenther kept riding horses in a field adjoining a school yard. The horses were penned in by a wire fence which met the legal requirements for fences. The school children would customarily feed and pet the horses. One day Brownie, a seven-year-old with no prior vicious propensities, bit 11 year old Sharon Leipske on the ear as she was standing by the fence, causing damage to her ear. The trial court held for Mr. Guenther since there was no reason for him to know of Brownie's vicious tendencies and was therefore not negligent. The Wisconsin Supreme Court affirmed stating that without evidence that Brownie had previously bitten anyone, Guenther was not negligent for Brownie's action. The court stated that owners of animals are only liable for damages caused by an animal due to traits of which the owner has knowledge. The court in essence allowed Brownie "one bite" and from then on Guenther had knowledge of Brownie's vicious tendencies.[65]

Marie Young was walking with her father down Rainier Avenue in Seattle when a chimpanzee attacked her and mangled her right hand. William Estep was the owner of the chimp which was not on a leash when it attacked Marie. The court awarded Marie $750. The Supreme Court affirmed the judgment since the evidence showed that Estep had knowledge of the dangerous propensities of the chimp, was negligent in not leashing the animal, and witnesses stated the girl did nothing to provoke or enrage the chimp.[66]

Dorothy and Carl Villari were strolling along a sidewalk on Cladran Drive in Clinton, Maryland, when a growling dog started coming towards them. Dorothy, attempting to protect herself, moved behind her husband but caught her heel and twisted her body. She caught herself before she fell, but felt a searing pain go down her back to her foot when she twisted. The dog did not touch or bite either of the Villaris. The incident occured in front of Roy and Winifred Slack's home. The dog belonged to the Slacks. Dorothy was in traction for a month and then returned for another month and had two of her vertabrae fused. She incurred over $20,000 in medical bills. She sued for those injuries and Carl also sued for loss of consortium. The jury awarded Dorothy $42,500 for damages and lost wages, and Carl $2,500 for loss of consortium. The appellate court reversed holding that the dog, Gideon, which had strayed onto the sidewalk in front of the Slacks' home was not "at large" within the meaning of the county leash law; Winifred could not be said to have violated the leash law where Gideon momentarily evaded her as she was transfering him from a fenced in area to her home, and she was not negligent; because the Slacks had no prior knowledge of Gideon's propensity to attack others, they couldn't be held strictly liable. A strong dissent was filed claiming that the court had ignored the purpose of leash laws, and overlooked caselaw which would show the Slacks were negligent.[67]

In Wyandotte, Michigan, seven-year-old Dawn Rickrode was attacked by Violet Wistinghausen's cat, Maynard. Dawn received stitches on her forehead, and retained a scar. The trial court held for Violet stating that Dawn had failed to show Maynard had vicious propensities. The Appeals Court reversed holding that the evidence was sufficient of Maynard's tendency to attack human beings, and it was a question for the jury to determine Violet's liability. They also held that Dawn only need to show Violet's failure to exercise ordinary care in restraining Maynard to prove negligence.[68]

An owner of a domestic animal can also be liable for injuries caused by them if he is in some way negligent or if the animals caused injury in an area where they should not have been allowed to go.

In some areas there are laws which overrule these common law principles and make owners of dogs liable for injuries which they cause in certain circumstances.

War story: John Paul Moore leased a 20-acre tract of land to David Lindeman. Moore wanted a tenant who had a few horses because the horses would maintain the premises by keeping down the underbrush. Lindeman began operating a riding stable which provided riding lessons, trail rides and boarding of horses. There were 12 to 14 horses boarded there. Moore soon found that 1100 trees had been damaged from the horses eating the bark, and sued Lindeman and several of the owners of the horses boarding at the stables. However, the case ended up going to trial against only one of the horse owners, a Kay McElveen. The lower court dismissed the case. The appellate court affirmed, holding that Moore did not prove that Kay McElveen's horses were the ones who caused the damage to the trees, and he therefore was not entitled to recover.[69]

Dangerous Animals

When an animal is know to be dangerous, whether it is because it was dangerous in the past, or because it is by nature dangerous (such as a lion), the owner is strictly liable for any injuries it causes. Strict liability means that the owner is liable even if he has done nothing negligent.

War stories: Jodrey's cat had gone upon McDonald's premises and killed his canary. McDonald sued Jodrey and won. The County Court held that the owner of a domestic animal is not liable for every depredation which it may commit and is only liable for the results of its known mischievous tendencies. Since this cat had no known mischievous tendencies, Jodrey was not liable for the canary.[70]

In West Hartford, Connecticut, Richard Doerfler, age 11, was delivering papers when he was bitten by Mrs. Redding's miniature poodle. The boy handed the paper to Mrs. Redding who warned him to keep away from the dog. The boy then put his hand on the back of the dog's head, and the dog bit him. The trial court found Mrs. Redding liable. The appeals court affirmed after finding that the boy was not trespassing when he was attacked, the boy did not do anything which would naturally antagonize or torment the dog, and it was not natural for the dog to attack merely because of a petting. The court stated that the fact that the boy touched the dog after being warned to stay away might be held to be contributory negligence, but this would not bar Mrs. Redding from being liable for the damage.[71]

Misty Butler and another person rented a home from Donald Matthews in Jacksonville, Florida. When Butler's nephew, Bryan Bessent came to visit he was bitten by Butler's dog, a mixed pit bull terrier and English bulldog. Bryan sued his aunt and the landlord. (Landlords presumably have more money *and* insurance!) The court held that the landlord was not liable since he did not know or have reason to know of the the dog's vicious propensity.[72]

In another Florida case Jacqueline Vasques, a child being cared for by the Trevino family was attacked by their pit bulldog. The landlord, Marcelino Lopez was held liable because he was found to have known that the dog was vicious, and had the right to terminate the week-to-week tenancy at any time. The landlord's son had married the tenant's daughter and the landlord visited the home, where six "bad dog" signs were posted, at least twice a year.[73] [Word to the wise: Don't let people with pit bulldogs babysit your children, even if the price is right.]

In some states there are laws which protect a dog owner from liability if the owner puts a "Bad Dog" sign on his property.

War story: The Yorkes went over to Mrs. Noble's home/business to purchase some jockey silks. Mrs. Noble told the Yorkes to ignore the "Beware of Dog" sign because the dog was secured. Unfortunately, the gate was not secured, and the dog bit Mrs. Yorke's finger. She sued for damages. The trial court held for Mrs. Noble because she had displayed a "Bad Dog" sign in a prominent place on the premises and under Florida law was therefore immune from liability for damages resulting from a dog bite. The Appeals Court reversed. The Florida Supreme Court affirmed the Appellate decision stating that immunity would not extend to a dog owner who affirmatively directed a business invitee to ignore the "Bad Dog" sign on the premises.[74]

When the dangerous animal constitutes an annoyance to neighboring property owners, it may be ruled to be a nuisance and ordered removed from the property.

War story: Robert and Stephen Rich owned the lot adjoining John Olmstead in Hobart, New York. The Rich's kept and hived bees. John Olmsted brought suit to enjoin the Rich's from keeping the bees since they would swarm and sting the Olmsteds and their guests. Olmsted claimed the bees were a nuisance since they kept him from enjoying his property. The lower court found a nuisance and granted an injunction along with six cents monetary damages. The Supreme Court affirmed holding that the Rich's were not necessarily entitled to a jury, the large number of bee hives indeed constituted a nuisance and the case was a proper one for a permanent injunction.[75]

In some cases persons other than the owner of an animal may be liable for injuries caused by it.

War story: In Laredo, Texas, a carnival was running in the parking lot of the H.E. Butt Grocery. An elephant escaped from the carnival and ran loose for two miles where it ran into the backyard of Elsa Perez. The elephant trampled a swing set, crashed through a concrete wall and ran to an adjoining yard. Mrs. Perez was fearful for her children's safety as well as her own, and suffered a miscarriage due to the shock. The grocery claimed it was not responsible as it was not the keeper of the animal. The court held that the grocery had obtained the carnival as part of a marketing scheme to gain economic benefit and therefore could be held liable. The court also held the elephant had been negligently restrained, and Mrs. Perez could obtain a monetary judgment against the grocery.[76]

Trespassing Animals

When an animal trespasses onto one's land, one is permitted to use as much force as is reasonably necessary to drive off the animal. If an animal is vicious and liable to cause harm it is legal to kill it, but if it is not doing anything wrong one may not kill it in vengeance for previously trespassing.

War stories: William Ihde owned some goats who truly believed the grass was greener on the land of Edward Doornbos and regularly strayed onto his property. Doornbos finally put the animals in a corral on his land and claimed them for himself as a lien to compensate him for the damage the goats had done to his land. The trial court held for Doornbos. The Montana Supreme Court affirmed holding that the value of the goats was not disproportionate to the damage caused by them and that the lower court was warranted in finding Doornbos justified in retaining the goats to satisfy his claim for damages.[77]

Clay Helsel sued Henry Fletcher for intentionally killing his pedigreed Persian cat. The court awarded Helsel $150, which was the value of the cat. The Supreme Court of Oklahoma reversed for new trial, holding that since this particular cat was a suspected chicken-stealer, Fletcher was justified in killing it when he found it lurking around his chickens. The court held the jury should be instructed as to that rule, and stated that if Helsel wanted to let his animals roam free, he did so at their peril.[78]

Ed Thomas had a dog who would go to Lemon Minyard's farm at night and suck the eggs there. Minyard finally shot and killed the dog. Ed Thomas then held Minyard at gunpoint and demanded $20 or else Minyard's cow and yearling. Minyard, having no money and greatly fearing for his life, turned over a cow and yearling to Thomas.

Thomas was convicted of robbery of the cow and yearling and appealed. The Mississippi Supreme Court affirmed the conviction holding that since Thomas' only claim against Minyard was for unliquidated damages for killing the dog, if there even was liability for killing the dog, and since Minyard did not owe Thomas an honest debt, it did not have to decide whether the collection by force or intimidation of a debt honestly believed to be due constitutes robbery. The court mentioned that Mr. Minyard was black and that Mr. Thomas was white and it is interesting to note that this happened in Mississippi in 1933.[79]

In Hennepin County, Minnesota, Edward Mitzel sued Louie Zachman for damages caused when Zachman castrated two of Mitzel's bulls. The bulls had broken through the fence separating their two properties and apparently damaged some of Zachman's heifers. A jury awarded Mitzel $500 and Zachman appealed. The Supreme Court of Minnesota affirmed since Zachman had taken the law into his own hands, the evidence did not show damage to Zachman's heifers, and the testimony of a witness as to the value of the bulls before and after castration did not show the jury verdict to be excessive.[80]

Two bulls belonging to G.S. Goodman and known as Old Jake and Young Jake jumped fences and chased Mrs. Harris into her home. They then began consorting with the Harris cows. Mrs. Harris screamed for help, and J.L. Cadenhead came to aid her. He shooed at the bulls, and as they were leaving Cadenhead shot the bulls. Old Jake was shot so as to be unfit for breeding and Goodman sent him to the slaughterhouse. Young Jake died from the gunshot. A jury awarded Goodman $75 for the damage to the bulls. The Supreme Court affirmed, holding that though the bulls had frightened Mrs. Harris, one may not shoot a valuable domestic animal in punishment for a wrong already committed, even though one could shoot the animal while it was engaged in the wrong act.[81]

Kilo Bandito, a German Shepherd, was shot and killed by Curtis Bardwell. Kilo was shot in the head with a shotgun, and died several hours later after emergency surgery. Debbie Quave, Kilo's owner, filed suit against Bardwell for the deliberate and unjustified killing of Kilo. The trial court found Bardwell guilty of deliberately killing Kilo without provocation and awarded Debbie Quave $2,500 in damages along with the veterinary bill. The Court of Appeal affirmed, holding that the evidence showed the killing was unprovoked and intentional, the damage award was appropriate, and evidence of Bardwell's prior conviction for cruelty to animals was relevant and the lower court correctly admitted it.[82]

In some areas statutes may change these principles. For example there are laws in some states which allow people to kill any dog which is not licensed and collared.

War story: On November 1, 1926 Fred Struck came to the house of Mr. Mendenhall in Eldora, Iowa and shot his female rat terrier dog named Bird, which had five not-yet-weaned pups. On December 17th he returned, entered Mr. Mendenhall's home and chased the pups into the yard where he shot them also. One of the pups he threw into the air and shot as it fell. Struct's defense was that since the dogs did not have licenses they were not property and that under the law it was legal to shoot them. The jury bought it and said that there were no damages. The Supreme Court of Iowa said that it must reverse the verdict, citing the "brutality of these dog killers."[83]

Chapter 11 Blocking View, Light and Air

Another area where neighbors have often gotten into disputes is when one person blocks the view, light or air of another. Such cases have involved fences blocking people's windows, trees blocking their sunlight and billboards blocking other billboards.

In England there is a doctrine known as "ancient lights" which holds that people have the right to the light which has reached their property since ancient times. This doctrine forbids people from building structures which block the light which has since ancient times reached their neighbors property unless they somehow obtain the legal right to do so, such as by purchasing an easement. The law started right after the great fire of London in 1666 when much of the city had to be rebuilt.

However, in America nearly every court has rejected the doctrine of ancient lights. The rationale in this country is that the doctrine is an impediment to technological and industrial progress and that since the advent of electric lights it is no longer necessary. This position has allowed our country to have some of the largest business districts and highest skyscrapers in the world. Imagine how much trouble it would have been to build the Empire State Building if the owner could have been liable to every owner whose property was touched by the building's shadow.

The general rule in America is that people can build structures on their property without regard to the effect on their neighbors' needs or preferences for view, light or air. An exception to this is Georgia where a statute[84] passed in 1982 recognizes an easement for light and air. Here are some examples of cases on this issue:

War stories: The Mohrs owned an office building on Highway 20 in Fort Dodge, Iowa. In 1983, Midas Realty built a muffler shop which while complying with the zoning restrictions, blocked the view of the Mohrs' building to traffic approaching from the west on Hwy 20. Mohr sued Midas for unreasonable interference with his lawful use and enjoyment of his property. He also sought abatement of the alleged nuisance. The courts dismissed the suit.[85]

In Washington state Mr. and Mrs. Earl Collinson owned a nice home at 1939 Broadway on the western slope of Capitol Hill. They bought the home because of the view and they didn't think that anything could be built near them, but Mr. and Mrs. William Bain and Mr. and Mrs.

Flemming Sorenson built two multi-story condominium buildings below them on the hill which blocked their view. The Collinsons sued but the court held that blocking a person's view with a building which was otherwise legal was not a nuisance.[86]

A six-story building and a four story building were built side to side in a town in New Hampshire. The six story building had air conditioners in the fifth and sixth floor windows which hung out over the four-story building. The owner of the four story building decided to tear it down and build a six story building. This meant that the windows on the fifth and sixth floors of the six story building would be up against a brick wall (and, of course, would not be able to use their air conditioners. The owner of the six story building sued and the case went to the New Hampshire Supreme Court. Justice David Souter, later to become a United States Supreme Court Justice, wrote the opinion which said that the owner of the six story building had no right to stop the neighbor from building directly in front of her windows.[87]

Though the general rule is that a person has no right to a view over his neighbor's land, there are, of course, exceptions. The main exception regards "spite fences." This is a fence built by someone solely to harass his neighbor. When a court finds that a fence is merely a spite fence, then it may order it removed.

War stories: In August, 1888, the Morans and the Flahertys owned adjoining lots on the Northwest corner of Goodrich and Lagrave streets in Grand Rapids Michigan and the Flahertys began laying a foundation to build a home. The Morans were upset with the location of the home because it would block their view. According to court testimony Mr. Moran asked Mrs. Flaherty if the building was going to be built so close to the street and when told it was, asked, "Don't you know that you are going to injure the property on the street, and injure ourselves entirely?" Mrs. Flaherty responded, "We are building the house for ourselves, not for other people." To which Mrs. Moran replied, "Very well. We will build a fence for ourselves, and we will make it twelve feet high." The fence was built directly in front of the Flaherty's windows. The Supreme Court of Michigan held it to be a spite fence and ordered it to be taken down.[88]

Right off the Murdo exit from I-90 in South Dakota, near the intersection of U.S. 83 and 16, Richard Hullinger had maintained a billboard for business advertising purposes. The billboard was on privately owned land. Hullinger claimed that Walter Prahl had constructed a billboard which when completed would obstruct part of the view of Hullinger's billboard. The lower court dismissed. The South Dakota Supreme Court reversed, holding that if the placement of the billboard was malicious, then Prahl could be enjoined from erecting it since it would be a private nuisance. The court held that a property owner has a duty to use his rights thereon in a manner which does not infringe on the rights of another, and maliciously erecting a sign to block the view of another's sign was a nuisance.[89]

In some cases the court may find that a person had both a legitimate and a spiteful purpose for building something, and allow it to stay.

War stories: In Miami the Fountainebleu hotel stood north along the beach from the Eden Roc hotel. The owners didn't get along and the owner of the Fountainebleu decided to build an addition which would cast a shadow over the pool and sun deck of the Eden Roc during the middle of the day. The Eden Roc sued to stop construction, but lost since the court found that spite was not the sole purpose of building the addition.[90]

In Atlanta a building had a billboard on its side and a neon sign on its roof. The property owner next door put up a billboard blocking both signs. The building owner complained bitterly about his loss of business and the confusion the sign caused, but the court held that the new billboard was lawful and not a nuisance. One might wonder if it mattered that the sign complained of said, "For what shall it profit a man, if he shall gain the whole world, and his own soul lose." Might Georgia judges in 1955 have been swayed by the content of the sign?[91]

There is one other exception which should be mentioned because it may prove important in the future. It regards solar energy.

War story: A couple in Wisconsin had a home heated by solar panels and a neighbor started to build in such a way that the solar panels would be blocked. The case went to the Wisconsin

Supreme Court and the court issued a long opinion explaining that it knew that no court in America recognized
the right to access to sunlight, but stated that it thought it
was time for a change. It said that since energy conservation was important and would be more so in the future, it
was reversing its own past decisions to modernize the law.
Therefore the neighbor was forbidden from blocking the
sun from the solar panels.[92]

It will be many years before we will know if this case is an aberration
or a new trend. There are some who argue that the American doctrine
is passe and that the law should change.[93] However, other courts
considering the issue have not jumped on the bandwagon.

War story: In California a couple built a passive solar house which had
              large windows facing south to catch the sun. The neighbor,
              in violation of rules in the area planted a number of trees
              which blocked the sun from the couple's windows. The
              California appellate court which reviewed the case de-
              cided not to follow Wisconsin's policy. It cited differences
              such as the fact that in Wisconsin solar panels were blocked
              but here it was just a passive solar house. The court also
              said, as courts often do, that this was an issue for the
              legislature to change, not the court.[94]

It is possible that state legislatures will will enter the field and
declare public policy in this area. In New Mexico a Solar Rights Act[95]
was passed in 1977 which gives property owners a right to solar energy
based upon priority in time.

For those interested in keeping abreast on this area of the law there
is a publication called *Solar Law Reporter* which may be found at some
law libraries.

As mentioned earlier, one way to obtain the right to view, light or
air is through an easement. If a person owns a large oceanfront lot and
sells the half near the water. He can put an easement on the oceanfront
lot at the time of sale which will forever restrict the use of the lot. For
example, he can put an easement on the property saying that no
building may ever be built on the property higher than one story. This
way he can insure that his second floor view of the ocean will never be
blocked.

Chapter 12 Boundary Disputes

Because of the difficulties in accurately measuring land there are frequent instances where neighbors disagree about the location of their boundary. Because maps are flat and the earth is curved, paper descriptions do not always match the actual shape of the land. Considering that many surveys in this country are based upon government surveys up to two hundred years old, the problems are understandable.

When two parties cannot locate the boundary between their property the first step would be to have a survey done of the two parcels. Occasionally, a survey cannot determine the exact location of a boundary because the descriptions conflict. If this is the case the best solution is for the parties to mutually agree on a location of their boundary.

Of course each party would rather have his parcel as large as possible and it may be difficult to come to an agreement, especially when each person's deed seems to give him the larger piece. However, considering the cost of going to court to determine a boundary the reward for winning may not be great.

In a court action one person will lose the disputed area and have to pay his attorney's fee and the other person will gain the disputed area and have to pay his own attorney's fee, so actually the real winners of a boundary suit will be the attorneys.

Some less expensive alternatives to this would be either arbitration or mediation. Arbitration means turning the question over to a disinterested arbitrator who would make a decision without the delay or expense of the court system. Mediation means having a trained mediator work with the parties to help them arrive at a fair resolution.

If two neighbors do arrive at an agreement as to their boundary, they should have their agreement put in writing and then they should execute deeds clearing up any questions in the title. The usual way to do this is to have the proper legal descriptions drafted by a surveyor and then to have each owner "quit claim" any interest he may have in the other property to the other owner.

If the parties cannot agree on a solution or an alternative to litigation, they can have a judge and jury determine their rights to the disputed property. Many such disputes have been heard over the years and the courts have developed numerous rules with which to guide them in such decisions. Some of those rules are:

- The important consideration is to be the intent of the parties who divided the lands.

•If there is an ambiguity then it is to be resolved in favor of the person who received the ambiguous deed, rather than the one who conveyed the property with the ambiguous deed.

War story: In 1869 the executors of Henry Goulding conveyed land to Kelley and Blackmer in which the distances of the lot lines conflicted with the angles. Although there was purportedly a map of what was intended, and the description stated that their property included only 7770 square feet, the legal description was found to be the one giving them 9101 square feet.[96]

•Where the terms of the description conflict the court uses a hierarchy to determine which descriptions are controlling. That hierarchy is as follows:
1. Monuments
2. Clearly marked neighbor's boundary
3. A plat or a map prepared from a survey
4. Angles and distances of the description (angles are given preference over distances)
5. Area measurement

For example, if a description says that a person owns a piece of land comprising 40 acres bounded by four corner markers and the land surrounded by those markers is only 35 acres, then a court will probably determine that the person only owns 35 acres because the corner markers are considered to be more accurate than the measurement of the area. (However, if the person was lead to believe that he was buying 40 acres, he may be able to sue the seller for misrepresentation.)

War stories: After James Pilgrim sold a portion of his land it was discovered that the descriptions of the land he sold and the land he retained overlapped. While Mr. Pilgrim thought an old fox farm fence was the boundary, his lot as described was smaller than he thought. A surveyor attempted to reconcile them and did so as close as possible but Mr. Pilgrim's property was still not as large as he had intended. In a suit between the parties the court accepted the survey and disregarded Mr. Pilgrim's evidence as to his intent. It found that since the fence zig-zagged around trees and jogged by as much as 20 feet, it could not be taken as the boundary which was described in the deed as a straight line.[97]

In the early 1980s Elbert Sowerwine and Glenn Nielson got into a disagreement over the boundary between their ranches in Park County, Wyoming. Mr. Sowerwine felt that the boundary should be based upon a call to a river which had been described in the original 1883 field notes of the surveyor and Mr. Nielson felt that the boundary should be 660 feet further. The trial court ruled for Mr. Nielson and Mr. Sowerwine filed his own appeal with the Wyoming Supreme Court without using an attorney. The court noted that if the river was used as a monument all three other calls of the description would be off and if it was assumed that the river had shifted over 100 years then only one call would need to be corrected. It also noted that if it used the river as a monument many neighboring property descriptions would be changed. It affirmed the trial court's decision.[98]

When the heirs of O. L. and Ozie Allen Sanders had a disagreement with M. D. Williams over the boundary between their properties, they sued to establish the boundary as the one determined by their surveyor and for payment for their surveyor, plus $15,000 for mental anguish and $10,000 for depreciation for Mr. Williams use of their property. The surveyor had determined that there was a deficiency in the section and he apportioned the loss equally between the owners. The trial court upheld the survey but denied the $25,000 damages since they had presented no evidence to prove them.[99]

The marker for the quarter corner between land owned by the United States Government and John and Florence Citko was lost and the parties could not agree where their boundary was. The United States claimed that it should be reestablished by measurement (giving the government more land) and the Citkos claimed that there was enough evidence to establish where the original corner had been. A lawsuit by the United States was dismissed after the Citkos presented testimony of longtime residents that a well-worn path, a post, a rock pile, a fence and bearing trees indicated the location of the corner. [Interestingly, it was not until the witness's second deposition (and conversations with Mr. Citko's lawyer) that his memory was jogged.][100]

Bodies of Water

Where a legal description describes a property as running to a road
or to a non-navigable body of water such as a lake, pond or small river,
and the person conveying the property owns to the center of the road
or river, it is assumed that the conveyance includes to the center of the
road or body of water, and that the seller did not intend to keep the strip
in the street or river. However, this does not apply to governmental
units which convey property.

War stories: When the Town of Castleton denied Ronald Fucci a permit
to keep a trailer on his lot because the lot was not large
enough, it did not consider the underwater land owned by
him up to the middle of the channel. The court said that this
was an error and that the underwater land should be
included in calculating the size of his lot.[101]

In some areas local authorities have passed laws forbidding property to be divided without compliance with
numerous governmental requirements. Clever lawyers
can often find loopholes in these laws. In 1979 Island
County, Washington and the State of Washington filed suit
against a developer who allegedly subdivided land improperly. The Supreme Court of Washington, En banc,
affirmed the dismissal of the complaint on the ground that
the submerged land to the center of the lake could be
included in the size of the lots to make them five acres in
size and exempt from the platting requirement.[102]

Where a boundary is marked by river, stream or other body of
water, a change in the location of the waterway can change the boundary of the property. This is an ancient rule of property law. However,
over the years exceptions to the rule have been allowed, especially
when sticking to the rule would have been unfair.

One modern rule is that when a river *slowly* changes its course the
property line changes with it, but when it *suddenly* changes its course
the boundary line remains where it originally was.

War stories: A dispute arose between the Lethins and the United States
government because of a conveyance in 1887 to the U.S. of
land to be used as a Life Saving Station. The land was on
the Columbia River in Oregon. The government no longer
used the land for Life Saving, and the Lethins brought a
quiet title action. The District Court held that the govern-

ment did not have title to the land but that the government did have an easement regardless of the fact that the walkway on the easement was being used for marine studies instead of as a Life Saving Station. The court gave the Lethins title but reserved the easement for the government to gain access to the river.[103]

Donald Albrecht, a landowner in Teton County, Wyoming and the United States Government both claimed lands comprising 203 acres along the Snake River. Albrecht's property was based upon a claim to the meander line of the river but there was actually a long distance between his property and the river. This was the land in dispute. He filed suit in Federal District Court to quiet title to the land. In reviewing the case the court examined surveys and notes made in 1901. From the notes it appeared that the surveyor made a gross error by measuring Fish creek instead of Snake River. The court ruled that in the case of such an error it would not apply the rule that a measurement to a meander line always conveys land to the edge of the water.[104]

When some people began cutting timber on Billie R. Weber's side of Jones Creek, he and and Mr. Johannes got into a disagreement over their boundary, which was said to be the creek. Mr. Johannes said that the real boundary was a dry stream bed quite a distance from the existing stream. However, the court ruled that when a stream meanders slowly over time the boundary between the owners moves with it and only when the stream changes course suddenly do the boundaries remain in the original locations.[105]

When Lee Evinger bought "Tract C" in Section 13, Township 48, Range 30 in Missouri he received a deed which gave him all land "east of Sin-A-Bar Creek." But the creek was not in the quarter quarter of land which he purchased, so he assumed that he owned the entire east half of it and began farming it. There was a dry creek bed on the land and Dale Walkup and his predecessors in title had been farming the land east of the creek bed for many years. He sued to regain possession of the land. Mr. Evinger claimed that the creek was a monument on his deed and it had moved he would be entitled to the land east of the new location. The court looked at aerial photographs of the area

and all of the deeds in the chain of title and concluded that
since the land between the channels remained unaltered
the location of the stream must have changed "avulsively,"
and therefore would not have changed ownership of the
land. It also noted that since Mr. Walkup and his predecessors in title had farmed the land and paid taxes on it for
many years they would have owned it by adverse possession anyway.[106]

Adverse possession

There is an ancient principle of property law that if a person
wrongfully holds onto another person's property long enough, then he
can gain ownership of it. This is called adverse possession.

The way it works is that the Statute of Limitations forbids owners
from suing to regain their land if they wait too long to do so. This is
based upon the rationale that after a certain period of time it is too late
to gather all the evidence and witnesses to prove a case in court. It also
has the effect of making it easier to get clear title to property.

War story: James Chisholm conveyed his 44 acres of land south of
             Fairbanks, Alaska to both Charles Taylor and James Stewart.
             Taylor and Stewart recorded their deeds. Stewart's family
             lived on the land while the Taylors moved to Oregon. The
             Stewart's daughter, Alaska Linck brought a quiet title
             action. The lower court granted Alaska the sole ownership
             of the land. The Supreme Court of Alaska affirmed holding
             the Alaska and her parents had cultivated, protected and
             cared for the land while the Taylors did not. The court held
             that since the Stewarts had paid taxes and dealt with public
             agencies as if they were the owners for at least 19 consecu-
             tive years, and that if the Taylors had visited the land they
             would have observed the changes made by the Stewarts,
             that Alaska Linck had established title by adverse posession
             under color of title. Affirmed.[107]

There are five legal requirements for adverse possession. For a
person to gain title to a piece of property through adverse possession he
must:

- Openly and notoriously take possession
- Hold exclusive possession of the property
- Hold possession continuously
- Hold possession without the owner's consent
- Hold the property for at least the period of time stated in the statute

Of course each of these points has been litigated numerous times and has been analyzed by several courts.

Open and Notorious Possession

Possession of the property must be open, notorious, visible, and exclusive. It must be open, notorious and visible to the owner of the property in order to cut off his rights. It must be exclusive in that the person claiming possession cannot be sharing it with the owner or with other members of the public.

War story: Where a company took possession of a cave which extended under another person's land, the possession was not considered to be "open and notorious" to allow a claim of adverse possession.[108]

Exclusive Possession

Exclusive possession means that possession to the exclusion of the true owner of the property. The adverse possessor may be more than one person, such as husband and wife, and may share the possession such as by renting it to a tenant.

War story: In a case where the original owner of a strip of land mowed the land regularly, the person claiming adverse possession could not claim his possession was exclusive.[109]

Where two people own a piece of property together there can no be adverse possession unless one physically ousts the other. Merely taking over the duties and possession of the property is not enough.

Continuous Possession

The possession must be continuous. If a person claiming by adverse possession abandons the property for a period of time, the period of possession starts over. However, if the property is only suitable for periodic use, such use may be considered continuous.

War story: Some time prior to 1932 a house was built on the Hood Canal in Mason County, Washington on the wrong lot. Through some mistake it was built on the lot next to the one on which it should have been built. Over the years the property was sold several times and each time the sellers transferred possession of the house but deeded the lot next door. Eventually the real owners of the property on which the house was located, the Howards and the Yearlys, filed suit to have themselves declared the owners. The occupants of the house at that time claimed that since they and their predecessors had occupied the house for years, they had acquired title to the property by adverse possession. The actual owners pointed out that the land was a summer house and that it was therefore not occupied continuously as is required for adverse possession, and they won the case. However, the occupants appealed and the ruling was reversed. The appeals court ruled that when a property was a summer beach house, continuous occupancy could consist of occupancy every summer, not all year round. The Washington Supreme Court declined to review this ruling.[110]

If the owner openly and notoriously regains possession of the property, then this ends the continuous possession and the adverse possessor must start over.

Without Consent

It is said that an adverse possessor must hold possession to the property "hostile" to the owner. This means that the person must be in possession without consent of the owner. In some areas the courts require that the adverse possessor must have some basis for his claim to the land, but most states allow any squatter to make a claim.

A majority of the states use an objective test, looking at the actions of the possessor, to determine if the possession is adverse. But other states use a subjective test, looking into the mind of the possessor to see if he has a good faith belief that he has title to the property.

War story: When John Mercer died he had no will and his land passed to his widow and children. Shortly later one of his children died without a will and her interest passed to her husband and children. John's widow and children deeded the property to his son, Fred. His daughter's widower also conveyed his interest and his children's interest to Fred. Thirty-four years later the parties realized that the latter deed was not effective to convey the children' interest. Fred filed suit to clear his title and the court said that he could not claim adverse possession because nothing was done affirmatively which would serve as notice to the children that he was claiming adversely.[111]

Statutory Period

Adverse possession is governed by state statutes. The time period in the various states may vary from seven to 20 years or more.

Additional Statutory Requirements

Some states have laws which impose other requirements on adverse possession such as that the adverse possessor must have paid the taxes on the property during the period, that he have some sort of deed to the property before making the claim or that he have a good faith belief that he is the owner of the property.

Chapter 13 Buildings and Structures

There are several ways in which a building or other structure can cause problems for neighbors. It may be dangerous, unsightly and lower the value of the neighborhood.

A building or structure which is merely unsightly is much more difficult to remedy. While many areas have attempted to regulate the appearance of property, it has been harder to justify these laws in the courts. While safety is generally accepted to be a legitimate governmental concern, beauty (which, of course is in the eye of the beholder) has not been.

If the problem which is causing a property to be unsightly is also dangerous, such as junk attracting rats or peeling paint which might contain lead, it may be possible to get a health or building inspector to take action. Otherwise, it will not be easy to take legal action.

War stories: Xoral Oliver and her daughter, Carol Borges, were the owners of three lots in Richmond Annex adjoining Richmond, California. Over a period of years they built various structures on the land and piled lumber, waste and rubbish. The property was near "several attractive residences" and apparently some of them contacted the district attorney who filed a complaint against the owners. The judge visited the sight and declared the structures to be a nuisance ordering them to be removed within 90 days. On appeal the court affirmed the judgment and noted that while an unsightly condition does not constitute a nuisance, a fire hazard does.[112]

On September 25, 1919, John J. Worm and others filed a petition in Eastland, Texas and obtained an injunction against the building of a number of small homes by Eugene Wood. The petitioners claimed that the houses were to be shacks of the poorest quality which would be crowded together and rented to "negroes, Mexicans and a low class of white people." After taking testimony from both sides the injunction was dismissed and the court held that such housing was not necessarily a nuisance, though it could possibly become one. In any event, halting the construction was not proper.[113]

Unless a building violates a zoning rule or other law or a restriction on the property, there is no limit of how high it can be built.

In platted subdivisions the property restrictions often offer stringent controls on what types of structures can be built. As explained in the beginning of this book, such restrictions are voluntarily placed on the property by the original owners and each purchaser must comply with them. Purchasers are deemed to be aware of them, even if they have never actually seen them.

Often subdivision restrictive covenants will provide that anyone violating the rules will have to pay all costs and attorneys' fees in any lawsuit which must be brought to enforce the restrictions.

War stories: At 2712 and 2714 Harmon Road in Silver Spring, Maryland, lived adjoining property owners Sarah and Walter Slaird and Reinhold and Patricia Klewers. The Slairds had lived at 2712 Harmon Road for 21 years and had spent substantial sums of money in landscaping their yard. The Klewers had lived at 2714 Harmon Road for about a year, and had installed a pool. The Slairds alleged the pool was a nuisance because it caused an unpleasant odor, the chlorinated water splashed onto their property causing damage, and the pool lights as well as loud noises generated by its use kept the Slairds from enjoying their own property. In addition, the pool allegedly changed the elevation and sloping of the Klewers property causing water to drain off into the Slaird's yard. The court ruled for the Klewers, since the pool had been constructed in accordance with building code requirements and sufficient evidence showing a nuisance was not shown by the Slairds.[114]

William M. Wells, III, bought three lots and a partially completed house in Sea Pines Plantation Subdivision on Hilton Head Island. He received a set of construction plans which had been approved by the Architectural Board of Sea Pines Plantation. Wells then proceeded to erect a flagpole, a jacuzzi, and a satellite antenna on the roof along with other unapproved structures such as a beach walkway, shower, fence, gate and trees. The trial court ordered Wells to remove the items as he was in violation of the restrictive covenant. The Supreme Court of South Carolina held that the restrictive covenants were enforceable; the covenants were not arbitrarily or discriminatorily enforced; the flagpole, jacuzzi, and satellite dish were prohibited by the covenant; and that Wells had breached the covenants by failing to obtain approval for landscape modifications and by obstructing the view of other lot owners.[115]

In 1981 in Bigantine, New Jersey, Joeseph Chaikin erected a 60 foot high windmill in an effort to conserve energy. The windmill was apparantly very loud and caused stress and anxiety to Joel Rose and his family. The Roses also were not able to enjoy the peace of their home. They sued hoping to enjoin the windmill claiming it was a nuisance and it violated zoning laws. The court weighed the utility of the windmill against the harm it caused and found the windmill to be a nuisance. The court held that the noise of the windmill was offensive because of its character, volume and duration; the windmill did indeed violate a zoning ordinance; and the ordinance reasonably advanced legitimate state purposes and did not violate Chaikin's due process. The court granted the injunction. [116]

Around 1880 Henry Yates was mayor of Newark, New Jersey and William Morris was the street commissioner. It was their duty as public officers to enforce and execute the city ordinances. Ernest Dreher erected a flag pole in violation of an ordinance requiring permission in writing by the street commissioner before erecting anything which would encumber or obstruct any street, highway, lane, alley, dock, wharf, or other public place in Newark. Yates and Morris removed the flag pole from Broad street after giving notice to Dreher. Dreher sued for trespass. The court affirmed the lower decision for Yates holding that Dreher's allegation that proper notice had not been given to him was such that no issue could have been raised by it. Since Yates acted according to the city ordinance, Dreher had no recourse.[117]

When J. Howard Rowley built a duplex in a Planned Unit Development in Utah County, Utah, a controversy arose as to placement of the two driveways. Some of the other owners objected to the use of one parking space near the street for an access to the driveway. However, Mr. Rowley had the driveway poured before the controversy was resolved. Thereafter, while the Rowleys were out of town the homeowners' association constructed flower boxes in front of the driveway. In the inevitable lawsuit between the parties the court agreed that a structure which has as its sole purpose the injury of a neighbor is illegal, but it found that since use of the parking area was illegal, the construction of the flower boxes was legal.[118]

When the owners of the building at 305-313 East 47th Street, in New York City began building an elevator tower and cooling system on their roof, Arnold and Karen Blair, owners of a duplex penthouse next door sued. In addition to claims that their light and air were blocked, the Blairs claimed that the housing of the elevator tower violated the law against fences over ten feet high. The court held that an elevator tower was not a fence, and that there was no other legal reason to stop the construction.[119]

Chapter 14 Businesses

Much of the litigation regarding businesses in residential neighborhoods has been eliminated by the practice of putting deed restrictions
on property and the proliferation of zoning laws. Imagine living in a
nice neighborhood and having someone open a slaughterhouse or a
garbage dump next door.

Today the issue of whether a business is legal in a certain
location is usually very simple. Either it is allowed by the zoning and
restrictions or it isn't. If it is legal, there is not much that neighbors can
do unless they suffer substantial injuries. If it is not legal, the business
usually has few options since invalidating deed restrictions and obtaining a zoning variance are both expensive and time consuming.

One problem which often comes up today is that of a business
legally in a business zone, next to a residence in a residential zone. The
business may be producing only the normal level of noise and annoyances
for its type, but that level may be too much for the residents next door.

In most cases of this type the residence owner has few options. Only
if the business is unusually obnoxious for its type and if it substantially
injures the neighbor, is there a chance of winning a legal action.

War stories: In December, 1925, Burke & Trotti Inc. opened a funeral
home at 428 Kirby Street in the Parish of Calcasieu, Louisiana. A neighbor, Lucious L. Moss was not pleased with this
as he felt it decreased the value of his property and caused
him the loss of over $8,000 in rents. He sued to restrain the
company from conducting the business, but the courts
held that in the absence of a zoning law prohibiting it, the
funeral business was legal, though the area had a residential character. [120]

On October 1, 1959, a Winn-Dixie supermarket opened on
the corner of East Calhoun and Baker Streets in Sumter,
South Carolina. Six weeks later Mr. and Mrs. L. E. Winget,
who lived in the house directly behind the store on Baker
Street filed suit against the store. They complained about
the trucks unloading produce and picking up trash at
night, large exhaust fans blowing toward their home,
floodlights shining on their home and crowds of people
and automobiles. The court declined to order the store to
close but it awarded the homeowners $5,000 in damages.
The store appealed to the South Carolina Supreme Court.
The court held that since the store was lawfully in a
business zone it did not have to pay for the depreciation in

value of nearby residences. It said that the fans and floodlights could constitute a nuisance and that there should be a new trial to let a jury decide if they were.[121]

In the late 1940s, Stevenson Packing Co., located in a residential area of Nebraska City, Nebraska, decided to add meat slaughtering to its other activities. This caused both noise, odors and a host of other unpleasantries. In a lawsuit by the neighbors the court noted that the slaughtering caused blood and animal parts to fall all over the place and that barrels of animal parts would be left outside. This attracted numbers of dogs and flies. The court noted "There were small flies and big flies, houseflies and blowflies of the most annoying and revolting kind." There were also hideous cries of anguish from the animals which apparently sensed their fates. The court also explained in detail how the animals were killed. Needless to say, the slaughterhouse was ordered to stop operations in the residential neighborhood.[122]

When James W. Killian built a building at 7436 Olive Street, St. Louis, Missouri, for use as a residence and dog and cat hospital his neighbors brought suit. The deed restrictions in the neighborhood said that the property should only be used for residences except that physicians and dentists could have offices in their homes. The court held that a veterinarian was not a physician or dentist under the restrictions and entered an injunction forbidding the property to be used as a dog and cat hospital. Mr. Killian appealed and lost.[123]

Another problem which can arise is where a homeowner in a residential area next to a commercial area wants to convert his property to commercial. Often his property is worth little as residential but would be worth a lot as commercial.

The problem for the courts is that if they let that person change his property use to commercial, then the person next door will be in the same predicament. If continued this could result in a domino effect. A related consideration is that the owner next to the commercial property would naturally have paid less for his property because of its location. By changing his use, the court would be revaluing his property at the expense of his neighbor.

For these reasons courts have been reluctant to allow changes in use for borderline properties, whether they were limited by restrictions or zoning.

Chapter 15 Cemeteries

A cemetery is not usually considered a nuisance. Therefore if it is not against the zoning laws, it is usually a legal activity.

However, there have been extreme cases where the condition of a cemetery has caused it to become a nuisance. Such cases are usually when it is near a residential area and in an unhealthy condition.

War stories: A. T. Knowles had operated a veterinary hospital at 29th Street NW and 17th Avenue in Miami, Florida, for several years when he was taken to court by Central Allapattae Properties, Inc. and the Buckingham Investment Co. They claimed that the burial of 300-400 dogs on the property and the barking of dogs was a nuisance. He claimed that they were merely interested in raising the value of their nearby property and that other neighbors were not disturbed by the dogs. The court held that "The decaying carcasses of some three or four hundred dogs buried on the three-acre tract in cypress boxes and placed three and one-half feet underground, is to say the least, a potential threat or menace to the health and welfare of the inhabitants residing in the immediate community."[124]

R. J. Lewis, the owner of the "Lewis Funeral Home" in Ashville, North Carolina bought some land in 1927 in Beaverdam Valley for use as a cemetery. The property was said to be located in the watershed area of Beaverdam Creek which was used for water by the city of Ashville. The Board of Health of the City filed suit to stop use of the land as a cemetery but its request was denied. The court found that Beaverdam Creek was not part of the Ashville Water Works, that they were already polluted, that dead bodies did not cause the pollution and that dead bodies had been buried in the area for at least 120 years. On appeal the Supreme Court of North Carolina affirmed noting that "the dead have to be disposed of in some way."[125]

Mary Young and others sued to enjoin Claud Brown from using his land as a cemetery. Mary Young and the other plaintiffs bought their land for residential purposes and alleged that the building of a cemetery in the area would constitute a nuisance. The area was about three miles from the Florence, South Carolina city limits. The lower court refused to dismiss the case. The South Carolina Supreme Court affirmed the lower holding and stated that while it is well established that a cemetery is not an automatic nuisance, it may be a nuisance depending on its location, manner and extent of use, and mode of burials. The court held that depreciation of property value, the depressing atmosphere or fact that it makes the neighborhood less attractive does not make a cemetery a nuisance. However, the endangering of public health will make it a nuisance. The court held there were enough facts to go to trial and let a jury decide.[126]

When a cemetery was started just 500 feet from the well they used for drinking water, some dairy farmers on the Fayette and Jessamine county line in Kentucky filed suit. All parties agreed that a cemetery is not a nuisance unless it endangers public health. The dairy farmers presented evidence that bodies contain germs and bacteria and that they would enter the ground water. However the court was persuaded by a professor of bacteriology from the University of Kentucky that the bacteria could not travel more than 50 feet and that the bodies would be disinfected. Therefore it found that the cemetery was not a nuisance and was legal.[127]

Chapter 16 Children

Yes, Virginia, some people do consider children to be a nuisance. However, the courts seldom, if ever, take their side and in most cases restrictions against children are considered to be "against public policy." It is only in extreme cases that courts rule against children.

If the children happen to be doing something particularly American, like playing baseball, don't even try to stop them. As one legal article put it, "One attempting to interfere with the games of children, particularly where the national sport of baseball is concerned, is likely to find himself in a not too popular position. For this reason, clients seeking to bring an action for nuisance against a playground operation should be discouraged except where it can be shown with particular clarity that an intolerable interference with the use of the client's property arises from the playground operation."[128]

Playgrounds

War stories: Since 1952 the Pee Wee Baseball League used Thompson Field in Kalispell, Montana for little league baseball games. In 1963 lights were installed so that night games could be held because some of the parents could not get off work early enough for day games. Some of the neighbors were not happy with this. They claimed that the noise, lights, dust, foul language, heavy traffic and balls flying into their yards were a nuisance. Three couples, the Kasalas, the Colliers and the Carlsons filed a suit and the court ordered the games stopped. However, the city and many residents were not happy with this ruling and they appealed. The Supreme Court of Montana reviewed the case, and the fact that 24 other people who lived near the park said that there was no serious problem in the area, and reversed the order stopping the games.[129]

Mrs. Hennessy's property was located across the street from a city playground in Boston. A great number of times balls from the playground broke windows in her garage. She sued and the court ordered the city of Boston to erect and maintain a fence to protect her property.[130]

Foster Homes

War story: In the 1970s, Abbott House, a not-for-profit corporation licensed by the state of New York to care for neglected and abandoned children leased a house in White Plains, New York from Gennaro Ferraioli to be used as a group home for foster children. In the home it placed 10 foster children with a married couple and their own two children. The couple was paid a salary and had all of its expenses paid by Abbott House. The City of White Plains sued the owners of the property, saying that they were violating the zoning ordinance requiring that the property be used only as a single family residence. The trial court and the appeals court agreed with the city, but the owners appealed to New York's highest court. Lawyers from three additional child welfare agencies jumped into the fray filing briefs. In order to save the day for the foster children, the court pointed out that the zoning ordinance did not define what a single family was. It decided that in this case a couple, their two children and ten foster children could be considered a family.[131]

Housing

In 1988 the Civil Rights Act was amended to forbid discrimination against children in the rental or sale of housing.[132] The law provides for penalties of up to $10,000 for the first offense, $25,000 for a second violation within five years and $50,000 for three or more violations within seven years. In private actions unlimited punitive damages are available.

The law does not apply to properties of four units or less if the owner lives there or to single family homes if the owner owns three or less and if there is not more than one sale within 24 months.

Also exempt from this law are certain facilities for the elderly. However, local ordinances may also forbid discrimination against children. In Miami, Florida, a county ordinance against age discrimination makes it impossible to build housing for the elderly!

Chapter 17 Chimneys

Chimneys present special problems because unless they are taller than surrounding structures they will not work properly. The way they work is that air passing across the top of the chimney creates a vacuum pulling the smoke out. If a neighboring building is taller and blocks the wind the smoke may not properly ventilate, or it may blow into the taller building.

Because of this situation some areas have laws which require owners of new buildings which are taller than neighboring chimneys to pay the cost of making the chimneys taller than their building. One area where this is the law is New York City. Of course neighbors have gotten in lawsuits over the exact requirements of the law.

War stories: In 1968, Mr. Spitzer owned a 12 story building at 1182-1184 Broadway built in 1887 and Mr. Siegal owned a 16 story building at 1186 Broadway built in 1907. The smaller building's chimney was rusted and in a dangerous condition to the taller building. Under a 1939 law of the city of New York, Mr. Siegal was responsible to maintain Mr. Spitzer's chimney. Because the chimney benefitted the taller building and the chimney law did not infringe the owner of the taller building's constitutional rights, he was guilty of the violation and the owner of the smaller building was not.[133]

When it built a building in the Bronx, the owner built a metal smoke stack on the shorter building next door. Over the years the smoke stack rusted and didn't work as well and caused damage to the neighbors building. The neighbor sued for replacement of the smoke stack and for repair of the damages. The court ruled that while John McNulty & Sons Holding Co., the owner of the taller building, was liable for repairing the smoke stack, it was not liable for other damages which the Graus had allowed to happen by not taking action sooner.[134]

Chapter 18 Churches

Believe it or not, some Americans have even considered churches to be nuisances. Sometime noise was the concern, other times it was property values. Like many other types of activities, a church is a legal activity, even in a residential area. However, in some cases it can become annoying enough to the neighborhood to constitute a nuisance.

If a church does not violate zoning laws it will probably not be considered a nuisance unless the annoying activity is quite extreme.

War story: Before it was able to build an open tabernacle on land next door, the First Baptist Church of Nashville, Arkansas was sued by some neighbors living in expensive homes nearby. They claimed that the value of their homes would be diminished 50 per cent. Their doctor testified that some of them were of nervous temperament and that in case of sickness the the conditions caused by the tabernacle would be very bad on them. The court ruled that if there was enough noise to cause a nuisance it could be enjoined, but that the construction could not be enjoined.[135]

Even if a church causes property values to decrease it will not be considered a nuisance.

War stories: When members of an organization called "Church of God," sometimes referred to as "Holy Rollers" prepared to erect a church in a residential area, several of the neighbors filed suit. They claimed that the church would be unusually noisy, some of them had ill health and needed quiet and that the church would lower their property values. The church claimed that its work would result in a benefit to mankind and the betterment of the community and that they were no louder than the Baptists or methodists. The court refused to stop the church.[136]

In 1903 or 1904 the Spencer Chapel Methodist Episcopal Church was built on Block 236 in what was a predominantly Black area of Muskogee, Oklahoma. Over the years whites began to move into the neighborhood. During the 1920s, after the church burned down, the trustees of the church contracted to build a modern, $25,000 church. However, thirteen whites in the area filed a suit claiming that it was an attempt to build a negro church in a white area, and they obtained an injunction against the building of the new church. The church appealed to the Supreme Court of Oklahoma which in October, 1924 reversed the decision. It held that churches are not normally nuisances and that enjoining the building of a negro church because of its effect on the white neighbors' property values was contrary to law, equity and good conscience.[137]

Chapter 19 Condominiums

Life in condominium developments is controlled by all five sets of rules, constitutional rights, specific laws, zoning laws, property restrictions and common law principles. The specific laws are usually contained in the state Condominium Act. This is the law which controls the division of property into condominiums. The property restrictions are usually contained in the Declaration of Condominium creating the condominium and also the bylaws and other rules and regulations adopted by the individual condominium. Where the rights of the parties are not spelled out in the statute or condominium documents, then common law principles will be used by judges to make decisions.

An explanation of the details of condominium law is beyond the scope of this book, and in fact could fill many volumes the size of this book. However, the legal principles which apply to people in condominiums and the ways to research those principles are the same.

If you have a problem with your neighbor in a condominium, you should first check all of the rules governing the condominium. These would include the Declaration of Condominium and all amendments to it, the bylaws of the association which runs the condominium and all amendments to them, and any rules or regulations promulgated by the condominium association.

You should have gotten some of these documents when you bought or rented your unit. If not, you should be able to get them from the association. In most states you have a clear right of access to these documents at all reasonable times. Be sure to ask to see all amendments. You may be able to see the declaration and its amendments and some restrictions in the records department of the courthouse, but the bylaws will probably not be recorded there.

If the answer to your problem is not found in these documents, of if your problem is caused by these documents, you should check your state condominium act. You can usually find it at your local library, or you may be able to obtain a copy from your state legislator (not your congressman or U.S. senator) or from your state capitol.

If you check your state's condominium laws you may find that your association is not following them or has passed some rule in violation of the state law. Keep in mind, though, that laws are not always interpreted to mean what they seem to say. The explanation of a law may be ten times as long as a law. To find out more about what the condominium laws mean you should go to a law library at a courthouse or at a law school.

Two types of materials which help explain the law are the annotated statutes and legal encyclopedias. Annotated statutes are books which first print the laws and then list all of the cases and other information which have been published explaining the law. Legal encyclopedias are books which explain the present state of the law and then reference every statement with footnotes referring to laws and cases which apply. Not all states have annotated statutes or legal encyclopedias, so you will have to check with your own law library. There is also a national legal encyclopedia called *Corpus Juris Secundum* which explains general principles of American law and cites cases from different states. However, if your state has its own encyclopedia it would be better to use that.

Zoning laws also cover condominium developments, but it is unlikely that a matter covered by zoning would not be covered by an even stricter rule in the condominium act or restrictions. For example, if a person is operating a business out of his condominium in violation of zoning laws, it is probably also against the condominium restrictions. However, it may be easier to stop someone by calling a zoning inspector than taking legal action.

If there is nothing in the statutes or rules covering the situation, some relief may be found in the common law principles regarding nuisance, trespass and other matters discussed the other chapters of this book.

Chapter 20 Crowds

Ordinary crowds are a normal incident of city life and can be expected in places where business is conducted. However, in some cases particularly disorderly or offensive crowds may be illegal or may be stopped by a civil action.

Criminal laws which forbid loitering or "unlawful assembly" may be useful in dispersing crowds. By contacting your local police authority you can find out if there is anything criminal about the activity which bothers you. However, because of the constitutional right of assembly which we enjoy in this country, there is a limit in how far such restrictions can go.

If it is not possible to solve the problem through police action, there may be a civil remedy. If actions of a neighbor attract a crowd which causes substantial injury to you or your property, it may be considered a nuisance.

War stories: Way back in 1695 (thirteen years before George Washington's mother was born) a Mr. Betterton erected a playhouse in Lincoln's Inn Fields near Portugal Row in England. This caused a problem for residents of the row who couldn't get their carriages in or out of their coachhouses. This well-to-do group appealed to officers of the king who prosecuted Mr. Betterton and obtained a writ prohibiting the continuing the inconvenience.[138]

Many years later in England a similar commotion was caused by a Mr. Carlisle who placed in the window of his store three satirical effigies. These caused a crowd to gather which created a lot of commotion on the street annoying neighboring shopkeepers. In a court action in 1830 this was held to be a nuisance.[139]

During Mr. Carlisle's trial a story was told of a Mr. Very whose daughter worked for him in his shop. His daughter was so beautiful that every day three to four hundred people would gather in the street to look at her. Eventually she had to be sent out of town.

In New York in the 1880s a couple whose extraordinary long hair was a museum attraction, used their bay window in which to comb their hair and to promote their hair tonic. This attracted a crowd which blocked the entrance to a business in the basement of the building. (This is what happens when there is no TV to go home to.) The court ordered the pair to stop causing such a crowd.[140]

A restaurant at 1130 Griswold St. in Detroit, Michigan must have had fantastic food in the 1940s. Crowds would gather blocking neighboring stores. The crowds were so big that the stores' window displays were almost completely blocked from view. The restaurant was ordered to hire a guard to supervise the lines.[141]

Americans in the 1940s seem to have been in a feeding frenzy. Later that decade in West Palm Beach, Florida, Morrison's Cafeteria was the place to eat. It was so popular that lines would form out the front door. The lines became so long that they blocked the entrance to a neighboring drug store. In a court action by the drug store a court ordered Morrison's to put an end to the lines.[142]

When O'Sullivan's Italian Pub on the corner of Runnion and Main Streets in Fort Wayne, Indiana was in danger of losing its liquor license in 1979 it told the liquor control commission that it was hiring a police officer to maintain order in the neighborhood. It also passed out flyers in the neighborhood offering to help if there was a disturbance in the neighborhood. When a person was assaulted in a parking lot across the street from the pub on a day when the policeman was late for work, a court held that the pub could be held liable for the injury if a jury decided that that the pub assumed the duty of protecting the neighborhood.[143]

But not all judges have been sympathetic with neighbors who object to crowds. In some cases it has been held that if a person is carrying on a lawful business and a crowd gathers, it is not the business person's fault.

War stories: After World War II potatoes were in short supply in England and were being rationed. One shopkeeper obtained a supply and a line formed to his shop, blocking several other shops. In this case the court held that the shopkeeper was not responsible for the short supply of potatoes and would not be liable for the crowds.[144]

Beginning in 1946 the Taft Stadium Board of Control began allowing midget auto racing in Taft Stadium at 23rd Street and May Avenue in Oklahoma City. R. W. Smilie, a neighbor who lived a block and a half from the stadium was not pleased with the races. He filed suit complaining that cars parked in the area crowded the streets, blocked driveways and made it impossible for two cars to pass on the streets. He also complained about the noise and devaluation of property values. The court ruled for the stadium authority quoting other cases which held, "City streets are primarily ways for public travel, and public right of travel includes privilege of parking vehicles at sidewalk curbing for reasonable periods as required by reasonable exigencies of business or social intercourse, " and "these are the plagues of city dwellers."[145]

Chapter 21 Dangers

Where a dangerous situation exists on a piece of property, the simplest solution is to seek help through health, zoning or building officials. Codes in many areas are becoming so strict that anything remotely dangerous will probably be a violation

If the situation does not violate any regulatory code then the question of whether there is a civil remedy will depend upon several factors. One is whether the danger is to persons on the premises or off the premises. Another factor is whether the dangerous condition naturally occured on the land or was artificially created. A third factor is whether the situation is normally dangerous, or unnecessarily dangerous.

For dangerous conditions to persons off the premises, which are a natural condition of the land there is not always a remedy.

War story: Mr. Moore-Gwyn was tenant for life of the Duffryn Estate, Pontardawe, Glamorgan in Great Britain. On this property were rocks which were located upon a bluff and were liable to break away and fall. The Pontardawe Rural District Council claimed these rocks were a nuisance both to the public and to himself. On one occasion a five ton piece of rock broke away and fell down the slope crashing into a Mr. Jenkins home, causing damage. The cause of the fall was weather, not any mining or quarrying operations. The court held that Mr. Moore-Gwyn was not liable for damages caused by the rocks since the falling was due to natural causes. The court followed another case which held that a person using his land in an ordinary way will not be liable for any damage to neighboring property unless he is negligent in some way. The case was dismissed.[146]

When the dangerous condition is artificially created the courts will look to whether the condition is abnormally dangerous. Some activities, such as high voltage lines, foundries and mining operations are normally dangerous activities. They will usually not be stopped by a neighbor's complaint because they are considered valuable to society. If anyone were able to object to high voltage lines next to their property, then there probably would not be any anywhere.

However, where an activity is abnormally dangerous, it may become either a public or a private nuisance and may be stopped by governmental action or by a private law suit.

War stories: When Central Power Company began distributing electric power in Bucyrus, Ohio, the residents along Southern Avenue were upset that a 66,000 volt line was to run down their street. They filed suit, but the court held that high voltage lines are not a nuisance unless they are not constructed properly. Putting a pole in the middle of someone's driveway was actionable, however, and the owners whose driveways were blocked were entitled to injunctions.[147]

The Grand River Dam Authority entered into a contract with the City of Wagoner, Oklahoma to supply electricity to the city and to construct transmission lines. Knowing how eager some people are to file lawsuits, Grand River first filed its own petition with the Supreme Court of Oklahoma to request a ruling on the legality of its contract. The court ruled that its contract was legal and that the property owners adjacent to streets where the transmission lines would be built could not claim that the lines were a nuisance.[148]

After harvesting his crop of grass seed on 55 acres near I-5 in Linn County, Oregon, Kenneth Roth burned the field. Subsequently, the fire spread to other properties, including that of George and Agnes Koos, whose damages amounted to $8,017.00. It would be hard to tell by the record of this case that the amount involved was not much higher than many small claims cases. The Industrial Forestry Ass'n., the Oregon Seed Council, the Oregon Seed Trade Ass'n., the Oregon Rygrass Growers Ass'n., the Oregon Farm Bureau Federation and the Field Burning Defense Committee all sent their lawyers into the action and the case involved two appeals to the Oregon Court of Appeals and one to the Oregon Supreme Court. The trial court held that if the person burning the field was careful and the fire was caused by something such as an unexpected whirlwind rather than negligence, then there would be no liability. But the Oregon Supreme Court said that burning a field was an abnormally dangerous activity and where one of two innocent persons must suffer, it should be the one who engaged in the dangerous activity.[149]

Where Emigrant Industrial Savings Bank stored a large quantity of tanks of explosive gas under high pressure in a congested area of New York City, a court ruled that this could constitute a nuisance.[150]

On October 25, 1935, some children were playing around a road improvement project funded by the WPA in Newcomb, Tennessee. The road crews had failed to tightly close some drums of asphalt and the children were putting sticks in the barrels and playing with the substance. When one child attempted to throw a lit match into one of the barrels it caused an explosion killing two children and seriously burning a third. In a suit against the county, the judge awarded the families of two of the victims $6,000 and $2,000. On appeal to the Tennessee Supreme Court the judgment was reversed and the case dismissed. The court said that it would like to find a remedy for the families but that there was none since the barrels were not a nuisance without the negligent act of the road hands in failing to tighten the caps.[151]

Four days before Christmas, 1916 a fire started at the Pierce-Fordyce Oil. Assn. in Abilene, Texas when an employee lit an oil stove and left it unattended for half an hour. The fire ignited 12,000 gallons of kerosene and 300 gallons of gasoline on the premises and this mixture ran out of the building and into the street. As it flowed down the street its path was blocked by an earthen dam thrown up by employees of the Producers' Oil Co. After reaching the dam it flowed toward some residences and set them ablaze. Gilbert McGuffey lost his houses and their contents in the fire. He sued the Pierce-Fordyce Oil. Assn. but lost because the court held that the earthen dam was the cause of his fire. On appeal the court held that the storage of dangerous materials could constitute a nuisance and that he was entitled to a new trial on that basis.[152]

John Brownsey was visiting his friend, Fitzsimmons, in Hudson County, New Jersey on February 5, 1936, tinkering with an automobile in the yard, when a four foot by eight foot icy mass over eight inches thick slid off the roof of the neighbor's garage and seriously injured him. The court held the neighbor liable because the structure of the roof was not a natural one and the sliding of the ice was foreseeable.[153]

Situations where there was a condition which was dangerous only to persons who enter a piece of property usually come up only after someone is injured. For adults this situation can be avoided by never entering the dangerous property. However, if a dangerous situation exists on a neighbor's property, it may attract children who are not wise enough to avoid it.

Unfortunately, if the situation does not violate a specific law, there is probably not a civil remedy for it.

War story: James Kilts was killed when a platform at the top of a water tower he was working on gave way and he fell 80 feet to the earth. Lena Kilts, James' wife, brought suit for wrongful death against the board of supervisors who authorized the erection of the tower, Stevens & Ziesse the contractors building the tower, and the Grand Rapids Bridge Co. a subcontractor who furnished material. The jury returned a verdict against the Bridge Co. for $5,000. Lena appealed. The Michigan Supreme Court affirmed, holding that the board of supervisors, likewise, was not liable; the water tower was not a nuisance since it did not pose an impending danger to the public.[154]

The best advice that can be given is to warn the owner (and the tenant if the property is leased) of the hazard and to point out that children are attracted to it. This should be done in a letter sent by certified mail. If the letter is sent by an attorney it will be even better. The letter is important because once a person is on notice of these things there is a greater chance of holding him liable. Possibly the letter alone will be enough to convince the owner or tenant to remedy the situation.

Dangerous Buildings

A building or structure which is dangerous is the easiest problem to solve. Whether it is in danger of falling down or causing risk to children who play in the area, the remedy is to call building, health or zoning officials. In most cases it is a violation of some code for the structure to remain in a dangerous condition.
Even if the structure does not violate some specific code, it still may be considered by a court to be a nuisance. If it is a danger to the public at large it may be a public nuisance and if it is a danger just to the neighbors it may be a private nuisance.

War stories: While Stella Gvoic was in Europe, a building she owned at 308-10 Woodward Avenue, Detroit, Michigan, was found by the city inspectors to be in imminent danger of collapse. The city took action to begin the demolition itself, but but before it could do so the building collapsed and damaged the property at 302-4 Woodward Ave. owned by Fred Oxenrider. He sued Ms. Gvoic for the keeping of a dangerous condition constituting a nuisance. However, the court ruled that the actions by the city in taking control of the building relieved her of her liability.[155]

The Andersons owned property at 10550 Avenue M. in Chicago. Mr. Mitchell was building on the adjoining property. On November 17, 1926, the north wall of the building Mitchell was erecting collapsed and part of it fell onto the Andersons' property doing considerable damage. The court held that the falling of the wall raised a presumption of negligence on the part of Mr. Mitchell, and that Mr. Mitchell must then overcome that presumption. The court held that Mr. Mitchell was not required, though, to prove that the accident could not have been prevented by the use of ordinary care. It would be enough to overcome the presumption of negligence if Mitchell gave proof merely sufficient to rebut the inference that he had not used due care.[156]

When Ole McDonald's Farms, Inc. built its sewage oxidation pond on its property in East Baton Rouge Parish, Louisiana, it built it a few feet from the property line of its neighbors, the Androwskis. Since the law forbid a residence within 200 feet of such a pond, this meant the Androwskis could not use much of their land to build a subdivision. In a lawsuit the court ruled that the Androwskis were entitled to damages.[157]

John Bertch was the owner of a boathouse and fishing tackle on the banks of the St. Joseph River in Elkhart, Indiana in July, 1902 when a 50 x 80 foot ice house, 30 feet high, toppled over and knocked it into the river. It was then washed over the nearby dam and lost or destroyed. Mr. Bertch sued the St. Joseph Ice Company for maintaining the building in a dangerous condition. But his complaint was dismissed because he did not allege that his boathouse was legally where it was and if he was trespassing on the land he would have no right to collect.[158]

Chapter 22 Easements

In some situations, property owners need or desire to make use of property owned by a neighbor. The need will usually be for physical access to the property, but it can also be for water rights, electrical lines, a better view or some other benefit. When neighbors disagree on the extent of these rights, they often end up in court where their rights are determined by common law principles of easement developed over several hundred years.

An **easement** is the right of one party to use land owned by another party. For example, a person whose property is not on a road may have an easement across another property to use as access to the road.

There are several categories of easements. Easements can be "appurtenant" or "in gross." Appurtenant means that the easement is a benefit to another particular piece of land. The easement for access just mentioned would be appurtenant. An easement in gross is one which can benefit anyone without relation to a piece of property, such as an easement giving someone the right to use a lake for fishing and recreation. When an easement is appurtenant, the property which owns the easement right is said to be the dominant estate and the one subject to the easement is said to be the servient estate.

An easement can also be either "affirmative" or "negative." An affirmative easement means that the holder of the easement can do something on the other person's land, such as cross over it. A negative easement means that the servient estate is not allowed to do some act, such as build higher than a certain height.

Under English common law there were only a limited number of types of easements, such as for access to property, for water, for light or for air. But American courts have recognized easements for all kinds of things. Some examples are easements for scenic view, for grazing cattle or for the right to flood land.

Creation of easements

There are four traditional ways that easements can be created, by express grant, by necessity, by implication and by prescription. In addition, easements may be created by laws passed by the states

An easement by express grant can be created by a deed or a will. For example one property owner may pay another for a deed of an easement over his land. Or, someone deeding property to another person may state in the deed that he reserves an easement to himself and his heirs. A person leaving property by will may create easements as part of the disposition of his property.

An easement by necessity is recognized where a person has no other access to his property. For example if a piece of land located on a road is divided into front and back halves, and the back half has no other access to a road, then a court would rule that the parcel in back has an "easement by necessity" across the front parcel for access to the road.

An easement by implication is one which is implied from the circumstances, even though it has not been put in writing. This would be similar to an easement by necessity, except it would be required that the easement area have been used continuously prior to the severance of the properties.

An easement by prescription is one which is created by constant use of property over a long period of time. This is similar to adverse possession as discussed in the chapter on boundaries. The basic rule is that if a person "open and notoriously" uses another's property without permission for a long enough period of time, that person can acquire some legal rights to the property.

In extraordinary cases state legislatures have created easements to protect traditional rights.

War story: When the idea of property ownership was introduced to Hawaii, a statute was passed to protect the ancient gathering rights of the native Hawaiians. Under the law, certain Hawaiians can enter the private property of others to gather certain leaves and herbs. When William Kalipi attempted to assert his rights against land owned by Hawaiian Trust Company, Ltd. his claim was denied because he no longer lived in the area and the rights only belonged to those who lived adjacent to the land.[159]

Scope of Rights

Disputes often arise when one party wishes to expand or limit the use of an easement. This can happen when the holder of the easement wants to start making a much greater use of the easement or when the owner of the servient property wants to use his property in a way which will limit the rights of the easement owner.

The court decisions on easements over the years have usually recognized the principle that easements are limited to their original uses except that they may be expanded by reasonable development and modernization.

War stories: An easement was acquired by prescription across the property of the Boston & Maine Railroad for access to a house and stable. Later two additional buildings were built on the property, each with two dwelling units. Suit was brought against the railroad to restore the path the people used across the easement. The court noted that although most cases hold that the rights in an easement gained by prescription cannot be enlarged, in this case the change was not in kind of use, but in quantity of people. It held that the people had a right to continued use of the easement.[160]

When Will Brown and his wife bought a lot next to their property so that they could build a new residence straddling the two lots their neighbors, Fred and Hattie Voss placed logs and a fence across an easement the Browns had across their property. The Vosses claimed that using the easement to access the additional parcel was beyond the scope of the easement. The Browns sued and won the right to use the easement. The Vosses appealed and the judgment was reversed. The Browns appealed to the Washington Supreme Court and the original opinion was reinstated. The Browns were given the right to use the easement even though they then owned an additional lot because there was no additional burden placed on the Voss property. The easement would still be used only for access to a single family home.[161]

Shady Shore was a subdivision on Lake Huron described as "the most beautiful of all Port Huron's beautiful beaches." The lots were large and intended for expensive single family dwellings. There was no public roadway through the plat for access to the beach as it was the intention that the beach would be exclusively for the use of the lot owners. Each lot owner held an easement for access to the beach. Richard Foreman and others bought three lots and subdivided them into 26 lots. They put up a sign welcoming people to the beach and sold several of the lots. The cottages built on the lots were rented out for short periods of time and the people visiting the beach would make commotion on the beach which would annoy the residents of the neighborhood. The Supreme Court of Michigan found that this increased the burden on the easement beyond that contemplated at the time the easement was created. It was meant for three families to have access to the beach, not 26. The court approved a permanent injunction against use of the easement.[162]

When the state highway department purchased a lot behind Grace Cameron's property on North Street in Carlisle,
Kentucky with plans to use its easement across her property to move trucks and equipment she sued. The suit was
dismissed. The court noted that the easement had been
used for animals and farm machinery and said that "as the
passage of time creates new needs and the uses of property
change, a normal change in the manner of using a passway
does not constitute a deviation from the original grant, and
modern transportation uses are not restricted to the ancient modes of travel.[163]

In the late 1930s the California-Michigan Land & Water Co.
began competing with the city of Pasadena, California for
customers in the area between Arcadia and Pasadena.
When the company began laying water pipes with the
permission of the property owners in the same five-foot
strip of land where the city had its easement, the city
complained. It said that the company could not put its
pipes where it had the easement. The court didn't buy the
argument and the city appealed to the Supreme Court of
California. The court noted that easement law allows an
owner to make any use of his land that does not interfere
with the rights of the easement holder. It held that the
owner could grant rights to others to use the area covered
by the easement and also held that if the city ever needs to
use the entire space of its easement it could then take legal
action.[164]

Melvin Kelly and Florence Jaris owned 6.05 acres of land in
Jefferson County, Missouri. The deed granting them the
land also granted them an easement to the county road.
The easement ran across the land of Lee and Katie Schmelz.
When Mr. Kelly and Ms. Jaris attempted to have the electric
company install poles and wires in order to get electricity,
the Schmelz's refused to allow the poles across their land.
Mr. Kelly and Ms. Jaris brought suit to enjoin the Schmelz'a
from interfering with the installation of the poles and
wires. The district court denied relief. The Appeals court
held that the Schmelz's had not shown that the placing of
the poles and wires would result in any damage to them,
their refusal to permit the electric company to erect the
poles and wires effectively precluded plaintiffs from obtaining electricity,andtherefore the actions constituted an

interference with plaintiffs' use of the easement. The court granted the injunction.[165]

Walter Ward and Robert McGlory owned adjoining tracts of land which were once part of a single tract. When the tracts were divided, Robert McGlory was given an easement for a right of way since his land was inaccessible to the public road. Seven years later, in 1955, McGlory erected two poles supporting electric wires about ten feet from the roadway on Ward's land. Ward opposed this but took no action until several years later when he sued to require McGlory to remove the poles. The lower court judge held the easement granting a right of way conveyed by implication the right to erect poles and maintain electric wires. He dismissed the case. The Supreme Judicial Court of Massachusetts reversed, holding that the poles violated the terms of the easement since they were not specifically granted and were ten feet from the roadway which was the easement. They held the poles constituted a trespass. The court also held the Mass. Electric Co. responsible for trespass of electric current across Ward's land.[166]

The owner of the land subject to the easement can still use the land for any purpose that does not affect the rights of the owner of the easement.

War story: In New York about a hundred years ago a gentleman purchased a 40 x 900 foot easement over the land of Charles Roberts for use as access to his country estate. The land was rocky and had to be cleared. After it was cleared Mr. Roberts began using it to carry produce and farming utensils. This caused deep ruts in the road. Mr. Roberts also set some stones in the road which obstructed passage. The court ordered him not to use the easement in such a way as to interfere in its use for carriages.[167]

Transfer of Easements

The general rule is that easements appurtenant are automatically transferred with the dominant property when it is, and that easements in gross usually cannot be transferred.

Easements in gross usually cannot be transferred because they many end up in the hands of numerous parties and heirs of parties which would make it difficult to clear title to the land. An exception to this is that easements of a commercial nature may be transferred. Also, in a few jurisdictions all easements may be freely transferred.

An easement appurtenant cannot be severed from the land and transferred to a third party without the consent of the land the easement crosses.

Termination of Easements

In most cases an easement is permanent and will last forever. However, there are certain circumstances under which an easement can be terminated. Some of these are mutual agreement, abandonment, merger, prescription and forfeiture.

War story: A parcel of land in Atherton, California owned by Mr. and Mrs. Walton Gould had access by way of an easement over the land of Mary Crimmins and others. The Goulds also owned a larger parcel next door, but that parcel had access through another road. When the Goulds subdivided the two parcels into 29 lots they made the sole access to the property across the easement. In legal action by Ms. Crimmins the court ruled that the Goulds could not expand the use of the easement by adding all of the lots of the second parcel, and that by dedicating the subdivision roads to the public the Goulds lost their right to use the easement.[168]

Chapter 23 Electromagnetic Waves

Radio, television, telephone and other electromagnetic waves are a relatively new topic for the legal system to deal with. However, principles used in related areas have been used when problems with these matters have come up.

Generally, like the situation with view, light and air, courts have found no rights to the reception of electromagnetic waves. An owner of property can build upon his property without worry about the effect on TV or radio reception at neighboring properties.

War story: When Sears Roebuck & Co. began building their 110-story headquarters in Chicago, surrounding property owners were concerned that it would disturb their radio and television reception. The Illinois Supreme Court ruled that unless there was a law against it, a landowner had a right to construct a 110-story building. Television reception was not a right protected by law.[169]

When a person produces electromagnetic waves and these cause a problem for the neighbors, this is a completely different situation and the waves produced can be deemed a nuisance.

War story: After Page County Appliance Center in Shenandoah, Iowa noticed that the reception of its televisions had suddenly deteriorated, it discovered that at the same time a new computer system had been installed at the neighboring Central Travel Service office. The computers were manufactured by Honeywell, Inc. and placed by ITT Travel Services. After installation of the computers several of the televisions no longer worked properly. Honeywell technicians made several service calls to investigate the problem, but it turned out to be a design problem and not a service problem. The appliance store was told that Honeywell was "way over budget" on the computer and "if you don't like it you can move." The appliance store filed suit and won. The court rejected the argument that the televisions were an extra sensitive use of the property and precluded a finding of nuisance.[170]

Chapter 24 Encroachments

An encroachment exists where a structure on one person's property crosses the property line onto the neighboring owner's property. An encroachment may be as small as a roof edge hanging one inch over the line or as big as an entire house being built on the wrong lot.

War stories:When Mary Cox built a poured concrete wall on her property in Hammond, Indiana, no paper was used to separate her wall from the adjacent building. Therefore the concrete ran into all of the cracks and crevices in her neighbor, Mr. Weis' wall. In 99.999% of the cases this would have gone unnoticed forever, but as fate would have it, the street in front of the properties was widened and Mr. Weis needed to have his two-story brick building moved back. After all preparations were made, including a new foundation it was discovered that the two buildings were stuck together. Weis sued to force Ms. Cox to remove the concrete, and the court ruled that concrete filling the cracks in a wall would constitute a trespass. However, since the court believed that Mr. Weis knew about and allowed the concrete to be poured in that manner, it did not order the trespass to be removed.[171]

When the Wells Amusement Co. in Anniston, Alabama added an amusement center to its property, it used the wall of a neighboring building against which to attach its roof. Apparently, the company wanted to avoid the cost of building its own wall and was using the side of the building as the interior wall of its amusement center. The court held that this was an encroachment and it was ordered removed.[172]

If an encroachment is left unchallenged for a long enough period of time the owner of it may acquire a permanent right to maintain it. This is called a right by prescription. It is similar to adverse possession and often the time period required is twenty years.

In some areas there are laws regulating the rights of the parties in the case of encroachments. For example in New York there is a law which states that if an encroachment is of six inches or less no court action can be brought more that one year after the encroachment starts.

An encroachment has been considered as both a nuisance and a trespass, but it more technically falls into the definition of a trespass. As a trespass it entitles the owner to monetary damages, whether he has suffered any actual losses or not. (See chapter 46.) This also means that the doctrine of de minimis (the law is not concerned with trifles) does not apply. An encroachment of one inch is considered serious.

War story: In order to protect his property in Pulaski County, Arkansas from water running off his neighbor's property, E. L. Glendenning had a 140 foot long stone and cement wall built. Unfortunately, 26 feet of it encroached a few inches onto his neighbor W. B. Leffingwell's property. Mr. Leffingwell filed suit to require removal of the wall. The trial judge ruled that there was an encroachment, but that it was minimal and that Mr. Glendenning should not have to go through the trouble and expense of removing it. The Supreme Court of Arkansas disagreed, saying that the doctrine that the law does not concern itself with trifles does not apply to invasion of real estate. It ordered the wall moved.[173]

An owner whose property is encroached upon has the right to personally remove the encroachment as long as he doesn't cause any additional damages.

War stories: The Bijou Theater in Racine, Wisconsin had a gutter which projected over the property next door. When the neighbor, Jens P. Christensen, made plans to build a taller building he asked several times that the gutter be removed. Finally, his workmen had to remove it and in doing so an opening was left in the roof which allowed rain and snow to get in. Mr. Christensen was not liable for the damage because the work had been done properly and he had a right to remove the gutter.[174]

Before Jacob Guttenkunst began excavation for his cellar, he gave notice to his neighbor, Theodore Lapp, who had a stone cellar wall next door. During the excavation it was discovered that a stone from Mr. Lapp's wall projected into Mr. Gutenkunst's property. Mr. Lapp agreed to pay $30 for removal of the encroachment. During the work Mr. Lapp's wall collapsed causing $1068 in damages. In a lawsuit for the $1068 damages Mr. Guttenkunst countersued for $30 and for his additional costs in removing the debris from the fallen wall. A jury ruled for Mr. Guttenkunst and awarded him one cent. On appeal the court held that Mr. Lapp had

the duty to shore up his own wall and that Mr. Guttekunst
was not liable for the collapse of the wall unless he was
negligent in the work he agreed to do for $30.[175]

If the owner does not wish to or cannot remove the encroachment,
he can bring a court action. This would be a civil action and he could
not get government help, such as the sheriff.

In the court action the owner could force the encroachment to be
removed or he could seek monetary damages.

War stories: In 1924 Isaac E. Brody built a concrete block garage on his
property with a concrete roof and a large driveway. It was
built in such a way that water from the roof and driveway
poured onto his neighbor Bessie Marcus's property. She
hired a surveyor who discovered that the garage was built
about two inches over the property line. She sued asking
that he be forced to remove the garage from her property,
stop draining water into her yard and to not park more
than two cars in his garage. The court ordered that Mr.
Brody stop the water from draining on her property, but
since her two inches of property were worth $5 and moving
the garage would cost $500, it held that he would not have
to move it if he paid her $5. She appealed and the Supreme
Court of Massachusetts held that the garage was trespassing and must be moved. But it said that parking three cars
in the garage was not a nuisance.[176]

Ben Schwartz owned a lot at 920 F Street in Washington
D.C. The adjoining lot was home to the Atlantic Building.
Part of the rear wall of the Atlantic Building was built upon
Schwartz's lot. When Schwartz began to erect a building
on his lot, he sought to use the Atlantic Building's wall as
a party wall. The defendant agreed, but later notified
Schwartz that the wall was not a party wall. When Swartz
dug trenches in order to build his own wall, he discovered
that the footing of the wall encroached upon his land about
two feet along the length of the wall. Schwartz began using
the wall as a party wall, and sued to force defendant to
remove the encroachment. The court held it would not
force defendant to remove the footing since Schwartz
elected to use the wall as a party wall. They held he could
remove the footings, without impairing the wall, at his
own cost.[177]

A concrete bulkhead built by Nelie Parks on her property in Seattle, Washington, settled a few inches onto the property of her neighbor George Wells. He filed suit and was awarded $1 in damages, and Ms. Parks was ordered to move the bulkhead within 60 days. On appeal she argued that it was doing no damage but would be very costly to remove, so the legal maxim *de minimis non curat lex* (the law does not concern itself with trifles) should apply. The court held that on a city lot an irregular lot could result in serious building complications and that the maxim should not apply.[178]

When Sol Gerber built a laundry and dry cleaning establishment next door to William Gerring's residence at 333 Meigs Street in Rochester, New York, Mr. Gerring had several complaints. Among them was the fact that footings encroached between 0.1 foot and 0.38 foot, the windowsills encroached and the windows encroached two feet when they were opened. The court ordered Mr. Gerber to remove all of the encroachments except for the footings more than one foot below grade.[179]

After buying a lot on Redwood Avenue in Sacramento County, California, Fred Phillips discovered that his neighbor Charles Isham's carport and hedge encroached on a 4.5 foot triangle of his property. He brought a suit for removal of the encroachment. The court refused to order removal but ordered Mr. Isham to pay him $250 to purchase the property from him. Not wanting to sell the property he appealed. The appeals court noted that where there is great hardship in removing an encroachment it will not be ordered, but held that in this case there was no extreme hardship. It noted that while Mr. Isham's driveway would not be wide enough for a car, he could still use the alley for access to his lot.[180]

When the Odd Fellows Lodge in Lane County, Oregon and the owner of the surrounding property and Fisherman's Wharf discovered that their buildings overlapped on each others' properties they exchanged five-foot strips of land. However, the surveyor did not notice that the lodge was built at an angle and that it encroached a few inches at one end. A subsequent owner of the surrounding property noticed that the eves of the building encroached even more and that the building leaned against his building. He filed suit and the court ordered the lodge to jack up its building to stop the leaning and to remove the eaves, but it declined to order that the entire building be moved to eliminate the encroachment on the rear of the building because the cost would be great and the benefit would be small.[181]

Usually the person who is liable for an encroachment is the owner of the property. But in some cases if a contractor or tenant cause the encroachment and the owner was blameless, then the proper party to sue would be the person who caused it.

War story: Max Wahl owned a building in Madison, Wisconsin in the 1920's when Beecroft Building Co. contracted to build a theater on the lot it owned next door. The contractor subcontracted the excavation and masonry work out to John H. Kelly. After excavation part of the soil caved in and when the concrete was poured it extended onto Mr. Wahl's property. In a suit against the owner, contractor and subcontractor, the court held that while the contractor would not have any liability to the adjacent owner, the subcontractor could be liable if his negligence caused the encroachment.[182]

Chapter 25 Excavations and Support

It is an established principle of American property law that a landowner has a duty to maintain lateral support to adjoining properties. This means that you cannot dig a hole on your land if it will cause your neighbor's land to cave in. If you do need to dig a hole, such as an excavation for a basement, it is your duty to shore up your neighbor's property and keep it from caving in.

A limit to the duty to provide support is a rule that one only has to provide support to the land in its natural condition, not to any extra weight placed on it by such things as buildings. This rule has resulted in many court cases fighting over whether the weight of a building caused the cave-in or whether it would have caved in even without the building. The number of cases on this issue show how difficult it is to determine what caused the cave-in. In most cases expert engineers must be called in and the jury must decide which one is more believable.

An exception to this exception (Who said law was easy?) is where the excavator was negligent. If an excavator carefully shores up a building when he is excavating, and it settles anyway, he is not liable. But if the owner can convince a jury that the excavator did something wrong, or that he didn't do enough to shore up the building the excavator can be held liable. Thus more experts and lawyers are needed.

War stories: In the 1950s Mr. & Mrs. Chang lived on a sloping lot in Hawaii. To level their property they built an eighteen foot high retaining wall. Years later the wall collapsed causing personal injuries and property damage to Joseph and Catherine Fung who live on the slope below them. The Changs were held liable for the damages when the court ruled that a property owner has the responsibility to see that his retaining wall is built properly.[183]

In 1964, Mr. and Mrs. William H. Noone became aware that their home on the side of a mountain in Glen Ferris, West Virginia was slowly slipping down the side of the mountain. The cause of the slippage, they felt, was the failure of their neighbor down the hill, Marion T. Price, to maintain a retaining wall which had been built around 1919. The wall was four feet high, was entirely on the neighbor's property and it had fallen into disrepair when she had bought her property in 1955. The Noones spent $6,000 to repair their house and sued Ms. Price for $50,000 for failure to provide support for their property. (Lawyers like to start with big figures so that you will feel better about giving them the smaller figure.) Their case was dismissed but the Supreme Court of West Virginia took their appeal. It ruled that if they could prove that the land would have subsided even without the weight of their house on it, then they could collect. Otherwise they could collect nothing.[184]

After buying some lots on a terraced hillside north of Hollywood Blvd. in Hollywood, California, De Witt Mortgage and Realty Co. excavated one of the lots 20 feet to bring the level even to that of its other lots. A few days after the work was done the adjacent lot caved in and lost two-thirds of its area. The owner of the lot, Charles F. Harper Co. sued and was awarded $200 in damages (It was 1926). The court ruled that even if the person excavating his lot was not negligent, he can be held liable for damages caused by his removal or lateral support for a neighbor's land.[185]

Emilie McCabe sued the City of Parkersburg for trespass and sought to recover damages caused by the undermining and sloughing away of her lot and the settling of her house allegedly caused by the city's collection of large quantities of rain and surface waters through its sewage system, which allowed the waters to be cast upon her property. The jury returned a $4,000 verdict in Emilie's favor. The Appeals court reversed, finding reversible error in the judge's instruction that it was the city's duty to keep storm sewers in a condition as not to permit water in them to escape and damage others' property. The court also held that a city only owes its citizens reasonable care in avoiding damage to others' property when maintaining its sewerage system. The court stated she was entitled to recover only temporary damages measured by the cost of repairs and expenses. They set aside the verdict as it was excessive and the jury considered damage to the house, which it should not have done in reaching its decision.[186]

Mr. and Mrs. Athan T. Falangus hired a contractor and an architect to build an apartment building on property they owned on Queen Anne Hill in Seattle, Washington. The contractor, Mr. Kirsh, was negligent in failing to brace the adjacent property and damage was caused to two adjacent buildings. The adjacent owners won a judgment against both Mr. Kirsch and Mr. Falangus and their spouses. Because the constitution of the state of Washington requires compensation for the damaging of property, it did not matter that Mr. and Mrs. Falangus were not negligent. They were liable as the owners who had the work done, even though the negligence was the act of an independent contractor.[187]

In Lynchburg, Virginia, were adjoining lots, each occupied by light wooden buildings. After a fire had destroyed his building, Camillus Christian built a three-story brick store in its place. A.A. Tunstall later removed his wooden store to make way for a large and expensive building. He notified Christian to protect his property from any injury that might result due to the deep excavation. Christian claimed the excavations would destroy the foundation of his building and got a court order enjoining the excavating within ten feet of Christian's foundation. Tunstall appealed. The court held that Christian possessed no right to support for his building from the soil of the lot next door; that the fact Tunstall did not object to Christian erecting his building did not estop him from denying Christian's right to support for that building from Tunstall's soil; that Tunstall must use reasonable care in erecting his building, and that he would be answerable for all damage done to Christian's land if he did not use care; and that the notice Tunstall gave was reasonable. The order granting the injunction was reversed.[188]

John Hacker was excavating for erection of a building next to a two-story building owned by A. F. Jones and E. L. Shaw when the wall on their building fell. They sued but the court found that they were not entitled to any damages. Important to the court were the condition of the wall, the fact that the owners knew of the excavation but did nothing to brace it themselves, and that the excavators took ordinary and usual measures in their work.[189]

Grading the land is not quite so drastic as excavating it, but still has the potential for causing problems for neighbors.

War stories: W. J. Sime and Lisbeth S. Jensen were owners of adjacent homes on Chicago Avenue in Minneapolis in the 1940s. The land on which the homes were built sloped from Mr. Sime's to Ms. Jensen's and Mr. Sime raised his further, adding top soil and sod. Ms. Jensen removed the part of the slope which was on her side and left an upright earth bank. This bank crumbled and when Mr. Sime hired workmen to fix it they trespassed upon Ms. Jensen's land during a birthday party she was having. The parties could not come to an agreement over the proper slope and eventually wound up in court. The court ordered that a retaining wall be built at a cost of $90 and that Ms. Jensen pay for one-third of the cost. Being a person of principles, she appealed to the Supreme Court of Minnesota. The court ruled that where a party raised the level of his land he must bear the full cost of building a retaining wall.[190]

In preparing to build a house, Albert DiFilippo raised the grade of his lot on Horace Street in Providence, Rhode Island. Later, when it rained, large amounts of dirt and debris washed onto the property of his neighbors, Mr. and Mrs. Guido Tortolano. In a suit Mr. DiFilippo was ordered to stabilize the fill and the Tortolanos were awarded damages in the amount of the damage to their property.[191]

Another problem related to excavating occurs when one party digs under the property of another. Since a property owner owns from the center of the earth to the heavens, any digging under the surface is a trespass, and it has usually been accepted that the owner is entitled to be compensated. However, some courts have found exceptions to this rule.

War stories: During the California gold rush, Maye and Yappen were owners of adjoining mining claims. Yappen mined over the dividing line and worked on a portion of Maye's mining ground. Maye sued to recover damages of $2,000 in lost gold and land damage. Yappen claimed he was ignorant of the locality of the dividing line and did not willfully ignore it. The court held ignorance was not an excuse or justification and evidence of such ignorance should not have been let in at trial. Yappen had means of ascertaining the line, and was guilty of negligence for not doing so. The court remanded the case for a new trial but held the true measure of damages would be the value of the gold-bearing earth at the time it was separated form the surrounding soil, not the value of the gold. If demand was made for the gold after its removal from the earth, then damages would be the value of the gold.[192]

After purchasing the right to mine coal on 39 acres of land owned by Martha E. Helton in Knox County, Kentucky, the North Jellico Coal Co. caused injury to and took coal from other parts of her land. In a law suit claiming $1,350 for injury to her land and $20,000 for coal, a jury awarded $50 for injury to the land and $450 for the coal. The company appealed arguing, among other things, that the coal was valued too highly. The court ruled that where a person takes coal through an honest mistake the amount of damages is the value of the royalty usually paid for the right to mine. Where a person willfully takes the coal the damages are the value of the coal, without subtracting the cost of mining.[193]

Back around 1916 in Edmonson County, Kentucky, L. P. Edwards discovered a cave on his land. Because it was near the world famous Mammoth cave he was able to operate a profitable business of providing tours and running a motel business. However, part of the cave was located under the land of his neighbor, F. P. Lee. Mr. Lee sued for his share of the profits since the tours of the cave were trespassing onto his land. The lawyers of the parties had a field day. The litigation went on for over eight years and included four published appeals. Before it ended Mr. Lee had died and the suit had to be continued by his administrator. In the end, Mr. Lee's estate was awarded a portion of the profits based upon the percentage of the cave owned by Mr. Lee which was displayed to the public.[194]

After Henry Boehringer filed a complaint to foreclose a mortgage on property he had sold to Amelia Montalto and others, she counterclaimed that he had breached his covenant of title since he did not make an exception to the rights of the Bronx Valley sewer commission to put a sewer 150 feet under the surface of the property. The court noted that in the past a person was considered to own "from heaven to hell," but it rejected the notion, saying that the title to property would only extend to a point beyond which the owner may not reasonably make use of.[195]

When the Railroad Commission of Texas ordered the injection of salt water into a gas field to force out the gas, some of the neighbors sued saying that the water would trespass under their property. The neighbors won but the

> Supreme Court of Texas reversed, saying that trespass
> does not occur from the injections.[196]

In situations where the mineral rights are owned by someone other
the owner of the land itself, the owner of the mineral rights has the duty
to support the surface of the land and not allow it to collapse.

It is also possible for a person to remove support from a neighbor's
property without even going near it. If a person takes enough water out
of his well the water under neighboring properties will also be withdrawn. This can cause the neighboring properties to settle. Under the
ancient principles of water law, a person could withdraw unlimited
amounts of water from his own property without liability for what
might happen to his neighbors.

However, this doctrine has come into question in recent years and
some courts have begun to modify it.[197]

If the settling of the land causes damage to structures on the land,
the person who withdrew the water (or oil) may be liable. However, if
a landowner later builds a structure on his land which causes it to settle,
the person who originally withdrew the water would usually not be
liable.

War story: Smith-Southwest and other landowners in the Seabrook
and Clear Lake area of Harris County, Texas brought
action against Friendswood Development and its parent
corporation, Exxon, alleging that severe subsidence of
their lands was caused by Friendswood's past and continuing withdrawals of vast quantities of underground
water from wells on Friendsood's lands. The lower court
granted summary judgement to Friendswood and Exxon,
but the appeals court reversed. The Texas Supreme Court
reinstated the lower court's verdict but held that from then
on the negligent withdrawing of ground water which
results in subsidence of others' land would allow recovery.[198]

In some localities zoning laws have been passed which prohibit
excavations such as quarries which cause a lot of dust, noise and
vibrations. Some of these laws have been upheld, but others have been
thrown out.

War stories: A tract of 348 acres of land owned by Valley Real Estate
Company in the area of Sunland and Tujunga, California,

had great value as a sand and gravel excavation but had no other value because of the soil and flooding. In spite of this, the area was zoned to prohibit such operation. The rationale was that people moved to the area for the clean air and climate and that this would be ruined by such quarrying. On appeal to the California Supreme Court the zoning was upheld. Over the dissent of two justices, the court said that it was not unconstitutional to deprive the owners of the value of their property.[199]

Since uncontrolled operations would put a ton of dust an hour into the air and even controlled operations would put a ton of dust a day into the air, the Zoning Board forbid quarrying in West Whiteland Township, Pennsylvania. But the Supreme Court of Pennsylvania ruled that since the quarry was a mile from any residences and there was no evidence as to what effect the dust would have on anyone's health, they could not ban quarrying.[200]

Oakland Township, Michigan, passed a law called the "Conservation of Natural Resources Ordinance" which required landowners to obtain permits before mining gravel or other materials. When Lyon Sand and Gravel Co. applied for a permit it was denied. The company sued and had the law declared unconstitutional. The court noted that there were no objective standards for issuing or denying a permit and the act of denying a permit in the area where there were other such pits would amount to a confiscation of the landowner's property.[201]

Under a federal law, the Surface Mining Control and Reclamation Act of 1977,[202] some excavations for mining are required to replace the surface of the land after the mining operation has been completed.

In many states the common law rights and duties of landowners have been modified by statutes. Some of these laws require the support of land and the buildings on it and some require a landowner to support his own buildings. Other laws have rules which only apply when excavations or foundations are made to certain depths.

Chapter 26 Fences

Even the lowly fence can cause innumerable problems between neighbors. It can be too high, too short, too ugly, in the wrong place or too dangerous. There can even be a problem if a person doesn't put up a fence at all.

Under basic principles of law, every property owner has a right to build a fence around his property, but no property owner has a duty to build a fence. However, there are numerous exceptions to this basic rule.

The most common exception is where there is a statute or ordinance requiring or controlling fences. In both rural and urban areas governmental bodies have found it necessary to regulate fences. In rural areas the perceived need is to keep grazing animals confined. In urban areas the perceived need can range from safety to aesthetics.

Rural Areas

In some states the laws allow for fencing districts and even fence boards. These groups make decisions on location and payment for needed fences. The idea is to fairly apportion the cost of keeping all the ranches or farms fenced. The districts often levy a tax or assessment on the different owners to pay for the fences. People who fail to pay the assessment can lose their property in foreclosure.

War story: When her mother died in 1926, Rosie Byrum inherited 50 acres of land in Jefferson County, Arkansas. During the depression the fence tax of 30 cents a year was not paid for 4 years and a suit was filed to foreclose the lien. In 1938 the land was sold for $4.84 to Robert Shelton. Shelton then took possession of the property from the tenant to whom Ms. Byrom had rented it. She filed suit asking the court to cancel the sale to Mr. Shelton. The court noted that the original assessment and the sale of the property had been in the name of the wrong party and the description of the property in the sale had been abbreviated so much that it was not a legal description of the property.[203]

Some areas have "fence viewers" which are people who go out to the land and decide which landowner is responsible for building or repairing which parts of a fence. Fence viewers may be elected or appointed and they must take an oath of office. When landowners in these areas have a dispute over a fence, they can take their problem to the local fence viewers for a decision.

War story: When the fence between Etta Butman's property at 194
             Chesnut Street, Chelsea, Massachusetts and the property
             at 192 Chesnut street deteriorated, the Fence Viewers of
             Chelsea were called in. At a hearing the fence viewers
             decided that the fence was "shaky, rotted away in many
             places, loose, improperly anchored to the ground and lacks
             stability against wind pressure creating a potential haz-
             ard." The fence viewers decided that Ms. Butman and her
             neighbor should each tear down half the fence and build a
             new one within 30 days. Apparently thinking that she was
             living in a free country, she filed suit. The local court
             disagreed with her so she appealed to the Supreme Court
             of Massachusetts. After reviewing the Massachusetts stat-
             ute and constitutional principles, the court decided that
             none of Ms. Butman's rights had been violated.[204]

In some areas the fence laws make clear what kind of fence is suitable and legal. Where there are no specifications in the law a fence must be strong enough to turn away ordinary livestock.

War story: One of the events of the summer of '42 which didn't make
             it into the movie of the same name was that some of Chester
             W. Bryson's cattle escaped into his field in Strafford County,
             New Hampshire, and destroyed some of his corn and hay.
             He filed suit against his neighbor, John E. Carroll, claiming
             that Mr. Carroll failed to keep part of their fence in repair.
             It was Mr. Carroll's responsibility to keep the fence re-
             paired, but he had previously told Mr. Bryson that he could
             not keep the fence repaired because there was a "fence
             breaker" in Mr. Bryson's herd. This was a cow which could
             break through almost any fence. The court ruled that Mr.
             Carroll was not liable for the damage because he did not
             legally have to make an impassible fence, only one strong
             enough to stop ordinary cattle.[205]

Where fences are required by law they may be placed equally on the land of adjoining owners. This is also true in areas where zigzag fences such as Virginia fences or worm fences are the custom. However, where more than half of a fence is built on one person's land without his consent, he is entitled to relief.

War story: Washington Rose and Albert Linderman were adjacent
            landowners in Michigan in 1907. When they got into a
            controversy over their property line Mr. Linderman called
            out the fence viewers to decide who was responsible for the
            fence. He then built a "stump fence" composed of tree
            stumps lying with the stump on his side and the trunk on
            the neighbor's side. The stump fence took up a strip of land
            five to five and a half feet wide. Most of the way, two thirds
            or more of the fence was on Mr. Rose's property. Mr. Rose
            sued and the trial court ruled that this was not illegal. He
            appealed to the Michigan Supreme Court and they ruled
            that the fence must be equally on each side of the boundary
            line.[206]

When a person builds a partition fence as required by law, he has
a right to enter the property of the adjoining owners as necessary to
complete the construction and may not be charged with trespass.

In some areas a person may be liable for triple damages for
destroying a person's fence.

War story: John Mayer and K & E Land and Cattle, Inc. were adjoining
            landowners in Elvira Township, Buffalo County, South
            Dakota. At a trapshoot in November, 1980 at the American
            Legion Club in Gann Valley at which "alcohol was freely
            consumed" Mr. Mayer and Kenneth Wulff of K & E got
            into a disagreement about the fence. Mr. Mayer then went
            home and tore out 165 feet of the fence with his tractor. Mr.
            Wulff repaired the fence at a cost of $199.60 and sued Mr.
            Mayer for triple damages and punitive damages. After a
            jury trial, Mr. Wulff was awarded $199.60 plus triple
            damages of $598.80 plus $7,000.00 punitive damages. This
            award was upheld by the Supreme Court of South Da-
            kota.[207]

Even if there is no law requiring a fence, owners of livestock are
required to keep their animals on their property. Therefore, persons
raising animals on their lands may be required to build fences to keep
them in.

War story: Donald Dasilva was injured when a horse wandered onto
            a public road from a boarding stable. The stable was on
            land owned by May L. Rotolante, but she had leased it to
            a tenant who operated the stable. Mr. Dasilva sued Ms.
            Rotolante as the owner of the land and won a judgment

against her. She appealed the judgment and it was thrown out. The court ruled that since Ms. Rotolante merely owned the land and had no custody or control of the horse, she had no duty to maintain a fence on the land. Because it was the tenant's horse and the tenant had control of the land, it would be the tenant who would be responsible for any injuries.[208]

Where there is some requirement to build a fence, a person failing to do so can be liable for injuries caused by his failure to do so.

War story: Fred Stallings and J. R. Adair had an agreement as to which parts of the fence between their properties in Hemphill County, Texas, each was going to maintain. Mr. Adair failed to keep his section in repair and his cattle trespassed onto Mr. Stallings land, causing damage to his crops. Mr. Stallings sued and was awarded $166 in damages.[209]

Urban areas

Fence laws are much more complicated in urban than in rural areas. There are often regulations as to height, composition and location. In some areas fences may even be forbidden. These rules may be contained in either local laws or in property restrictions.

Dangerous fences

Whether a person is liable for injury caused by his dangerous fence is determined by the law related to negligence. Under general principles of negligence law a person is not liable to trespassers, is required to warn guests of any known dangerous conditions and is required to provide safe conditions for business visitors to the property. Of course, there have been numerous exceptions to these general rules.

Where a fence is unusually dangerous, especially if it is built along a well-traveled road without warnings being posted, the owner may be liable for injuries to travelers.

War stories: Charles F. Gardner and others owned some land in Lasses County, California in the 1880s and enclosed it with a barbed wire fence. The fence posts were 36 feet apart and the first strand of barbed wire 24 inches off the ground. Some horses owned by F. C. Loveland came in contact with the fence and were seriously injured. Some of them died.

Mr. Loveland sued the owners for negligence and won. Gardner appealed to the Supreme Court of California and the court upheld his liability. The court noted that the wire was hanging loosely between the posts and that California law stated that a good fence would have the posts not more than eight feet apart and the first wire not more than eighteen inches off the ground. It said that property owners are not required to fence their land but if they fence it negligently they are liable for injuries caused by it.[210]

The Abilene Cotton Oil Co. was next door to Delk School House and church in Jones County, Texas, and shared a common road with them. Because of wandering cattle the company installed a barbed wire fence around the place on September 11, 1900. Part of the fence crossed the road and the manager of the company, John Guitar, stayed until 8:30 that night to warn people away. About 9:00, 20 year old I. J. Briscoe came riding down the road and rode into the fence killing his father's horse and crippling himself for life. In a suit against the company his father was awarded $385 for the horse and he was awarded $6,000 for his injuries.[211]

Leonard Herdt, Jr., a ten year old boy was leaning over the top board on a fence at 3874 Kosciusco Street, St. Louis, Missouri, adjacent to a rock quarry, when it came loose allowing him to fall to the bottom of the quarry. He "received serious and painful injuries by coming in contact with the stones below." His family sued the owner of the quarry but lost the suit because the court held that the boy was negligent. Evidence showed that he was a bright intelligent boy, had been warned repeatedly about the danger of playing near the quarry, had been driven away from it and had been whipped by his father several times for refusing to stay away.[212]

On February 13, 1922, seven-year-old Elizabeth Skalling was sledding near her home in New London County Connecticut. When her sled hit a rock she was seriously injured, including permanent scars to her face and the growth of a lump on her ear which required surgery. In a suit against Bridget A. Sheedy, the adjacent landowner, she claimed that she had been injured on a barbed wire fence. Ms. Sheedy claimed that she had fallen into a bush.

She was awarded $400 in damages, but Ms. Sheedy appealed. The appeals court ordered a new trial, holding that barbed wire was not a dangerous thing and that laws against barbed wire should not have been admitted into evidence.[213]

Sixto Hernandez was working as a migrant farm laborer near Anderson, Indiana in 1968, when the truck he was loading floundered in soft dirt spilling half a load of tomatoes.While retrieving the tomatoes, Mr. Hernandez came in contact with the fence on the neighbor's property. Because of a 110 volt electric charge in the fence, he was unable to release his hands for ten minutes and was seriously injured. In a suit against the landowners, Mr. & Mrs. James N. Jones, he was awarded $7500 compensation and $500 punitive damages.[214]

Flying fences

Where it was found that the owner of a fence had no knowledge that its fence was defective, and had not designed or constructed it, the owner was not liable when it blew away and injured someone.

War story: On November 1, 1977, Virginia M. Blodgett was walking on a public sidewalk near Second and Pacific Avenues in Bremerton, Washington, when she was struck and knocked unconscious by an 8- by 16-foot panel from a fence. The fence was from a construction site owned by Olympic Savings and Loan Association. She sued Olympic and the construction company and won. On appeal the court decided that since Olympic had nothing to do with design, construction or maintenance of the fence, and no knowledge that the fence was defective, it was not liable for her injuries.[215]

Chapter 27 Found Property

Nothing can start a bigger neighbor dispute than one neighbor taking something from the property of another. But in some cases, such as where the property has been lost by a third party, the finder may be considered the legal owner.

As the finder of lost property, a person gains some rights to the property. His rights are not superior to those of the true owner of the property, but they are superior to the rights of others.

Where something is found on property owned by another, the rights of the parties depend upon whether the finder was invited on the property or is a trespasser. If he is a trespasser, then the owner of the premises is usually entitled to keep what is found on the property. But if the finder was on the property at the invitation of the property owner, he can often keep the property.

War stories: Bridges was a traveler for a large firm with which Hawkesworth, a shopkeeper, had dealings. Bridges was in Hawkesworth's store when he found a parcel which contained bank notes of £55. Bridges left the money in Hawkesworth hands so that he might find the owner and return the money. Hawkesworth advertised in newspapers, but after three years no one had claimed the money. Hawkesworth refused to give the money to Bridges, and Bridges sued. The court reversed the lower holding for Hawkesworth and held that the finder of property had greater rights to the property than everyone but the true owner. When the money was placed with the owner of the shop, the shopkeeper was just an agent of Bridges who never intended to waive his title to the property.[216]

While in a barber shop owned by John Medina, David McAvoy found a wallet lying on a table. The parties decided that Medina should keep the pocket-book in case its owner returned. Medina was also going to advertise that he had the wallet. No one claimed it, and McAvoy demanded the money from Medina who refused to give it up. McAvoy sued to recover the money. The court cited the *Bridges v. Hawkesworth* case (above) and its rule that the finder of lost property had a valid claim to that property against all but the true owner, but distinguished the facts in this case. The court held this property was not lost, but voluntarily placed on the table by a customer who accidentally left it. Since the property was not lost, the court held that McAvoy had acquired no original right to the property, and held for Medina.[217]

The South Staffordshire Water Co. employed Sherman to clean out a pool on their property. Sherman found two gold rings in the mud at the bottom of the pool. The rings were given to the police who attempted to locate the owner. When no owner was found the defendant received the rings, and refused to turn them over to the plaintiffs. The water company sued for recovery of the rings and won when the court held that the possession of land carries with it possession of everything which is attached to or under the land. The court held that this would include articles found on the land by other people.[218]

In cases like these, some of the factors considered by the court are whether the property was "lost" or "mislaid" and whether it was embedded in the soil or on the surface. However, as discussed in Chapter 63, the findings in a particular case often are decided upon what the court thinks is the most fair decision based upon the facts. Thus, no matter how many cases you find defining lost property, if the court feels that the finder is not entitled to it, it will call it mislaid property.

In some states there are laws which spell out the rights to lost property. Some of these require that a certain notice be given and that after a period of time the finder can keep the property.

Animals which are wild (called *ferae naturae* by the courts) do not belong to anyone until someone takes possession of them. One can take possession by trapping or wounding them.

War story: Post saw a fox while on the beach with his dogs and began pursuing it. Pierson, knowing Post was hunting the fox, killed the fox and carried it off. Post sued and won, but the appeals court reversed. It held that pursuit alone gives no right of property in wild animals, and that ownership of wild animals can be acquired only by possession. Post had not established ownership because he had not taken possession of the fox.[219]

Chapter 28 Funeral Parlors

Funeral parlors may not be the most desirous types of businesses to have as a neighbor, but if they do not violate the zoning laws they will probably not be held to be nuisances. However, in a few cases have courts declared funeral parlors to be nuisances.

War stories: In the 1920s Roy Hatcher purchased some land in Wellington, Kansas, on which he planned to open a funeral home. When the neighbors heard of this they filed suit to stop him. Especially upset was a Dr. A. R. Hatcher who owned a hospital a few feet from the property. He felt that it would be too depressing for the patients to see a funeral home from the hospital window. At the trial, Mr. Hitchcock was asked about the mangled bodies he occasionally handled, the ones that smelled, and those run over by trains. He was asked why he didn't build the funeral home on the lots he owned next to his home. He said he thought about it but decided against it for personal reasons. The court ordered him not to open the funeral parlor near the hospital. He appealed to the Kansas Supreme Court and it said that while funeral homes are not always a nuisance, they can be in certain circumstances, such as this.[220]

Also in the 1920s, M. A. Jordan and a Mr. Fowler proposed to build a funeral home in an exclusive residential area of Chickasha, Oklahoma. W. H. Nesmith and other neighbors sued to stop them, claiming that their property values would be depressed, that there was a danger from infectious and contagious diseases, that disagreeable odors would be emitted from the building and would contaminate the air, and that the funeral activities would be depressing. In response, the defendants argued that they would be using the latest and most improved methods (of the 1920s) and that their business would not be a nuisance. They lost and took their case to the Oklahoma Supreme Court which had no sympathy for them, saying that in the last analysis the constant reminders of death impair the enjoyment of one's home.[221]

When Welch Laufersweiler began construction of a funeral parlor in Ft. Dodge Iowa, Dr. Emerson B. Dawson and other neighboring property owners filed suit for an injunction to stop the building. They claimed that it would be depressing to their families and that it would lower their property values. Five other doctors testified that it would be depressing. The Dawsons said that it lowered the value of their property from $26,000 to $16,000. The court issued the injunction, but it was overturned by the Supreme Court of Iowa which noted that the area was not purely residential. It was in a state of transition from residential to commercial and nearby were a filling station and a church where funerals were held.[222]

Back in the 1930s, B. J. Wooten and others erected a small building in a residential area of Atlanta and put on display tombstones and monuments which they offered for sale. The display resembled a graveyard. The neighbors, who were "average normal people of average normal sensibilities" objected. O. P. Grubbs and some of the other neighbors filed suit. They claimed that they were thrown into the thoughts of the horrors of the sick-room, the morgue, autopsies, embalming of loved ones, hearses and funerals and that they and their children passing through their formative years were caused to be depressed to the extent that their health and spirits were impaired. Also, their property values were diminished. Their suit was dismissed and they appealed to the Supreme Court of Georgia. The Supreme Court agreed with the trial judge that tombstones were not a nuisance. They asked for a second hearing but were denied.[223]

Chapter 29 Historical Buildings

Because buildings add character to a neighborhood, residents of the neighborhood often put great value in preserving the most historical structures in the neighborhood. Where people join together to purchase the structures there is usually no problem. They can do what they wish with it once they own it. Problems come up when people attempt to control property owned by others. This is especially so when the owner has other, more profitable plans for the property.

Where a local government designates an area as an historic district, it has been held that owners can be kept from altering, demolishing or building new structures in the area. This is done under the rationale that historic districts "promote the general welfare," which is a valid use of government power.

War stories: In order to preserve the character of its historic district, the City of Santa Fe, New Mexico, passed a law in 1957 requiring buildings to conform with the "Old Santa Fe Style" including a rule controlling the size of windows. In order to conform to the size requirements, building owners were required to use wooden dividers to make large panes appear small. After completion of their building, Gamble-Skogmo, Inc. removed the window dividers and were convicted of the crime of violating the building code. They appealed to the Supreme Court of New Mexico which held that the city had the power to require buildings to conform to their list of historical standards. The court also held that the fact that other buildings in the area had windows that violated the rules was no defense.[224]

In New Orleans the city government designated a certain area as an historic district and made it illegal to do any construction, alteration or demolition in the area without a permit from the Vieux Carre Commission. A Mr. Maher wanted to build an apartment complex in place of a Victorian cottage and was refused permission. He went to federal court over the issue and the court held that such a law was a valid exercise of government power. He argued that the law constituted a taking of his property and that he should be compensated, but this was rejected by the court.[225]

When a city designates one building as a landmark, rather than a whole area, and forbids any alteration to it, the issue is not so clear that there has not been a taking of the owner's property which should be compensated.

The landmark case in the area of landmarks concerns the Penn Central terminal in New York City.[226] In that case the owners wanted to build a huge office building on the site but were prevented by the city which designated the building as a landmark. The owners went to court and New York's highest court* ruled that the city's action was valid. It noted numerous factors as justification, such as the fact the owners could make a reasonable return on the property if they operated it efficiently, the claim that "society" gave value to the property, and the fact that the city gave the owners transferable development rights which it could use elsewhere in the city or sell to other property owners.

The owners appealed their case to the United States Supreme Court[227] and the New York decision was affirmed, although Justice Rehnquist, who has since become the Chief Justice of the court dissented. In his dissent Rehnquist stated that any substantial interference with property rights constitutes a taking of property and under the constitution should be compensated.

---

* In most states the highest court is the state Supreme court, but in New York the highest court is the Court of Appeals. The reason for this is that when the New York politicians gave out judgships as political favors everyone wanted to be a supreme court justice. Since the highest court in the state had a limited number of seats, and they were seldom vacant, there were not many political plums to hand out. To solve this they began calling the lower courts of the state the supreme courts, and were able to give out supreme court seats to all their cronies.

Chapter 30 Immoral Activities

What one person considers immoral another may consider to be the meaning of life. But where the government is concerned, any doubts are usually resolved in deciding a thing is immoral. And if it is immoral, it can be stopped.

There are numerous specific laws making nudity, prostitution, gambling, drug sales and the like illegal. There are also zoning laws which ban certain activities in certain areas. But citizens have also been successful in using civil lawsuits to rid their neighborhoods of offensive activities.

Disorderly Houses and bawdyhouses are two types of activities which have often been ruled to be nuisances. Bawdyhouses are in fact considered nuisances at all times and in all places. Slaughterhouses, rendering plants and chemical factories can be nuisances in certain cases, but these places are nuisances in every instance. Disorderly houses which are gambling houses are considered nuisances per se, but other types of disorderly houses, such as tippling houses and saloons are only considered nuisances when they annoy the neighborhood.

War stories: Mr. and Mrs. Magel owned a group of flats at 2708, 2710 and 2714 Arsenal Street, St. Louis, Missouri. Their neighbors were 24 different social clubs which operated a bowling alley at 2726 Arsenal St. In addition to causing great noise the members of the clubs exposed themselves from the open windows of the shower rooms and used loud, boisterous and obscene language. The Magels sued and the case dragged on into hundreds of pages of pleadings and testimony. In the end the courts balanced the interests of the parties and held that the clubs must reduce their noise and stop exposing themselves and using obscene language.[228]

In the early 1950s the prosecuting attorney in Seattle, Washington, filed a case to close down the Oxford Hotel for six months and to to sell the contents because he claimed three acts of prostitution and four offers to commit prostitution were committed on the premises. The hotel actually had a reputation as a decent, orderly respectable place and 80 of the 114 rooms were rented by permanent residents. The bellmen involved in the alleged crimes were immediately fired and the owners had nothing to do with their actions. The case was dismissed by the local judge but the prosecutor appealed to the state supreme court. It also agreed the case should be dismissed.[229]

In 1975 Sidne Enterprises, Inc. operated an establishment which allegedly featured topless and bottomless dancing. According to a plainclothes police officer, the women would undulate and gyrate as they approached the patrons and eventually brought their vaginas to within three inches of the faces of the patrons. The attorney for the establishment likened the performance to the ballet "Swan Lake." The court was unimpressed, deciding the activities were "lewd, gross and disgusting." Therefore the activities were deemed a nuisance and the city was entitled to an injunction.[230]

Also in 1975 a complaint was filed against the "Gaisha Bath House" at 4816 N. Western Avenue in Chicago. It seems that a Police Sergeant went to the bath house and after paying $25 he "was taken into a small room in the premises where a completely nude female offered to and did in fact fondle and stroke his penis." Similar conduct allegedly happened on other occasions. Six times the employees were arrested but the bath house stayed open, and the citizens of Chicago allegedly suffered irreparable injury from these activities. To save the city from this nuisance the Illinois appellate court allowed an injunction to issue since "masturbatory massage parlors" are "specialized houses of prostitution" and houses of prostitution are nuisances.[231]

At the Panama-California International Exposition in San Diego County, California, in 1916 a Joseph Weis operated an entertainment concession known as "Sultan's Harem" for which he charged admission. The local district attorney filed an action against him claiming that in his "Sultan's Harem" women exposed "their naked persons and private parts" in front of men, women and children and was granted an injunction. He appealed, saying that an injunction was not the proper way to enforce a criminal law. He lost, the court deciding that such a display was a nuisance.[232]

In 1889 a Ms. Toole was brought before the criminal court of Mecklenberg, North Carolina, and charged with the offence of singing a ribald, vulgar, obscene and profane song for a period of ten minutes while walking down the street. She argued to the North Carolina Supreme Court that since the profane sentence was used only once she should not be found guilty. The court disagreed, holding that even singing it once was a nuisance. We have been unable to locate the words to this song.[233]

Jesse J. Turner and another operated Circle Bar on a public highway about a mile from Anderson, South Carolina. In or about 1941 Mr. Turner and his partner were convicted of the crime of operating a "disorderly house." They appealed to the Supreme Court of South Carolina. Unfortunately for them, the court agreed with the trial judge that although dancing is usually an innocent amusement, and drinking may also be legal, dancing and drinking accompanied by swearing and drunkenness, and annoying the neighborhood with loud and disturbing noises was a nuisance.[234]

In some cases the government has gotten quite creative in finding reasons to ban activity it deems improper.

War story: Nude sunbathing was becoming a problem for some people at the Cape Cod National Seashore. Rather than pass a criminal law against it, the United States Department of the Interior passed a regulation banning nude bathing there due to the fact that it was a "natural environmental area." In 1975 twelve Massachusetts residents sued in federal district court. District Judge Freedman, in upholding the regulation, held that banning nude bathing was a good way to solve the problems of litter, sanitation and damage to the dunes and plant life. (Supposedly people wearing bathing suits would not create such problems!)[235]

Chapter 31 Injuries

The subjects of personal injuries caused either by intentional acts or negligence is beyond the scope of this book and each could easily warrant a book of its own. However, since neighbors occasionally do injure or even kill each other, a brief explanation of the law in these areas is included.

Both intentional acts such as assault and battery and negligent acts such as nuisance and trespass are part of the body of law called tort law. Torts are wrongful acts. Whether they are intentional or negligent, the law allows victims of wrongful acts to receive compensation.

Intentional Injuries

Intention acts which cause injury can include such things as battery and murder. **Battery** is any case were one person causes the touching of another person without permission. The touching may be a tap with the hand, shooting them with a bullet, or running over them with a car. Any unauthorized touching is considered a battery. Committing a battery can result in both a court action for damages by the person touched and a criminal charge, since battery is both a tort and a crime.

Since battery is most often used along with "assault" as in "assault and battery" it would be worthwhile to understand that term, too. An **assault** is an act of putting a person in fear of receiving a battery. Common examples of assaults would be pointing a gun at someone, or driving a car toward them and missing them, or raising your arm at them as if to hit them.

War stories: Back in 1669 an altercation took place which will forever be remembered in law books. During an argument one party put his hand on his sword and said "If it were not assize time,[*] I would not take such language from you." In a suit between the parties he was charged with assault, but he won the case. The judges ruled that since it *was* assize time, the other person had no reason to fear.[236]

In New Hampshire in the 1850s two men got into an argument and one pointed an unloaded gun at the other. He was successfully sued for assault since pointing a gun at someone would put that person in fear of receiving a battery.[237]

---

[*] The time that the judges were passing through town.

Murder is, of course, the unauthorized killing of another human. Murder would not include killing someone in self defense, in a war, as a law enforcement officer in the line of duty or as an agent of the state carrying out an execution.

Unintentional Injuries

Whether or not a person is liable for unintentionally injuring someone depends upon whether or not the accident was due to negligence and whether the injury was caused by some inherently dangerous activity. If it was neither of these, it may have been an "unavoidable accident" for which no one is liable.

Unavoidable Accidents

If an accident is judged to be "unavoidable" then the person who "caused" it is not liable for any injuries resulting from it.

War stories: If a person is riding a horse and someone else whips it and causes it to run over a person, the person who whipped the horse is guilty, not the person riding it.[238]

Because of a problem with dogs around their slaughter house in Sterling, Kansas, M. E. Richardson and Samuel Haston kept a Colts rifle handy. On January 31, 1898 at 9:00 a.m. D. Cleghorn, who was in charge of the place noticed dogs on the premises and got the rifle. When he fired at the dogs the bullet struck a sharp stone on the ground and deflected toward the highway killing Joseph Thompson who happened to be passing by. After four trials (one was reversed and two were deadlocked) Mr. Thompson's heirs were awarded damages. However, the award was thrown out by the Supreme Court of Kansas which ruled that the death was an unavoidable accident. It felt that shooting toward the ground was not negligent and that the unusual deflection by the stone was "inevitable misfortune" or an "act of God."[239]

Warren Kreis was working as a part-time police officer on Sunday, October 4, 1953 on the White Horse Pike in Berlin, New Jersey, when he was struck by a vehicle driven by Thomas Owens. In a law suit against Mr. Owens' estate (he had subsequently died) Mr. Kreis won an award of damages. However, on appeal a new trial was ordered and it was held that it would be proper to offer evidence that the accident was caused by Mr. Owens' heart condition and not any negligence on his part.[240]

Negligence

If an accident is caused by negligence, then the negligent person (and others such as his employer or partner) can be held liable for an injury caused by the negligence. Negligence is a subject which takes months to learn in law school, and depends upon numerous complicated principles of law. But the ultimate decision as to whether a person is negligent depends upon whether he was using the proper amount of care under the circumstances and whether his act was the actual cause of the damages.

One of the issues which must be decided when claiming a person was negligent is what the "standard of care" was for the circumstances. This is because the law has developed different standards for different situations. For example, if a person falls on your steps, you cannot know what your duty of care of the steps was until you find out what the status of the visitor was. Was he trespassing? Was he a dinner guest? Was he making a business delivery?

War stories: In the 1920s Helen Palsgraf was standing on the platform of the Long Island railroad waiting to go to Rockaway Beach. Another passenger was running to catch his moving train when he started to fall. Two train guards helped him on the train but in doing so caused him to drop a package he was carrying. The package, wrapped in newspaper, contained fireworks which exploded when they landed on the tracks. The shock of the explosion knocked down some scales at the other end of the platform hitting Ms. Palsgraf. She sued the railroad and won. Her verdict was upheld by the appeals court, but the railroad appealed to New York's highest court and her verdict was thrown out. In a landmark opinion by Chief Justice Cardozo, the court held that there must be some connection between the act of the party sued and the injury caused. In this case, any negligence in helping one passenger should not make one liable to another passenger at the other end of the platform from a package that did not appear dangerous.[241]

When Bryson Pillars took the first plug of his Brown Mule Chewing Tobacco it was fine, but when he took his second he began to feel sick. Not suspecting it was the tobacco, he took another and another until he bit into a foreign substance which "crumbled like bread," and caused him to foam at the mouth. Upon examination he discovered that the tobacco contained a human toe with the flesh and nail intact! He sued Reynolds Tobacco Co. and the distributor. At the time manufacturers of products were not usually liable to consumers for defective products since they did not have direct dealings with them. The only exceptions were for foods, beverages and drugs. He lost his case and appealed to the Mississippi Supreme Court. The court said that the tobacco company was right that tobacco was not a food, except for worms and goats, but decided that it would take a step forward for the health and life of the public and hold Reynolds liable. The court added, "We can imagine no reason why, with ordinary care, human toes could not be left out of chewing tobacco, and if toes are found in chewing tobacco, it seems to us that somebody has been very careless.[242] No word has ever been heard about the unfortunate whose toe it was.

Back in the '50s James Wells of New London County, Connecticut left a golf club lying on the ground in the back yard of his home for some time. Before he picked it up, his son, James, Jr. eleven years old used it to swing at a stone lying on the ground. In doing so, he hit his friend, Judith Lubitz in the jaw. In attempting to hold the father liable the girl's attorney argued that the father was negligent in leaving it around. The court disagreed, saying that a golf club was not so dangerous that leaving it around would make him liable.[243]

On April 15, 1953, 66-year-old Fannie Hope Guthrie and her husband went to the Winfield Sales Company at the Cowley County, Kansas, fair grounds. While sitting in a chair on the main floor, a six-hundred-pound steer suddenly fell through the ceiling and landed on her, causing painful, serious and permanent injuries. In finding the woman entitled to a trial, the court used the doctrine, *res ipsa loquitur*, meaning, the thing speaks for itself. The effect of this doctrine is to say, of course someone is liable when something like this happens.[244]

Dangerous activity

When persons engage in dangerous activities, they can be held liable for any injuries caused by their actions whether they were negligent or not.

War stories: A few years before the Pilgrims departed for Plymouth Rock, two soldiers were skirmishing with their loaded muskets in England. Ward's musket fired and injured Weaver. Weaver sued for trespass and assault and battery. The court held that in trespass Weaver could recover because every man is answerable in trespass unless it is judged utterly without his fault. Apparently Ward did not show that he had not committed negligence, and the court held for Weaver.[245]

R. L. Moore was hired to exterminate cockroaches and other vermin in the Sacramento Medico-Dental Building in Sacramento, California. On November 16, 1943 at midnight he released some hydrocyanic gas in the building. The next morning, Albert L. Luthringer arrived for work at the building at 8:45. The entrance he used to enter had no sign warning of the gas and while he was in the building he passed out. He was discovered later and taken to a hospital. In a suit against Mr. Moore he was awarded $10,000. The release of the gas was considered to be an ultrahazardous activity for which the actor would be strictly liable.[246]

On November 22, 1967 seventeen-year-old Carol J. House was driving home from her after-school job along Capitol Lake Drive in Olympia, Washington, when she encountered a pool of thousands of gallons of spilled gasoline. There was an explosion and she was killed in the fire. The source of the gasoline, it turned out, was a gasoline truck pulling an additional trailer unit filled with 4,800 gallons of gasoline, driven by Aaron L. Kuhlman. While he was driving toward Highway 101 he felt a jerk and noticed the trailer pull away from the truck. He got out of the truck and saw that the trailer crashed through a chain-link fence and had come to rest upside down on Capitol Lake Drive below. Then he heard a sound and the fire started. In a lawsuit the owner of the trailer presented evidence that it had not done anything wrong, and that the trailer had been properly constructed and taken care of. It also presented some evidence that Miss House had been speeding. The jury found the defendants not guilty and the appeals court upheld this finding. Miss House's parents appealed to the Washington Supreme Court which reversed the decision and held that a hauler of gasoline in a situation like this would be strictly liable (even if there was no negligence).[247]

Chapter 32 Jails and Prisons

Jails and Prisons, being operated by the government, do not usually violate other laws such as zoning ordinances. However, if operated improperly they may constitute a nuisance. In such cases court action by the neighbors may be able to remedy the situation.

War stories: Ella Pritchett was living in a nice home on one of the most desirable streets in Vincennes, Indiana, in 1902 when the county built a jail thirty feet away. It was a large jail which held an average of 40 prisoners. The prison also was used to house the insane. At times the prisoners would look down into the Pritchett home and "loudly scream, sing, swear, curse, and utter profane and indecent language." They would also pound on the bars and make loud and dismal noises. Mrs. Prichett sued, but the court held that the owner of a residence has no remedy for an injury from a properly built jail conducted in a proper manner. It said the noise from the jail was unavoidable and that the county has a duty to house criminals and the insane somewhere. It did concede, however, that allowing the prisoners to look into her residence was an invasion of her privacy and that the sheriff and the jailer may be liable for that.[248]

The Board of County Commissioners of Baldwin County, Georgia, decided to build a convict camp north of the city of Milledgeville. The residents of a nearby subdivision went to court to try to get an injunction against building the camp. The court declined to issue the injunction and the Supreme Court of Georgia agreed, saying that a prison or convict camp was not a nuisance unless it was not operated properly and could not be stopped before it was built.[249]

Arthur Pharr filed suit against the North Carolina State Prison Commission to force them to stop allowing criminals to wander the streets and to halt construction of an expansion to the Camp Polk Prison northwest of Raleigh. The judge noted that escapees and discharged prisoners committed serious crimes in the area and issued the injunction. However, Mr. Pharr's victory was short-lived since the state supreme court dissolved the injunction because he had failed to allege that the prison commission had acted fraudulently or in an arbitrary manner and had not found any ordinance prohibiting prisons in the area.[250]

Chapter 33 Lights

Like many areas of neighbor law, lights are usually legal unless they cause a substantial injury and there is no overriding justification. The courts balance the interests of the parties. Of course, when baseball or Christmas is involved, the balance may be tilted against the person complaining.

War stories: A race track was built across from a drive-in movie theater in Portland Oregon. The lights for night races made it difficult to see the films. In a lawsuit against the race track the court noted that the movie screen was especially sensitive to light and that it had to be specially recessed from the moon and star light and had to have other special barriers to make it useful. Therefore, the court found it to be unusually sensitive and that the lights at the race track were not a nuisance.[251]

In 1937 A. B. Kurbitz, owner of a professional baseball club, leased Bengal Field from Lewiston High School in Lewiston, Idaho for use by the "Lewiston Indians" for night baseball games. G. H. Hansen and other nearby property owners sued, claiming that their homes were being flooded with excessive light, and that the games caused excessive noise and trespass of balls and people onto their properties. Their suit went up to the Idaho Supreme Court which held that they were entitled to an injunction limiting the lights, hours of the game and other factors which interfered with their enjoyment of their property.[252]

When the Louisville Board of Education decided to install lights at the Manual High School stadium for night football games in the 1940s, Roy J. Klein and others representing more than 300 nearby homeowners filed suit to stop the installation. They won their case before the trial court judge but the school board appealed. The appeals court noted that Mr. Klein's home had already increased in value from $6,650 in 1924 to $13,000 in 1946 and that "The Youth of a Nation are the trustees of Posterity." It held that in a case like this the lighting could not be stopped before it was even used. Only if it proved to be an actual nuisance could it be enjoined.[253]

Since 1977 Alvin C. Copeland had maintained an elaborate Christmas display on his residence at 5001 Folse Dr. in

Jefferson Parish, Louisiana. Each year the display grew in size and popularity. It included lights and music amplified through loud speakers. By 1983 the neighbors claimed it was becoming a nuisance, causing restricted access to their homes, noise, public urination, property damage and a lack of on-street parking. The local sheriff instituted a traffic control plan using seven deputies and portable toilets, and the parish limited the display to a period of 30 days and only until 11 p.m. in the evening. The neighbors felt that this did not eliminate the problem and filed suit. Mr. Copeland counterclaimed that the restrictions abridged his constitutional rights. The local court refused to stop the display and the neighbors appealed. The appeals court held that the display should not be stopped but that the regulations were reasonable and not unconstitutional. The neighbors appealed to the Louisiana Supreme Court which held that the display did cause real damage in a residential area and was not just an inconvenience. It entered an injunction against the display.[254] [Mr. Copeland, the owner of Popeyes Famous Fried Chicken, Inc., merely moved the display to his corporate headquarters.]

In 1929 A. J. Weber opened a root beer stand across from a nice residence at the corner of Avondale and Preston streets in Dallas, Texas. O. H. Mann, the owner of the residence, claimed that in the 20 x 24 foot space of the root beer stand there were large glaring lights which reflected into his home and a red neon sign. In a law suit against Mr. Weber, he also complained about noise dust and obnoxious odors claiming that the stand was a nuisance. The jury came back with a confusing verdict saying both that Mr. Mann was and was not injured by the stand. The trial court ordered Mr. Weber to install lights with colored or shaded globes of a lesser candle power than 25 kilowatts and to not operate his radio. In an appeal by both sides the court noted that a 25,000 bulb "would make a most dazzling light" and that the matter should be reconsidered by the judge.[255]

In the 1920s Frank Shepler lived at 1221 Santa Fé Avenue in Wichita, Kansas. Across the street and across the railroad tracks Kansas Milling Co. built a number of grain tanks 60 feet high and painted them white. When the afternoon sun would shine on the tanks it would reflect upon Mr. Shepler's property causing him great annoyance. He filed suit claiming that the light reflected from the tanks rendered his house unsalable, untenantable and no longer fit for residential purposes, reducing its value by $1,800. His suit was dismissed when the Supreme Court of Kansas held that "The law does not in every instance provide directly for compensation or financial redress for every damnum a man may sustain as a member of an organized community."[256]

When the city of High Point, North Carolina constructed a million-gallon, 184-foot high water tank and painted it a bright silver color, the reflecting sunlight caused a problem for the owners of property on the southeast corner of Salem Street and Bridges Street. The parties sued and won but in two separate appeals to the North Carolina Supreme Court the city won a ruling that limited the owners rights to compensation.[257]

The Shelbourne, Inc. operated a hotel of 121 rooms on the Boardwalk at Michigan Avenue in Atlantic City, New Jersey, in the early 1920s. Crossan Corp. owned property southwest of the Shelbourne. It rented its roof to R. C. Maxwell Company which contracted with Colgate Company for operation of a sign on the roof. The sign was 66 feet high, 72 feet long and weighed 20 tons. It had 1084 15-watt lights and 34 75-watt and 100-watt lights. A new wing of the Shelbourne faced the sign and the lights shined into some of the bedrooms. Shelbourne sued complaining that the lights devalued its rooms and were a nuisance. The court held that such light would be a nuisance to persons wanting to sleep, but that since the Shelbourne had a loud band playing until midnight, the guests wouldn't be able to sleep until then anyway. So it ordered that the sign not be used after midnight.[258]

Faye Ward Born, a neighbor of a treatment facility operated by Exxon Corporation in Escambia County, Alabama was bothered by the light and odor emanating from a flare stack at the facility. She filed suit claiming that it was both a nuisance and a trespass. She filed a suit and took it as high as the Alabama Supreme Court. But the court held that light and odor would not constitute a trespass in this case and that if it was a nuisance, she had waited too long to sue since the statute of limitations was only one year.[259]

Chapter 34 Noise

Noisy neighbors can be the most annoying aspect of having them. When we are not allowed the quiet we need for sleep and relaxation it can affect many aspects of our lives including our health. However, not all noise is a nuisance. Courts have ruled that no one is entitled to absolute quiet in the enjoyment of his property.[260] The level of allowable noise is that which is customary to the community. Thus the amount of noise considered a nuisance in a quiet suburban community may be considered normal in an industrial area.

War stories: In November, 1924, Sadie Abend bought a house at 765 S. 16th Street, Newark, New Jersey. Next door was a vacant lot and beside that a laundry. The laundry grew and built an addition on the lot. The additional business resulted in increased noise, as well as vibrations, smoke and soot. In deciding to enjoin operation of the laundry between 7 p.m. and 6:30 a.m. the court quoted an older case, "Mankind needs to sleep for a succession of several or more hours once in every twenty-four hours, and nature has provided a time for that purpose, to wit, the nighttime, and by common consent of civilized man the night is devoted to rest and sleep, and noises which would not be adjudged nuisances, under the circumstances, if made in the day-time, will be declared to be nuisances if made at night and during the hours which are usually devoted by the inhab-itants of that neighborhood to sleep."[261]

A mill was operated about a mile outside of Grand Rapids, Michigan around 1950. The neighbors sued because they couldn't stand the noise and smell. But the mill won and the court said that no one is entitled to absolute quiet or air uncontaminated by any odor.[262]

The Meadowbrook Swimming Club in Jones' Falls, Mary-land, enlarged its premises in 1935 by adding an outdoor dance floor with amplifiers to enhance the volume of the music. The jazz orchestras hired to play music did so from 9 p.m. until midnight, six nights a week, and many resi-dents in the area complained in writing. Meadowbrook ceased using the amplifiers and cut back to dancing only four nights a week. Nevertheless, the noise was very annoying and the neighbors sued to enjoin the outdoor

dances. The club was ordered to find a way to keep the
music from disturbing the neighbors.[263]

Some activities in modern society cannot be performed without
noise and the courts take this into account when deciding if a noise is a
nuisance. For a noise to be considered a nuisance it must be considered
"unreasonable" and annoying to a person of "ordinary sensibilities." If
a person is unusually sensitive to noise, the fact that he was upset would
not make the noise a nuisance.

War stories: In the early 1940s Bobbe Ernst of 219 Sagamore Road in
Brookline, Pennsylvania, would play her marimba for long
periods of time and so loudly that it disturbed the whole
neighborhood. She also would play songs intending to
disturb particular neighbors. For example, when Horace
Griffith Collier entered or left his home, Bobbe Ernst would
play "Jingle Bells" on the marimba because Mr. Collier
resembled Santa Claus. She would also play "When Irish
Eyes are Smiling" to annoy Leo Kelly, and play "Anchors
Aweigh" to annoy a naval officer living in the neighborhood. Mrs. Broadbelt, an elderly woman, was greeted with
"Little Old Lady" whenever she entered or left her home.
The court held that while playing the marimba is not
generally a nuisance, because Bobbe Ernst had played it so
loudly and for such long periods of time and at unreasonable hours, it had injured her neighbors and was a nuisance. The court forbade her from playing at certain hours
and strictly limited the number of hours she could play in
one day. The court also forbade her from playing "Jingle
Bells," "When Irish Eyes Are Smiling," "Anchors Aweigh,"
and "Little Old Lady" with the intention of annoying and
disturbing her neighbors.[264]

Frank S. Minard was keeping some roosters at his residence at Municipal No. 540 Kings Highway, Shreveport,
Louisiana in the 1940s which were not appreciated by at
least two of his neighbors. Mrs. Leonora Myer and her son
Jacob S. Myer were living at No. 554 Kings highway and
could hear the roosters quite well each morning. They
claimed that they were awakened each morning at five
o'clock a. m. (four o'clock Standard time) by the roosters
(especially the big red one) which continued at fifteen
minute intervals until six-thirty a. m. After several complaints to Mr. Minard did not solve the situation they filed

a lawsuit asking the court to order him to stop his roosters from awakening them and for $500 each in damages. However, the court did not see it there way, and ruled that the crowing of a rooster at the break of day would not be a nuisance to persons of ordinary sensibilities and normal habits and tastes. Sounds like a problem of night people versus day people.[265]

In 1972 Congress decided that noise was becoming a growing danger to the health and welfare of the country and passed the Noise Control Act. It is contained in Title 42, United States Code, Sections 4901 through 4918. It provides for both criminal penalties and citizen suits and covers railroads, motor carriers and others.

Occasionally, when a nuisance action fails, a person will attempt to sue on the basis that the noise has trespassed upon his property. This theory has not been successful as courts have held that noise and vibrations are not "things" which can trespass.

War story: In 1969 Interlake Steel Co. purchased a plant in Lodi, California, which operated eight hours a day and expanded the operations to 24 hours a day. The continuous operation of a punch press, shearing machine and other equipment disturbed 22 retirees who lived nearby. They filed a nuisance suit but lost because a California law forbid suits attempting to stop businesses lawfully operating in a proper zone. They filed a trespass suit and took the case before the entire California Supreme Court. The court agreed with the lower courts that trespass is not the proper remedy for noise and vibrations. But it also held that a nuisance action would be possible if the parties sought monetary damages rather than an order stopping the operation of the business.[266]

Chapter 35 Obnoxious Behavior

Some behavior does not fit into any of the other categories in this book, and yet is it a bother. It is not necessarily noise. It is not odor, though it stinks. And it is not sights. But it is obnoxious. The following cases illustrate better than could be explained, the type of behavior to which we are referring.

War stories: One night in February, 1928 after J. T. Wilkins had gone to bed, Dennis Wilson and five others came to his house in Scott county, Arkansas, and called him to come out. He came to the door and was told he had been stealing hogs and that if he did not leave the community within ten days they would put a rope around his neck. Although he had just bought a farm and spent $50 improving it, he did as they said and left town. But he sued them for causing him mental suffering. Wilson and the others each said he was home on the night in question, but the jury believed Wilkins and his seven-year-old son. He was awarded $100. This was upheld by the Supreme Court of Arkansas which said that although mental suffering is usually not allowed without physical inury, there was an exception in cases where there is an intent to cause mental suffering.[267]

For three years Connie Burnett had been doing certain things which disturbed her neighbor J. Frank Rushton in Duval County, Florida. These things included operating her lawn mower in an unnecessarily noisy manner at an early hour of the morning close to Mr. Rushton's bedroom, making obscene gestures toward his family, focusing a light on his residence at night and inciting her dog to bark boisterously to annoy him. Mr. Rushton filed suit and was granted an injunction and damages of $500. On appeal the Supreme Court of Florida upheld the verdict even though it was claimed that Mrs. Burnett was not mentally well and held that her husband was also liable for acquiescing in and condoning her conduct.[268]

After Thomas Medford rented part of his apartment to Joseph Levy, their wives did not get along. The Medfords filed a suit against the Levys claiming that they were creating a nuisance by slamming doors, singing loudly, talking impolitely to Mrs. Medford, frequently cooking cabbage and onions with the kitchen door open, purposely spilling water on the stairs, sweeping dirt under doors and throwing it over transoms, throwing old boots, shoes, socks and other objectionable things into the yard and doing other dreadful acts. In the trial court the Medfords won and were granted an injunction. The Levys appealed to the West Virginia Supreme Court. The court noted that some ordinary things which are not usually serious may constitute a nuisance when done maliciously. But it also noted that the Levys made claims that the Medfords engaged in similar conduct, and said that when there is a domestic quarrel between two women, the court should not protect one against the other.It said that the case was one of rare occurrence and that it hoped that no such case would appear again.[269]

Mitch and Brenda Melvin, living in Illinois in the 1980s, began receiving numerous items through the mail which they had not ordered. These were followed by bills for the items. In a lawsuit they alleged that an Eric Burling intentionally ordered these items and that such actions constituted an invasion of their privacy. The trial court dismissed their case, but the appeals court, after reviewing the history of the developing law of privacy decided that the facts alleged by them would constitute a claim for invasion of privacy which could be presented to a jury.[270]

An ordinance passed by the city of Hope, Arkansas, made it unlawful to construct any residence without connecting it to a sewer. James H. Bennett, who was building a residence did not want to have toilet facilities in his home. He wished to equip it with "toilet facilities of the out-door type" and filed a suit against the city. He lost but appealed to the Arkansas Supreme Court which held the law unconstitutional. It said that a residence was not necessarily a nuisance and that under state law the city could not require someone who was more than 300 feet from a sewer to connect to it.[271]

In Stowe, Vermont, Victor and Mary Coty, Dorothy Nelson and Anton and Pamela Flory formed a committee to oppose the building of a motel on an open meadow near their property. Norman and Raymond Ramsey refused to sell the meadow to the committee, and established a rather large pig farm on the land instead. Also, sixteen truckloads of chicken manure were dumped on a narrow strip directy across from the Nelson and Flory properties. The trucks also managed to get the Flory driveway and the road covered with manure. The police issued a temporary restraining order, and one of the truck drivers said that now the Ramseys had gotten even with the committee. The neighbors sued claiming the pig farm was a nuisance. The lower court held for the neighbors and awarded the Cotys $40,000 compensatory and $80,000 punitive damages; Mrs. Nelson $70,500 compensatory and $150,000 punitive damages; and the Florys $77,000 compensatory and $150,000 punitive damages. The Supreme Court of Vermont held that the pig farm substantially interfered with the neighbors' use of their properties and was a nuisance; the farm was a nuisance due to the odors, flies and offensive animal husbandry practices; the evidence showed that Norman Ramsey acted with actual malice in establishing the pig farm and dumping the chicken manure but the evidence did not show that Raymond Ramsey had acted with malice; Raymond could be liable for compensatory but not punitive damages; Norman could be liable for punitive damages and the court sent the case back for redetermination of punitive damages based on culpability and financial status; and the $380,000 in punitive damages was not excessive considering the spitefulness involved in maintaining the pig farm and dumping the manure.[272]

Chapter 36 Odors

Obnoxious odors have often been held to be a nuisance. The factors to be considered in deciding whether a smell is obnoxious are whether the smells are unusual for the location and whether they would offend someone of ordinary sensibilities. For example, fish hanging in the sun to dry might be normal in a seaside market, but if a fisherman took them home to a residential neighborhood and hung them in his yard every day it would probably be considered a nuisance.

War stories: In 1611 a man in Norfolk County, England built a hogsty near enough to his neighbor's house that the smell upset the neighbor. The court found that this constituted a nuisance.[273]

In 1905 a person had a hen house near enough to another dewlling in Bridgewater, Massachusetts that the owner claimed it was difficult to rent. The Massachusetts Supreme Court ruled that to an ordinary citizen of Massachusetts, poultry odors should not be offensive.[274]

In the 1890s Oscar R. Hundley a lawyer in Huntsville, Alabama, bought a lot and had a two-story brick office building built on it. Behind him Daniel T. Harrison built another building and added a tobacco drying house to their property. Mr. Hundley and the other tenants of his building complained that the smell from the tobacco was sickening, pungent and abominable. They sued but lost. They appealed to the Supreme Court of Alabama which saw their side of the case, holding that it was a nuisance.[275]

Nettie Carroll operated a kennel about a mile outside of Grand Rapids, Michigan. It was in an area with several commercial establishments and about a quarter mile from about 20 homes. Roy De Longpre and others brought a suit against Mrs. Carroll and her husband claiming that the kennel was a nuisance to the area because of the smells and noise. They provided evidence that it was a nuisance and she provided evidence that it was not. The judge visited the kennel and found the testimony about the problems was exaggerated. He also noted that Mrs. Carroll installed a gas incinerator which remedied the problem with the odors and ruled that he would not order to stop operating the kennel. Mr. De Longpre appealed to the Supreme Court of Michigan which held that it would not reverse a judge's ruling unless he made a legal error, which this judge had not. It also ruled that no one is entitled to air utterly uncontaminated by any odor whatsoever.[276]

When Mr. and Mrs. Kenneth P. Tubbs lived on West Chestnut Street in Kokomo, Indiana in the 1940s, they were very much disturbed by their neighbors, Mr. and Mrs. Hedrick, who would deposit in the street in front of the Tubbs' house, rotten apples, chicken feathers, rubber, old rags and other garbage which they would burn. After this went on for three years, the Tubbs sued, asking that the court order the Hedricks to stop, because the noxious offensive odors were annoying and discomforting to them and causing damage to their premises. The court ordered the Hedricks to stop and they appealed. The appeals court upheld the injunction, saying, "Unpleasant odors, from the very constitution of our nature, render us uncomfortable, and, when continued and repeated, make life uncomfortable. To live comfortably is the chief and most reasonable object of men in acquiring property as the means of attaining it, and any interference with our neighbor, in the comfortable enjoyment of life, is a wrong which the law will redress."[277]

In Wilmington, Delaware, the residents of Westhaven development brought an action against Domenico Roggero to enjoin him from storing 360 tons of horse manure on the land next to Westhaven. They claimed the manure gave off an extremely offensive stench, contaminating the air of the neighborhood; that flies germinated in large numbers and swarmed around Westhaven homes; and as a result, many families had been made uncomfortable and sick, and living in Westhaven had become unbearable. The manure was stored outside during the spring and summer for use in Roggero's mushroom houses. The court held that the manure had substantially impaired reasonable comfort could constitute a nuisance; the fact that Roggero's mushroom houses and manure storage had been going on for twelve years before Westhaven was built would not keep the residents from obtaining injunctive relief; the residents had met the burden of establishing their case by clear and convincing proof. The court granted the injunction.[278]

Jasper Cropsey owned a house on 44th street in New York
which he had been leasing out for $59.00 a month until
Cornelius Murphy began boiling fat on the adjoining lot,
after which he could not lease the house. The fat-boiling
caused unpleasant and unhealthy odors. In a lawsuit
against Mr. Murphy, the court held for Mr. Jasper and
awarded him $250.00. On appeal the court refused to
dismiss the damages, although they considered them excessive, because Jasper had proved a nuisance.[279]

Elisha Ruckman sued to recover damages to his lands
caused by a bone and offal boiling establishment erected
by and belonging to John Green upon his lands in New
Jersey. Ruckman's lands were in New York on the pali-
sades on the Hudson River, 1,300 acres of which were in
New Jersey, 200 acres in New York. Ruckman claimed the
gases and smells from the boiling establishment impaired
the use and enjoyment of his land so much as to prevent its
sale. The lower court dismissed Ruckman's case, but on
appeal the court ordered a new trial so that Ruckman
might be able to introduce evidence showing a nuisance.[280]

One of the few things which is almost always considered a "nuisance per se" is garbage. This means that it is a nuisance wherever and
whenever it becomes annoying. When odors are caused by accumu-
lated garbage, it is usually easy to take action to stop it.

War stories: In 1898 the city of Grand Rapids, Michigan, passed an
ordinance which was later amended, regulating the collection of garbage and requiring those doing so to be licensed.
Such services were to be provided by the Grand Rapids
Garbage Holding Company. Some years later a Benjamin
Vink was caught hauling garbage without a license. This
garbage was claimed to be "mushy and wet" barrels of
food including "clamshells, celery, beans (cooked), egg-
shells, cabbage, etc." and was alleged to have fermented
and to smell. Mr. Vink claimed that it had not fermented
and did not smell and that he provided a better service of
hauling garbage. He lost the case and appealed to the
Michigan Supreme Court. However, the court rejected his
appeal saying that garbage was a nuisance.[281]

Robert Lightner was feeding 600 hogs on his farm with
garbage obtained from the city of Dayton. The garbage

was in various stages of decay and produced noxious odors. Many complaints were lodged concerning the odors and a health officer investigated, found the condition created a nuisance, and ordered Lightner to abate the nuisance. Lightner did not obey the order and the health commissioner brought suit. The court held that the system of garbage distribution employed by Dayton should be discontinued, the practice was unsanitary and posed potential health risks, the feeding of garbage to the hogs constituted a nuisance, and ordered it stopped.[282]

Chapter 37 Party Walls

A party wall is a wall on the boundary line of two properties which is used by both owners. Each party owns half the wall and has an easement on the other half of the wall. The wall is usually placed equally on each side of the property line.

Party walls have been used since ancient times. They are typically found in large cities and areas where row houses are common. The use of a party wall between two properties saves the cost of building a separate wall for each building. Walls can become party walls by agreement between the parties, by statute or by continued use.

In some areas statutes have been passed which define the circumstances under which a wall becomes a party wall. In other areas landowners can create a party wall by written or oral agreement, or by using a wall as a party wall without any agreement or understanding. If a person owning a large piece of property deeds parts of it to two different persons and the dividing line between the parts of the property is a wall, this can create a party wall.

Once a wall legally becomes a party wall, party wall law controls how it may be used and what the rights of the parties are. A wall remains a party wall until the two owners agree that it shall no longer be a party wall or until it decays or is destroyed. But neither owner has the right to destroy the wall without the other's consent. A destroyed party wall can be revived by rebuilding it.

A person building a party wall must make it strong enough to hold up buildings on both sides of it. There is no right to put windows in a party wall.

It is legal to build chimney flues in a party wall, but if they are located on both sides of the property line, then both owners can use them. It is legal to put a sign on one's own side of a party wall, but it is not legal to put one on the other person's side.

Nothing may be built which projects over the other owner's side of the party wall. In many areas it is legal to extend and thicken a party wall or to replace it with a better wall. However, it is not legal to make it thinner. In some states owners are required to contribute to the cost of building a party wall. Some examples of party wall disputes follow:

War stories: When Benjamin Auerbach and others began to extend a party wall between their property and that of Frank Cappelletti in Washington, D. C., Mr. Cappelletti filed suit in federal court to stop them from extending the wall and for damages to his property. In examining the law of the District of Columbia, the court found that the rules for construction of party walls were issued by George Washington and were still in force. One rule allowed a property owner to build a party wall extending onto his neighbor's land.[283]

When the Old St. Nicholas Hotel on Fourth Street in St. Louis, Missouri built an extension wall on its building and supported it by placing a girder in a party wall with the Nelson House next door. The walls both caved in. The owner of the hotel was liable since the wall was known to be old and weak and he had not provided additional support.[284]

Mary L. Yeakel and Mr. & Mrs. John Driscoll were owners of adjacent parcels of land in Allentown, Pennsylvania, and each owned one-half of a double home on the properties. The home was constructed in the 1930s and contains a party wall separating the two residences. In 1979 the Driscolls made some improvements to their property including replacement of part of the party wall with a fire wall. Ms. Yeakel filed a suit against them asking that the court order the fire wall removed since it encroached several inches onto her property and caused water problems in her basement. The court decided that removal of the wall would do Ms. Yeakle no good and would be a hardship on the Driscolls.[285]

Richard Blackmer and Montcalm County, Michigan, owned adjoining buildings which shared a common wall until a 1981 fire destroyed Mr. Blackmer's building. An engineer recommended to Blackmer that the party wall was unsound and that it should be demolished. The county refused to agree since the wall was providing some support to its roof. Blackmer sued for damages resulting from the delay in rebuilding caused by defendant's refusal to remove the damaged wall. The lower court dismissed his action. The Appeals court held that an owner of an easement right in a party wall had no obligation to agree to destroying the wall and that as long as the wall provided some support to defendant's building, plaintiff had no right to destroy the wall, and was under a duty to refrain from doing so.[286]

When the owner of property next to a party wall began making use of it for the construction of a building, the owner of the existing building sued, saying that the beams should not extend more than half way through the wall and that sewer pipes should not be installed in the wall. The Supreme Court of Iowa agreed.[287]

The city of La Crosse, Wisconsin, brought a suit against Jiracek Companies, the owner of a dilapidated building to order it be razed. It also joined Marc Arenson, the owner of the building next door which shared a party wall with the condemned building, asking the court to order him to pay the cost of strengthening the wall. The court noted that some states disagree, but that in Wisconsin the owner of a building sharing a party wall must pay for the support of the wall.[288]

Chapter 38 People

There are no laws in this country controlling the types of people who live in different neighborhoods. Such laws would violate the equal protection clause of the United States Constitution and many state constitutions as well. However, some private restrictive covenants which regulate the types of people in a neighborhood have been upheld, and some zoning laws have had the effect of controlling types of people who move into an area.

Many years ago it was not unusual for restrictions to be placed on subdivisions which stated that the properties could be transferred to "only to persons of the Caucasian race" or "not to persons of the Negro or Mongoloid races." In 1948 the United States Supreme Court held that the courts in this country could not enforce these covenants.[289] To get around this the courts started awarding monetary damages against anyone violating such covenants. Then in 1953 the Supreme Court ruled that courts could not grant monetary damages for these types of violations either.[290] It reasoned that the government of the United States cannot aid an individual in an act which would be unconstitutional for the government to do.

At that time there was no law against property owners voluntarily enforcing such a prohibition. However, the subsequently adopted civil rights and fair housing acts have made such restrictions illegal.

One type of control which has been upheld by the courts has been the right of some homeowners groups to control the sale of other units. This has often been held to be legal for condominiums and for cooperative apartments, but when applied to homes it has been rejected as an illegal limit on the salability of property (a restraint on alienation.)

War stories: In 1940 Mildred and Dayton S. Lauderbaugh purchased land in Wayne and Monroe Counties, Pennsylvania, including Lake Watawga. When they divided and sold the land as lots, they put a restriction on the property that all purchasers must be members of the Lake Watawga Association and that other members of the Association would vote to determine whether a prospective purchaser could become a member. In 1958, after her husband passed away, Mrs. Lauderbach filed a suit to declare the restrictions void so that she could sell some of the land to persons who were not members of the association. The defendants in that suit filed another suit against Mrs. Lauderbach to

stop her from conveying the property to anyone not belonging to the association. They won and she appealed to
the Pennsylvania Supreme Court which held that the restrictions were void because they restricted the ability of
people to freely sell their land and that members of the
association could by whim deny any person the right to buy
property.[291]

In 1924 Houston Properties Corp. built a fifteen story
apartment building at the southeast corner of Fifth Avenue
and 97th Street in Manhattan. It organized the building as
a coop and organized a company called 1158 Fifth Avenue,
Inc. to own the building. Those purchasing shares of stock
in the corporation were allowed to live in the apartments.
In March, 1938 Mrs. Belle C. Harriss, who owned several
shares of the stock and used one of the apartments, offered
to sell her stock back to the corporation at a loss, but it
refused to purchase it. She then transferred it to a corporation owned by her husband. In a lawsuit between the
parties the court held that restrictions on the right to sell
stock in a cooperative apartment house in New York are
valid.[292]

To avoid the problem of causing an illegal restraint on alienation,
some associations have instead created a right of first refusal to a
homeowners group to purchase a property which is to be sold to
someone they find objectionable. This has often been held to be legal.

War story: York Center is a subdivision in Du Page County, Illinois,
just south of Lombard. It has seventy-two families, all of
which are members of the York Center Community Cooperative, Inc., their neighborhood association. Under the
rules of their association, no member could sell their interest until the cooperative had an opportunity to bid and any
interest sold on the open market could be bought back by
the association. When William Gale and others refused to
convey their interests to the association it sued. The Illinois
Supreme Court held that while restrictions controlling the
right to sell property are usually void, where they are
reasonable and useful in attaining accepted social ends, as
in this case, they would be legal.[293]

Another type of controls which has the effect of controlling the
people in a neighborhood is restricting the property to single-family

residences. This can be done by private property restrictions or by zoning laws. Such restrictions and laws are usually upheld, but some courts have weakened them by broadening the definition of "family."

War stories: An ordinance of the Village of Belle Terre limited land use to single family dwellings and defined family as people related by blood, marriage or adoption or no more than two unrelated persons living and cooking together. When a homeowner rented a house to six unrelated students the village prosecuted them and won in the Federal District Court. They appealed to the Court of Appeals and the law was found to be unconstitutional. But the village appealed to the United States Supreme Court and the usually liberal Justice William O. Douglas joined Justices Rehnquist, Burger, Stewart, White and Powell in holding the law to be valid. The court held that the law was reasonable and that it bore a rational relationship to a permissible state objective.[294]

Mrs. Inez Moore lived in East Cleveland with her son and two grandsons who were first cousins. In 1973 she was convicted of violating a city ordinance which limited occupancy to a single family. Under the rationale of the above case her conviction was upheld by the Court of Appeals, but on appeal to the United States Supreme Court the law was held to be unconstitutional. The difference, the court held, was that in this case the law dictated living arrangements within families, and made it a crime for a grandmother to live with a grandchild. It noted the sanctity of the family in America and said that the history and tradition of the country compel a larger conception of the family.[295]

In 1980 the New York City/Long Island County Services Group leased a home at 3 Johns Hollow Road in the Hamlet of Crane Neck for use as a home for eight severely retarded adults. In addition to the residents there were 16 staff persons working at the property. This upset other residents in the area since the property had restrictions on its use limiting it to single-family residences. The neighbors filed suit and the trial court found that such use of the property was not use as a single-family residence. The appeals court reversed, finding that in New York eight severely retarded adults and 16 staff members could constitute a family. The case then went to New York's highest court which said that such a group was not a single family, but that it didn't matter. It held that when the state wants to do something important like providing a home for retarded persons, it can ignore private deed restrictions.[296]

Some areas have attempted to use zoning to exclude certain people from the area. This is done by requiring that lots or homes are of a certain (large) size, or banning multifamily or publicly subsidized housing.

Generally, federal courts have not forbidden such exclusionary zoning, but several state courts have held them to be illegal under state constitutions.

One consideration which is looked at is whether the zoning has an exclusionary purpose, or merely an exclusionary effect. For example, if the purpose of a zoning rule is to discriminate racially, then it will be held invalid. If it is found that there is a legitimate purpose to the rule, but that it inadvertently has a discriminatory effect, then it is usually held to be valid.

War stories: In the early 1970s the local chapter of the NAACP and others brought a suit against the Township of Mt. Laurel, New Jersey, complaining that its zoning plan excluded low income individuals from the township. The township was a nice area with expensive homes. The Supreme Court of New Jersey ruled that under the state constitution, the township had a duty to provide for a fair share of the region's low income population. Eight years later the township was again brought before the New Jersey Supreme Court with a complaint that nothing had been done by the township to allow low income individuals to move into the area. In an opinion of over one hundred pages complete with several pages of maps, the court laid out a detailed plan of changes in zoning, incentives for builders of low income housing and special judges to administer the program, in order to force the towns in the area to accept low income housing.[297]

A nonprofit housing developer contracted to buy land in Arlington Heights, Illinois to build low-income housing, contingent upon rezoning of the property. The rezoning was denied and the company sued, claiming the reason for the denial was racial discrimination. The United States Supreme Court held that the fact that the zoning had a racial impact was not the sole matter to consider. For the zoning to be invalid, there must have been proof of a racially discriminatory intent or purpose. In this case there was a legitimate purpose other than racial discrimination.[298]

The Cleburne Living Center brought suit against the city of Cleburne, Texas, in federal district court because the zoning law did not permit it to start a group home for the mentally retarded. The suit ended up in the Supreme Court of the United States. The justices of the court filed three different opinions. [Is it any wonder why lawyers can't figure out what the law is?] A majority of the justices ruled that mental retardation was not a suspect classification which requires a strict scrutiny, but that the law violated equal protection anyway, since there was no rational basis for excluding the home from the area.[299]

Zoning laws have also been able to control some other uses of property.

War stories: LeRoy Moore applied to the Mayor of Statesboro, Georgia, for a permit to build an apartment building on some land within the city. It was denied and he was informally told that if he lowered the density from 15 units per acre to 10 units per acre it would be approved. But it was again denied. He filed suit and the court held that when a applicant complied with the applicable codes, the mayor and council of Statesboro did not have any discretion as to whether or not to issue a permit. The area was zoned residential, and there was nothing prohibiting apartment buildings in a residential area.[300]

When a boat shed was built in a residential area in Tuftonboro, New Hampshire, the residents filed a suit saying that the increased truck traffic was dangerous to their children, their property values were diminished and that the gasoline in the boats was dangerous. The court noted that there were no zoning laws in the town and that such a business was not a nuisance and that the harm was not substantial or unreasonable.[301]

The Arkansas Release Guidance Foundation operated a halfway house in Pulaski County called New Life House which it said would exclude criminals whose offenses

involved sex, drugs and alcohol. However, it turned out
that there had been at least one person there convicted of
carnal abuse and another had been removed for activities
related to alcohol. A suit was filed by the Halfway House
Opposition Committee," a group of neighbors opposed to
the halfway house. The committee won both in the trial
court and before the Supreme Court of Arkansas which
held that where a halfway house reduces property values
and causes neighbors a real and reasonable fear for their
safety, it would be a nuisance and could be stopped by the
court.[302]

Chapter 39 Phone Calls

It has often been held that verbal harassment is not actionable, that is, one cannot be sued for it. However, in cases where a person uses a phone to harass another person, especially where the harassment is shocking to the courts, they have made exceptions to the rule and allowed the harassed party to recover.

The persons in the following cases probably were not neighbors, but the holdings of the courts would apply just as well in neighbor situations.

War stories: On October 27, 1916 Mrs. Cora Brooker was working as a night operator in Barnwell, South Carolina. A. E. Silverthorne called the exchange asking for a connection. Mrs. Brooker had trouble making the connection and according to her, Mr. Silverthorne said "You God damned woman! None of you attend to your business. You are a God damned liar. If I were there, I would break your God damned neck." In a law suit, Mrs. Brooker claimed that she was so shocked that she was unfit for work and had to take sleeping medicine. She said that she continued to suffer in health, mind and body on account of the abusive and threatening language. Mr. Silverthorne denied using such language and his wife and a lineman of the telephone company who happened to have been listening in also testified that they didn't hear him use that language. Despite this, the jury awarded Mrs. Brooker $2,000 in damages. On appeal to the Supreme Court of South Carolina the court reversed the jury and said that such words would not have bothered a person of ordinary reason and firmness.[303]

Ms. Housh, a supervisor of music in the public schools of Dayton, Ohio in the 1950s, got behind in payment on a bill to Dr. L. A. Lydic in the amount of $197. He turned the bill over to Doctors Business Bureau, a collection agency. According to Ms. Housh, the collection agency called her six or eight times every day at her home and work, as late as 11:45 p. m. over a period of three weeks. They also called her supervisors and called her at work as many as three times in 15 minutes. She sued for invasion of privacy and the Supreme Court of Ohio said that she was entitled to relief.[304]

Myrtle L. Wiggins rented out rooms in her residence to tenants. As she explained it, in May of 1955 an agent of Moskins Credit Clothing Store called and asked to talk to one of her tenants. She refused to call the tenant to the phone and told the company not to call again. The calling party became abusive and, using vile and opprobrious language told her he would call whenever he wished. For three months thereafter agents of the company supposedly continued to call her, even late in the evening, using language "unfit for the ears of a lady." She sued in federal district court in Columbia, South Carolina. In differentiating this case from cases where insulting words were held to be harmless, the court noted that the use of the telephone invaded Ms. Wiggins home, causing a nuisance.[305]

When Arzalia got behind on money she owed to Signature Loans, Inc., the company's employees called her employer, Ruby Savage, as many as 15 times a day demanding that she pay the debt and made visits, demanding payment in person. Mrs. Savage became nervous and sleepless, and eventually had a heart attack. In a suit against the company and its president, W. Lee Moore, Jr., she was awarded $500. On appeal, the defendants claimed that they had a right to be unreasonable, but not to be outrageous, and that they were not outrageous. The court held that the efforts were harsh, unreasonable, harassing and negligent and that Mrs. Savage was entitled to the award.[306]

According to Rose, when her husband got behind on payments to Statewide Finance Co., she began getting calls demanding payment. In December, 1964, she was in Griffin Hospital in Derby, Connecticut for an operation. While she was in the recovery room after the operation the company continued to harass and annoy her. When she sued for invasion of privacy the company tried to have the suit thrown out, but the Circuit Court of Connecticut held that under these facts she would have a claim.[307]

Chapter 40 Practical Jokes

There is nothing that can be done legally about harmless practical jokes. There is no law on the books making it illegal to make a fool of someone. However, where the joke causes actual harm there are a couple of possible remedies available.

Where the joke causes some injury or damage to property, the remedy can be either criminal or a civil action for damages. Where the harm is some sort of emotional injury, recovery is not as simple, but several cases have recognized a right to recovery.

War stories: The wife of Thomas Wilkinson was told by a Mr. Downton that her husband had been in an accident and was lying at The Elms publichouse with both legs broken, but it was not true. She suffered a shock to her nervous system and became seriously ill. A jury awarded her £100 plus traveling expenses. The judgement was upheld on appeal because defendant had willfully done an act calculated to cause physical harm, and the cause and effect of the harm was sufficiently close.[308]

Carrie E. Nickerson, a maiden nearing the age of 45, lived in Webster Parish, Louisiana. Although she had been in an insane asylum 20 years earlier, she had found employment as a soap saleswoman and was successful. While travelling her route, she was told by a "negro fortune teller" that some of her relatives had buried some gold. Having heard a family tradition that a large amount of gold had been buried by her ancestors, she believed it. With the help of some relatives and friends she began digging on the land of John W. Smith. After much digging uncovered nothing, Mr. Smith's daughter, Minnie, along with William "Bud" Baker and H. R. Hayes came up with the idea of burying a "pot of gold" for them to find. They took a copper pot, filled it with rocks and dirt and buried it with a note stating that it should not be opened for three days after it was found. When it was found Miss Nickerson planned a big celebration at a local bank for the opening of the pot and even invited a judge from a nearby town. At the opening ceremony she was so humiliated that she flew into a rage and died within two years. Her heirs continued her lawsuit against the perpetrators of the joke after her death and were awarded $500 in damages. The Supreme Court of

Louisiana said that had she lived, it would have awarded her even more for her humiliation.[309]

In order to get a woman to a hospital to have her committed for mental illness, the deputy sheriffs of Maricopa County, Arizona, told her that her seven-year-old child was critically injured in an automobile accident. When she got there she was disrobed in front of the deputies and confined to the psychiatric ward. She sued for emotional distress and invasion of privacy. The Supreme Court of Arizona held that the deputies were not liable for her having been disrobed by the hospital employees, but that she did have a claim against them for emotional distress.[310]

According to Vicky Halio, a native of Turkey who had become a United States citizen and was living in New York, she had been keeping company with Eli M. Lurie for two years, expecting to marry him. Without telling her, he married another woman. When she found out, their relationship ended. He then mailed an envelope addressed to Mrs. Vicky Halio, a poem entitled "An Ode to Vicky" in which he referred to her as "The Tortured Turk" and taunted her, claiming he was "wise to her game," and stating that through the coming years she would be an object of derision and the subject of amusement. This allegedly caused Miss Halio mental distress and physical illness. She sued and a New York appellate court held that she did have a valid claim.[311]

Chapter 41 Privacy

In most states there are four types of invasion of privacy recognized by the law. Two of them, using someone's likeness for commercial purposes and placing someone in a false light in the public eye, usually do not apply to neighbor relations. These usually involve the news media or businesses.

The two types of invasion of privacy which may come up between neighbors are the right not to have one's solitude or seclusion intruded upon and the right not to have one's private facts disclosed. In some states, such as New York, these rights are spelled out in the statutes, but in other states, such as New Jersey, they are part of the common law developed by judges.

Peeping Tom. One type of invasion of one's privacy is the "Peeping Tom." This may be someone coming up to your window and peeking in, or looking across from another window with a telescope. For these situations the best solution is not a legal one, it is keeping one's curtains closed. In some states there are laws against "window-peeping," but there are also laws against indecent exposure. If you complain about a person watching you undress, they may charge you with exposing yourself in an open window.

As for suing someone in civil court for peeping in one's window, privacy rights are a growing area of the law. Rights which were rejected years ago are now being recognized and the time may be right for a court to award damages in such a case. However, no record has been found of any court doing so thus far. In fact, even some laws against window peeping have been thrown out.[312]

One early case of invasion of privacy involved a jail which was built such that the prisoners could look into a nearby residence. This is mentioned in Chapter 32. The other cases used in this chapter do not all specifically involve neighbors, but the principles used in the decisions would apply as well to neighbor situations.

War stories: William D. Souder filed a workman's compensation claim and his employer hired Pendleton Detectives, Inc. to investigate whether he was really injured. They followed him around, peeped in his windows and watched him with binoculars. Mr. Souder sued and the court held that since the agency had a legitimate right to investigate a claim he could not collect unless the detectives violated a specific law while investigating him.[313]

In the 1930s Kenneth and Elihu Heath operated a public beach on the West shore of Lake Washington at the southeast corner of the Sand Point Naval Air Station in Seattle, Washington. Some of the other homeowners on the lake were upset because of noise, vulgar language and intoxicants used at the beach and because two row boats at the beach were used by some people to row along the shore and observe their yards and look into their residences. However, in a lawsuit against the Heaths, the court ruled that this would not constitute a nuisance and that since this was the only beach in the area it would not be shut down.[314]

Entering the premises. Where a person invades your privacy by coming onto your property or into your house there is a much better case for recovery. The reason is that there is also a trespass which is a much more easily recognized wrong. If the person touches you at the same time, that makes it an even stronger case since it involves battery.

War stories: In Michigan about 1880 a Dr. DeMay brought an unmarried friend, Mr. Scattergood with him when he visited Mrs. Roberts who was pregnant. While they were at the Roberts' house, Mrs. Roberts delivered her baby and Mr. Scattergood assisted in the delivery. Some time later Mrs. Roberts discovered that Mr. Scattergood was neither a doctor nor a medical student and became upset that he had been there at her delivery. She sued the doctor and won, since the doctor had brought the stranger into her home at a most personal time of her life.[315]

A patient on his deathbed in Maine and the patient's wife told his doctor that he did not wish to be photographed. The doctor photographed him anyway and in doing so lifted his head on a pillow. In a law suit after the patient's death the court found the doctor liable for both invasion of privacy and assault and battery.[316]

However, in some cases a person, such as a landlord or repairman, may have a right to enter your apartment.

War story: Delores Novel sued her landlord for invasion of privacy for entering her apartment and taking pictures. Her case was dismissed and she filed her own appeal without a lawyer.

The dismissal was affirmed. The court held that in New York no common law right of privacy exists and the only privacy rights are provided by statute. The New York statute on privacy only concerns the commercial exploitation of one's personality.[317]

Disclosing private facts. People with whom we live in close proximity often become acquainted with intimate details of our lives. A person can be held liable for disclosure for these details if the following conditions are met:

The details are private or secret facts

The disclosure is a public one

Making the disclosure would be offensive to a reasonable person

One limitation to this is that persons who are in the public eye, such as movie stars, politicians, directors of organizations and others in positions of authority, have less of a right to privacy. This is because they are considered to have placed themselves in the public eye, and in many cases details about them are of necessary concern to the public.

When one leaves another in charge of one's property, for example, by renting it out, then that person has a right to permit others to make it public.

War story: When Oscar and Johanna Merz were in Borneo, Indonesia, they rented their home in Georgia to Mark and Donna Plants. While the property was leased to the Plants, Professional Health Control of Augusta filmed four television commercials on the premises. The Merzes sued Professional Health Control, claiming, among other things, that such filming on their premises was an invasion of their privacy. They lost. The courts held that by leasing their house they gave up any expectation of privacy, and that the filming of a commercial in their home was not an intrusion on their seclusion or solitude or into their private affairs. They asked the appeals court for a second hearing, and asked the supreme court of Georgia to hear their case, but were denied in both instances.[318]

Chapter 42 Radioactivity

Leakage of radiation from a nearby facility can be one of the most frightening events in a homeowner's life. Besides the devastation to property values, there is the risk of cancer and future birth defects.

The law regarding radioactivity is in most respects controlled by the Atomic Energy Act of 1954. While state law determines general principles of liability, many of the ultimate issues are determined by federal laws and regulations.

There have been several instances of neighbors of nuclear facilities attempting court action and many of the legal issues have been settled. The courts have ruled that the Federal government has the exclusive power to regulate radiological hazards. However, the states are allowed to regulate hazards caused by a nuclear facility which are not of a radiological nature. This means a state court could declare a facility a nuisance for any reason other than one based upon a radiological hazard.

War stories: Wendell Marshall, a resident of Midland County, Michigan, sued to stop the construction of a pressurized water nuclear power plant on the Tittabawassee River, one mile from Marshall's home. Marshall claimed the nuclear power plant would be a private and public nuisance jeopardizing the health of Marshall, depreciating his property value, and interfere with his use and enjoyment of his property. The lower court held for Consumers Power Co. The Court of Appeals held that state courts could not consider the allegations dealing with the possibility of nuclear accident, as that was the federal government's domain. State courts however, could consider the allegations of nonradiological hazards from the plant, and that if a state court did find a nuisance to exist it could require the plant to abate the nuisance, but could not prohibit construction of the plant. The court held that Marshall had failed to show a present or definite future nuisance, and affirmed the lower holding.[319]

When a large number of fish were killed by a discharge of cold water by a nuclear power plant owned by Jersey Cent. Power & Light Co., the New Jersey Department of Environmental Protection sought and won a judgment holding the company responsible. However, this was reversed by the

New jersey Supreme Court which held such a judgment would infringe on the subject of radiological hazards. It noted that the shutdown was required by rules of the Atomic Energy Commission because of a coolant leak.[320]

In 1973 Good Fund Ltd.—1972, a limited partnership with a general partner based in Texas, decided that Colorado was a good place to invest and bought some land in Jefferson County, Colorado, near the Rocky Flats Nuclear Plant. As it turned out, the investment was a poor one since the land was contaminated by plutonium, americium and uranium and was unfit for either residential or commercial development. Feeling that this awful state of affairs must be someone's fault other than their own, they called in the lawyers, and thus began a series of lawsuits involving the sellers of the property, Dow Chemical Co., Rockwell International, the United States Government, the State of Colorado, Great Western Venture and others too numerous to mention. After over six years of litigation, the Federal District Court in Colorado held that since there was no showing of violation of any Environmental Protection Agency standards,the issues were preempted by federal law, the issues involved were largely political, it had no power to take action. The court noted that the owners of the land could show nothing more than potential harm from the radioactive chemicals on their property and that this was not a trespass.[321] The case was appealed to the United States Court of Appeals for the Tenth Circuit which reversed the ruling. The court held that this case was similar to the Karen Silkwood case and that state law was not preempted by the Atomic Energy Act in cases like this involving negligence, trespass and nuisance. It noted that in cases like this there was no administrative remedy available.[322]

Chapter 43 Sights

Until recent years government attempts to control the look of a neighborhood have generally not been seen favorably by the courts. When the United States Supreme Court first approved zoning laws in 1926[323] it held that if the objectives of zoning were the health, safety, morals and welfare of the citizens it was valid.

The first crack in the rules was when cases began to accept aesthetics as one of several objectives which could form the basis for a zoning scheme. As governmental regulation has become more acceptable in more and more areas of our lives, the courts have held that aesthetics could be the sole basis for a zoning regulation.

War stories: The city of Baltimore, Maryland was so successful in limiting the size of signs in the Charles Center area that it decided to try to achieve uniformity in the whole downtown district. In 1970, just before the expiration of a five-year moratorium in the sign ordinance, Mano Swartz, Inc. and nine other firms filed suit attacking the validity of the ordinance regulating signs. The trial judge ruled that the ordinance was invalid and the city appealed. The Court of Appeals of Maryland agreed that since the sole purpose of the ordinance was aesthetics, it was not a permissible use of the police powers.[324]

The county of Monterey, California, passed a zoning ordinance which required removal of billboards within one year. National Advertising Co., which owned several billboards in the county, brought suit against the county to keep it from enforcing the law. The trial court agreed with National and found the law to be unenforceable. The County appealed and the Supreme Court of California held that the law could be enforced as to 31 billboards which the company had fully amortized under the IRS regulations, but that it could not be enforced as to 11 signs which had not been amortized. The court said that there was nothing wrong with the fact that the company would have to pay about $139 per billboard to remove them.[325]

The city of San Diego enacted an ordinance banning many types of billboards and signs in the city, for the purpose of eliminating hazards to pedestrians and motorists and to improve the appearance of the city. The ordinance prohibited most types of signs except on-site commercial signs. Several companies engaged in outdoor advertising sued and the trial court ruled the law unconstitutional. The appeals court agreed but the Supreme Court of California reversed, holding the law to be valid. The companies appealed to the United States Supreme Court which reversed the California Supreme Court. It held that while the controls of commercial signs were valid, the ban on non-commercial signs was invalid under the First and Fourteenth Amendments to the U.S. Constitution.[326] (Now, if the California Supreme Court didn't know what the law was, how can you, or your lawyer expect to?)

In some cases special laws have been passed to combat sights which were especially disturbing to the city fathers.

War story: To protest the high taxes of the city of Rye, New York, Webster and Marion Stover erected a clothesline, filled with old clothes, in front of their house on the corner of Rye Beach and Forest Avenues. During each succeeding year they would add another clothesline, including underwear, old uniforms, tattered clothing, rags and scarecrows. By 1961 there were six clotheslines, three on Forest and three on Rye Beach. In August, 1961 the city passed an ordinance prohibiting clotheslines in a front or side yard abutting a street and prosecuted Mr. and Mrs. Stover for maintaining their clotheslines. The city won in the trial court and the Stovers appealed, claiming that the law infringed upon their constitutional rights. Both the county court and New York's highest court sided with the city.[327]

If an unsightly property is not against a zoning law or building code there is probably not much that can be done in civil court. In order to constitute a nuisance it would have to cause substantial injury to a nearby owner.

War story: In 1923 the city of Indianola, Iowa, established a dump in an agricultural area within the city limits. Over the years it was enlarged by adding more land. In 1956 Ronald Mahlstadt purchased a large tract of land next to the dump and began developing it into a subdivision. Mr. Mahlstadt's own home was in the subdivision and just 120 yards from the dump. The dump was an open type and from the subdivision it was in plain view. Rats and flies were attracted to the dump and smoke was given off night and day from the burning of garbage and animal bodies. Mr. Mahlstadt filed suit and won an injunction ordering that the dump stop operations. The city appealed and the Supreme Court of Iowa ruled that as long as the dump put up a fence, stopped burning animal bodies and took action to reduce the rats and flies, the dump would be allowed to continue operations. The court found it important that the dump had been in operation for many years and that it provided an essential service to the community.[328]

Chapter 44 Smoke, Dust and Pollution

Traditionally, the only way to stop pollution was a nuisance suit. If it was a public nuisance the city could take action. For a private nuisance, affected citizens could go to court. But as we enter the age of environmental consciousness more and more remedies become available.

Besides zoning and land use laws there are specific pollution laws passed by the state and local government as well as the United States Congress. Now if the local zoning or health official cannot do anything, there are many other state and federal officials whose sole job it is to combat pollution. Additionally, many of the antipollution laws allow suits by private individuals.

Some of the federal laws which may be useful against a neighborhood polluter are:
Rivers and Harbors Act of 1899, 33 USC §§ 407, 411
Federal Water Pollution Control Act, 33 USC § 1365
National Environmental Policy Act of 1969, 42 USC §§4321-4335
Clean Air Act, 42 USC §7604
Resource Conservation and Recovery Act of 1976, 42 USC §6972
Comprehensive Environmental Response, Compensation and
    Liability Act, 42 USC 9659

After the passage of the National Environmental Policy Act many states passed their own environmental policy acts. These acts include such provisions as requiring environmental impact statements and allowing private suits.

Some state constitutions were amended in the 1960s and 1970s to include clauses providing for protection of the environment. Some of these clauses specifically allow for citizen suits to protect the environment and others have been interpreted to do so by the courts.

If there is a neighborhood pollution problem and one of the various government agencies cannot do anything, the nuisance suit is still an available remedy. The following cases will provide some guidance as to how courts look at nuisance suits for pollution.

War stories: Craven Bros. operated a carpet cleaning business, laundry and stable at 1443 Franklin Street, Philadelphia, Pennsylvania in a "good class" residential area. Mr. Rodenhausen who lived next door filed suit claiming it was a nuisance because of the dust and moths from the carpet cleaning and the stench and noise from the stable. The court agreed, finding that it seriously interfered with Mr. Rodenhausen's comfort and enjoyment of his house.[329]

A dye works was being operated in the 1930s on St. Charles Place in Chester, Pennsylvania which the neighbors claimed was a nuisance, causing smoke, soot and fumes. The company brought in witnesses from the neighborhood who testified that they hung waitress uniforms and chiropodist towels out to dry and they they were not affected by any smoke or soot. This convinced the court that it was not bad enough to be a nuisance.[330]

When the garbage dump in the city of Ann Arbor, Michigan, became objectionable and nearly full, the city began looking for another site. After three and a half years, it found a parcel with a ravine suitable for dumping about a mile north of the city. In February, 1941, the city began using the ravine as a dump. In May James C. Smith and other neighbors in the area filed suit against the city to stop the use of the land as a dump. The trial court ruled for the neighbors, enjoining use of the land as a dump, and the city appealed. The Supreme Court of Michigan reversed the decision and allowed the dump to continue. It noted that there was nowhere in the city for a dump and the surrounding county had made it illegal to start a new dump, so that the city had nowhere else to dump. But it ordered the city to eliminate the most objectionable features of the dump.[331]

In the 1950's the state health commissioner decided to crack down on the garbage dumps in Montgomery County, Ohio. Nine suits were filed, one of them against Cyril Grillot and others who operated the South Dayton Dump. The Supreme Court of Ohio noted that both dumping and burning of garbage had been a problem in the state for many years and that it is clearly a nuisance. The court gave the owners of the dumps just 30 days to complete their burning operations and then to convert to a sanitary landfill operation in which the garbage would be buried each day.[332]

Chapter 45 Trees and Plants

Plants have probably been one of the earliest sources of disagreements between neighbors. Trees have fallen on people and houses, they have blocked sunlight, they have clogged drains with their leaves and their roots have damaged all types of structures.

The problems encountered with plants usually fall into one of three areas, ownership, bothersomeness and dangerousness.

Ownership

The ownership of a plant depends upon where its trunk is situated. The owner of the land in which a plant is growing is the owner of the plant, and all the fruit growing on it, even if the fruit is hanging in another person's yard.

War stories: A row of hedge trees had been growing for about forty years one foot on Eugenie Wideman's side of her property line with Adrian Faivre when Mr. Faivre began in 1915 to cut some of them down. She sued for an injunction and for damages. The court awarded her $65 and ordered Mr. Faivre to stop cutting them down.[333]

In 1871 Dr. Hoffman's sister, Sarah, was picking cherries from branches of her brother's cherry tree. When she attempted to pick cherries from a branch which hung over onto Abner Armstrong's land, Abner told her to stop. When Sarah continued to pick cherries, Abner stopped her by using force, causing personal injury. Sarah sued Abner for assault and battery. The court held that a person upon whose lands a tree wholly stands is the owner of the whole tree, and is entitled to all its fruit, even if some of its branches overhang the lands of another. Abner was therefore liable for assault and battery.[334]

Mease and Dinius had agreed to plant hedges on the boundary line of their adjoining property at equal cost to each. Dinius had cut down some of the hedges, and Mease brought a court action. Mease claimed they had agreed to plant on the boundary line, but did not know if this had been done. Dinius claimed the trees were wholly on his land. A survey showed the trees were wholly on Dinius' land. The court held that Mease could sue for Dinius' breach of the agreement to plant on the boundary line, but not for trespass and diminuation of property value. They awarded Mease damages in the amount of his interest in the value of the trees.[335]

Where a plant is located directly upon a property line, it is jointly owned by both of the property owners. Each would also own any fruit on the plant. Neither one has the right to cut it down without the permission of the other. Only if the plants become a nuisance will the courts allow removal.

War stories: A row of large cottonwood trees sat on the boundary line between the properties owned by Mr. Musch and Mr. Burkhart in Iowa in the 1890s. One of them needed the trees for protection from winter winds. The other wanted them removed because they shaded his field and made it unproductive. The court held that the damage was insufficient to warrant the trees removal.[336]

William Lemon and Florence Curington owned adjoining property. Two trees planted on the Lemon's property before they bought it were causing problems because the roots had spread and were pushing against Mrs. Curington's basement so as to crack it and push the whole house inward. Mrs. Curington sued alleging the trees constituted a nuisance, and asked that they be removed. The court authorized the removal of one of the trees. The Idaho Supreme Court affirmed, holding that the tree whose roots were threatening the home of Mrs. Curington was a nuisance, but the other tree whose roots did not constitute a threat was not a nuisance. They held Mrs. Curington could remove the nuisance tree at her own expense.[337]

The Cookes and McShanes owned adjoining property which was divided by a hedge which had grown to about twelve feet high. Edward McShane cut the hedge to about six feet and Joanna Cooke sued for destruction of the hedge. At trial the court found for McShane. The Appeals court found that the trial court was in error in holding that McShane did not invade the rights of the Cookes since a lot of the hedge was on the land of the Cookes. However, since the Cookes at best suffered only nominal damages, a new trial would be a waste of time and the court affirmed the lower decision.[338]

Bothersome Plants and Trees

On the issue of what the remedy is for plants which are bothersome, such as trees which fill gutters with their leaves, the courts of our nation are divided into three camps. The different rules which they follow are called the Massachusetts Rule, the Restatement Rule, and most recently invented, the Hawaii Rule.

The Massachusetts Rule is that people who are bothered by encroaching roots and branches can cut them off at the property line themselves and should not be bringing such cases to court. The rationale is that tree growth is natural and the common sense solution is to just cut them.

The Restatement rule is so named because it is contained in the Restatement of Torts (Second) promulgated by the American Law Institute. Under this rule the Massachusetts approach only applies to "natural growth." If there is some damage due to an artificial condition created on the land, then the landowner can be held liable and the case may be taken to court.

A Hawaiian court recently rejected both the Massachusetts Rule and the Restatement Rule. This court felt that the Massachussets Rule was "simple and certain" but that it was not realistic and fair. It ruled that where overhanging branches or protruding roots actually cause, or there is immanent danger of them causing harm to property other than plant life, in ways other than by casting shade or dropping leaves, flowers, or fruit, then the endangered neighbor may require the owner to cut back the plant. If the owner refuses of if there is imminent danger, then one can have them cut and bill the neighbor. Also, one can always cut the branches to the property line at one's own cost.

In some states the courts seem to take into account the further factor of whether the damage or injury is serious.

Not all states have had a chance to issue court opinions on tree branches. Perhaps their lawyers can't take the stress of such litigation. So it is not known for sure how a similar case would be decided in all states. However, the following is a list of some states whose positions are known.

These states appear to follow the Massachussetts Rule. An asterisk (*) after the state means that there may be an exception in cases where there is substantial injury.
Alabama
Arizona*
Connecticut

District of Columbia*
Illinois
Iowa
Kansas
Kentucky
Massachussets
Nebraska
New Jersey
New York*
Ohio*
Rhode Island
Tennessee*
Vermont

These states seem to follow either the Restatement Rule or the Hawaii Rule in putting some obligation on the landowner.

California
Hawaii
Indiana
Louisiana
Mississippi
Missouri
New Mexico
North Carolina

The following are some noteworthy neighborhood battles over trees.

War stories: In the 1880s a party named Grandona sued a party named Lovdal in Sacramento county court claiming that the latter's trees were casting shade upon his land, injuring crops, filling his soil with roots and destroying the value of the land. The suit was dismissed, but on appeal to the Supreme Court of California the court held that when the branches of a tree are extending over the property line the owner may cut them off at the line or sue for damages and to force the owner of the tree to cut them.[339]

When Salvatore Loggia built a concrete patio in his yard in Suffolk County, New York, a tree belonging to Katerina Grobe, which was near the property line and just eight or nine inches from the edge of the patio, was just three inches in diameter. Eight years latter the tree was much bigger and its roots were causing damage to the patio. When he

complained to Ms. Grobe, she told him he could remove
the tree. Instead he sued her for trespass and nuisance for
$1500 damage to his patio. A previous New York case had
ruled that an owner does not have to resort to self-help
remedies for problems involving roots. However in this
case the court made an exception to the self-help rule since
the tree was planted before the patio was built and Mr.
Loggia could have easily cut the roots before they reached
his patio. The court also noted that Ms. Grobe had not done
anything intentional or negligent to cause the problem.[340]

In Louisiana the Civil Code, Article 688 prohibits a landowner from
cutting or removing branches from his neighbor's trees that have come
onto his property.

Dangerous Plants and Trees

In cases of dangerous trees the courts have made a distinction
between rural and urban areas. In urban areas persons in possession of
land (owners or tenants) have been held to have a duty to inspect their
trees and to be sure that they do not present a danger. In rural areas,
especially where persons own vast tracts of land, courts have held that
they do not have to inspect the trees and no not even have to remove
them if they are known to be rotten.

War stories: Bonnie Bell Taylor, who was driving down a road in
Claclamas County, Oregon, on a "dark and windy January
evening" sustained injuries when her car struck a tree
which had fallen across the road. She sued the county
which owned the road right-of-way and Marion Olsen
who owned the adjoining land. The trial court ruled
against her and she appealed to the Oregon Supreme
Court. The court ruled that while a landowner must take
reasonable care to prevent a risk from dangerous trees, the
fact that this tree rotted from the center and could not have
been noticed by a reasonable inspection, the county and
landowner would not be liable.[341]

On September 26, 1980, Daniel H. Ivancic was working on
his truck in the driveway of his parent's home on Prospect
Street in Fultonville, New York during a heavy windstorm.
About noon, a limb from a Maple tree on the neighboring
property fell and severely injured him. However, his suit
was dismissed because no evidence was presented that

indicated that there was any evidence that the tree was defective before the accident. The court ruled that in order to collect, the injured party would have to prove that the tree was in a dangerous condition, that the condition caused the injury, that the landowner realized or should have realized that the tree was dangerous and that there would have been enough time to correct the danger after the landowner realized it. Needless to say, Mr. Ivancic and his attorney were not happy with this result. They appealed to the highest court in New York and lost, asked for a reargument of the case which was denied and then tried to appeal to the U. S. Supreme Court and were denied a hearing there also.[342]

Chapter 46 Trespass

Trespass is one of the earliest concepts of English common law, probably because one of the first purposes of law was to protect rights in property. Trespass is the act of unlawfully entering another's property. In explaining trespass law nearly three hundred years ago a judge said, "The law bounds every man's property and is his fence."[343]

In Roman times people could not be sued for trespass unless they had been told not to enter the land. But the English took a different approach and ruled that a person could always be sued for trespass unless he had permission to enter the property.

An act of trespass includes any "breaking of the close," the invisible line surrounding a person's property. It includes walking onto a person's property, throwing things there, or even putting one's arm over the property line. Because one of the requirements for trespass is an intent to do the act, it does not include accidentally falling onto a person's land.

One rule of trespass law that is most important is that some *thing* must enter the property. Noise and vibrations cannot trespass, although they can constitute a nuisance.

It does not matter whether or not the trespass resulted in any harm to the landowner. In discussing nuisances the legal maxim, *De minimis non curat lex*, the law does not concern itself with trifles, is often mentioned. In trespass cases this maxim is not applicable. The ownership of land was considered so sacred that any interference with it was considered a serious offense. Even a harmless trespass was considered enough for court action. Part of the reason for this was the fact that entering a person's property regularly and continuously could result in obtaining rights to the property.

To explain why damages are awarded even if the trespass appears harmless, a court in 1835 said, "From every such entry against the will of the possessor, the law infers some damage; if nothing more, the treading down grass or herbage."[344]

A famous old neighbor dispute, which was mentioned in the introduction to this book, gave us some lessons in trespass law. In the late 1890s the Hannabalsons and the Sessionses, who were neighbors in Pottawattamie County, Iowa, were engaged in an ongoing feud. The Hannabalsons put up a fence between the properties which the Supreme Court of Iowa said was "sufficient to prevent passage of the dove of peace, [but] neither high enough nor tight enough to prevent the interchange of brick bats or the bandying of opprobious epithets." On May 30th, 1898 a scuffle took place across the fence between Mr.

Sessions and Mr. and Mrs. Hannabalson which is best described in the
original words of the Iowa Supreme Court:

> About this time [Mr. Hannabalson] discovered that a ladder
> belonging to [Mr. Sessions] was hanging upon a peg or block
> attached to the partition fence, and, conceiving this to be a
> cloud upon his title, he forthwith attempted to remove it, while
> [Mr. Sessions], seeing the peril in which his property was
> placed, rushed to its defense. Whether [Mrs. Hannabalson]
> herself laid violent hands on the ladder is a matter of grave
> dispute. She denies it, and says that the height and depth of her
> offending consisted in her leaning up against the fence with
> one arm quietly hanging over the top thereof, and in stimulat-
> ing her husband's zeal by audible remarks about the "crazy
> fool" who was bearing down upon them from the other side.
> She further avers that while occupying this position of strict
> neutrality the defendant assaulted her vi et armis, and with his
> clenched fist struck the arm which protruded over the fence top
> into his domain. [Mr. Sessions] denies the striking, and says
> that [Mrs. Hannabalson], instead of being a peaceable and
> impartial observer of the skirmish, was herself a principal
> actor, and that in aid of her husband she climbed upon some
> convenient pedestal, and, hanging herself across the fence,
> reached down, and with malice aforethought seized the ladder
> and wrenched it from its resting place. Thereupon, actuated by
> a natural and lawful desire to protect his property from such
> ravishments, and being goaded on by statements from the
> other side of the fence reflecting upon his mother and casting
> doubt upon his proper rank in the animal kingdom, he gently,
> and without unreasonable force, laid his open hand upon [Mrs.
> Hannabalsons'] arm, and mildly but firmly suggested the
> propriety of her "keeping on her own side of the fence." As is
> usual in cases of this kind the testimony of the principal parties
> is entirely irreconcilable, and, as is also usual, each is supported
> by partisan witnesses in a very emphatic manner. More than a
> year after the alleged assault this action for damages was
> begun, and [Mrs. Hannabalson] swears that, as a result of the
> blow upon her arm, she was during all that time been sick,
> weak, nervous, suffering great pain and anguish, and is to a
> great extent a physical and nervous wreck. On the other hand,
> some of [Mr. Sessions'] witnesses testify, in effect, that, what-
> ever may be [Mrs. Hannabalson's] bodily ills, they have existed
> for many years, while others tell us that since the alleged
> assault they have seen her performing outdoor labor with all

the apparent strength of an athlete. Her physician, who was a witness in her behalf, says that, while "she is not quite so fleshy as she was a year ago, she is still fleshy enough," and the jury, who saw her at the trial seem to have adopted his conservative estimate.

After seriously weighing the merits of the parties in this action the court ruled that by putting her arm across the fence, Mrs. Hannabalson became a trespasser, and this gave Mr. Sessions the right to use reasonable and necessary force to expel "so much of her person as he found on his side of the line." The court also noted that although the title of a property owner extends from the center of the earth to the heavens, "it is, perhaps, doubtful whether owners as quarrelsome as the parties in this case will ever enjoy the usufruct of their property in the latter direction."

The extent of property rights as they extend skyward has been limited since the advent of aviation as discussed in Chapter 7 of this book.

Some more recent, though less colorful incidents will help illustrate other principles of trespass law.

War stories: On November 24, 1978, Debbie L. Kenney went to visit her great-grandmother who lived in Omaha. Next door lived Robert J. Barna who owned a dog and enclosed his yard with a wire fence with 2- by 4-inch openings. While playing in the yard, Debbie reached through the fence three or four times and then was bitten by the dog. In a suit by Debbie and her father, Gerald L. Kenney against Mr. Barna, a jury awarded $607 in damages. The trial court granted a new trial saying that the amount was inadequate. But Mr. Barna appealed and the Nebraska Supreme Court noted that under Nebraska law a dog owner would not be liable to a trespasser who is bitten by his dog and ruled that a child could be a trespasser.[345]

Helen and Coralie Cobai owned a home in Crested Butte, Colorado, which was built in the 1930s and was within inches of the property line. Since the time it was built the local zoning rules were changed to require that homes be at least 7.5 feet from the lot line. In 1978 Michael Young and Cheryl Gannon built a house next door which was properly set back from the lot line, but which was built in such a way that snow from their roof would slide onto the Cobais' roof. The annual snowfall in Crested Butte is 300 to 500 inches, so the sliding snow was causing quite a bit of noise and some damage. The Cobais sued for trespass and were awarded $1 in damages and an injunction requiring Young and Gannon to keep their snow from trespassing. The court found it didn't matter that the Cobais' house did not conform to the zoning code but the other house did.[346]

In 1957 Chippewa County, Michigan, undertook some road reconstruction in the area of Ranger, Lakeshore and Tower Roads. In 1959 there was considerable rain in the area and water built up which was too much for the culverts which had been installed. At 6:30 a.m. on May 3, 1959 the pressure of the backed up water became so great that it washed away Tower and Lakeview Roads. As the rush of water continued toward Lake Superior it up-ended and hurled a summer cottage, killing Nancy Jean Herro who was residing there. A suit against the county for wrongful death was dismissed by the trial court, but the Supreme Court of Michigan reversed, saying that the county could be found liable for causing the trespass.[347]

Back in the 1920s H. J. Herrin owned a large tract of land in Lewis and Clark County, Montana, on both sides of the Missouri River. On September 18, 1924 William Sutherland traveled down the river in a boat shooting ducks and fishing. He also waded in a stream and went ashore. Mr. Herrin sued him for trespass and was awarded the sum of one dollar. Mr. Sutherland appealed to the Supreme Court of Montana (lawyers must have charged less in those days) and the court held there was not a trespass as long as he stayed in the navigable portion of the river, but that shooting over the land, wading in the stream and going ashore were all trespasses.[348]

When a landowner began filling his lot in Polk City, Iowa, with sand and gravel to bring it up to street level, it was piled against the wall of the adjoining building. This, the owner of the building claimed, was causing damage to her wall. She sued and won, obtaining an injunction against the materials being against her wall. The lot owner appealed to the Iowa Supreme Court but the injunction was affirmed. The court held that piling the sand and gravel against the wall was a trespass and that the lot owner should have built his own foundation against which to pile the fill. The court pointed out that "With a little neighborly consideration on both parties, this controversy could easily have been avoided."[349]

In May, 1939, metal signs were nailed to the side of a building adjacent to the home of Alvin A. Mawson at 310 East Thirty-Third Street in Salt Lake City, Utah. The signs were advertising signs for "Cleo Cola" and "Bubble Up." In a lawsuit against the manufacturers of the drinks advertised in the signs, LaVar Mawson, Mr. Mawson's five-year, eleven-month-old son claimed that he was trying to remove the signs from the wall which were trespassing on his wall when he sustained serious injury. He claimed that his arm, hand and fingers were bruised and contused and cut and crushed, and the muscles, ligaments and tendons thereof were cut and torn from their attachments, and he was caused to sustain great nervous shock. In a trial before a jury in Missouri, Mawson was awarded $7,000. However, the beverage company appealed and the court threw out the award. It held that where a child injured himself several days after an act of trespass, the trespasser could not be held liable for the injury. The court hinted that if the boy's lawyer had sued for negligence, he might have had a better chance of winning.[350]

When Whitney Company built a building next to that of Charles Sally, it allowed mortar and debris to fall into the thin space between the buildings which was on land owned by Mr. Sally. Some time when it rained, the debris caused the rainwater to build up in the space and to soak into Mr. Sally's building, damaging the wainscoting. Mr. Sally sued and was awarded $1,011.85 in damages. In weighing the merits of the case, the appeals judge said, "On the one hand, the law does not wish to punish too severely the careless man; on the other, it is he that is at fault in some degree when the damaged party may not be at fault at all."[351]

In order to sue someone for trespass, a person must first have **possession** of the land. Possession can include various types of interest in the land, but they must be legal interests such as ownership, a lease or an easement. If a landlord turns over possession of his property to a tenant, the landlord no longer has possession and cannot sue for trespass unless some damage is being done to his interest in the property. If the property being trespassed upon is vacant land, then owning title to the land is considered constructive possession.

War stories: Where Elizabeth Perry was in possession of some land in Cherokee County, South Carolina, with a life estate rather than full ownership she was allowed to sue her neighbor, Samuel Jefferies, for trespass for cutting timber on her land.[352]

When Arthur W. Evans bought property in Rockingham County, New Hampshire, in 1907 his wife refused to live with him unless the title was put in her name. He did so and she lived with him until 1910 when she left him. She then sold the standing grass on the property for $50 to Frank Watkins who came by to harvest it. Mr. Evans objected and eventually sued Mr. Watkins for trespass. Watkins defended the suit saying that he had bought the grass from the wife who was the legal owner. The court rejected this argument, saying that Mr. Evans was like a tenant at will on the land in his wife's land and that a landlord does not have the right to sell the crops sown by a tenant.[353]

On November 5, 1913, the African Methodist Episcopal Church entered into a contract to purchase two acres of land from W. A. Bass on Sparta and Milledgeville Road in Hancock County, Georgia. After the church had paid the full purchase price of $200, Mr. Bass refused to execute a deed and entered the premises, destroying trees and removing the steps of the church. The church sued to obtain the deed and for trespass. Mr. Bass argued that since it did not yet own the property, it could not sue for trespass, but the Georgia Supreme Court ruled otherwise, saying that a contract purchaser had an interest in land which allowed it to sue for trespass.[354]

After renting an acre of land in Jefferson County, Kentucky to a tenant, James Walden noticed that John D. Conn entered the land and built a fence on it. He sued for trespass and lost when the court held that once a landowner rents his property he is no longer in possession of it, which is a necessary condition for a trespass suit. The court held that he should have sued for damage to his reversion interest in the property.[355]

Trespass occurs when a person or a thing enters property without authority. If a person enters with authority, but then does some act which indicates that he never should have been granted authority to enter the premises, some, but not all courts have said that the person becomes a trespasser *ab initio* (from the beginning).

War stories: In 1610 Thomas Newman and five other carpenters went into a tavern owned by John Vaux where they had some wine and a loaf of bread. When they were done they refused to pay and Mr. Vaux sued them for trespass, saying that they had no right to enter the tavern if they did not intend to pay. The carpenters won the case because, the court said, they were not trespassing when they entered the tavern, so they could not become trespassers by *not doing something* later. The court said that the tavern owner should have sued them for the debt owed, not for trespass.[356] (This like many interesting old cases, is the result of a lawyer's mistake.)

Paul met Robert at a bar frequented by homosexuals, mentioned that he had $200 and asked him to come home with him. Robert went home with Paul planning to steal the money. The next morning Paul was found stabbed, covered with blood and strangled to death. Robert claimed self defense. The courts rejected this defense, saying that Robert was a trespasser *ab initio* and had a duty to retreat from the premises, not to stay and fight. Robert was sentenced to death.[357]

Thomas Rogers sustained fatal injuries when he was pulling a mower with his tractor and hit an anchor stake in the ground. The stake had been placed there by the Kent County, Michigan, Board of Road Commissioners when it installed snow fences, but it had not been removed when the fences were removed. Mr. Roger's widow sued the county but lost. On appeal the Supreme Court of Michigan stated that leaving the stake in the ground would constitute a trespass for which the board could be liable.[358]

If a person is asked to leave a premises because of discrimination for reasons such as race, that discrimination can be illegal under federal civil rights statutes. Therefore one may not be charged with trespass if one is asked to leave for racial reasons.

War story: In the early 1960s the refusal of some restaurants to serve Blacks resulted in sit-ins across the country. In many cases these sit-ins ended in the arrest of the participants under trespass laws. Several of the cases, from South Carolina and Arkansas, were appealed to the United States Supreme Court. The court held that the Civil Rights Act of 1964, under Supremacy Clause of the constitution forbid convictions for trespass in such situations.[359]

Where a property owner invites the public to enter his property, such as a shopkeeper or shopping center, the members of the public who enter are considered invitees. A special set of rules has been evolved regarding the rights of invitees.

War story: One night in 1979 Boris Navratil took a client out for a nightcap at the Split Decision on Bennington Avenue in Baton Rouge, Louisiana, and parked his car in the lot of Associates Financial Services nearby. When he returned to get his car it was missing. He called the police and discovered that it had been towed by Road Runner Wrecking Services under contract with Associates. Road Runner refused to return the car without payment of $57.50 for towing and storage. He refused to pay the bill and filed suit instead, and won. The Louisiana court held that unless warning signs are posted, towing a person's car away is illegal. It said that the landowner was liable until such time as he asked the wrecker to release the car and wrecker refused. From that point the wrecker was liable. It awarded Mr. Navratil $1,500 for loss of use of his car, $1,500 for depreciation of the car while it was not in his possession and $500 for shock, humiliation and inconvenience. The wrecking company had argued that he could have minimized his loss of the car by paying the towing bill, but the court didn't buy it.[360]

When a person sues someone for trespass and wins, he is entitled to recover the amount of the damage to his property. If there is no damage to his property he may still be awarded some damages as compensation for the trespass. He may even receive damages if the trespass resulted in a benefit to his property!

War stories:When a building company used a person's land to store equipment, the landowner was entitled to be compensated for the actual damage to his property plus the value of the use of his property.[361]

Two women were adjoining landowners in Johnson County Kansas in the early 1950's when one of them hired the Arborfield Tree Surgery Co. to top off three cedar trees on the property of the other. The trees were 20 to 25 feet high and about ten feet was cut off of each. The owner sued for trespass, claiming that she attached sentimental value to the trees, that they would not grow tall again once the tops were cut and that they were worth $150 to $200 each. After a trial by jury the question of the topped trees was put before the Supreme Court of Kansas which ruled that even without proof of any injury a landowner would be entitled to damages for a trespass and that a Kansas statute would allow triple damages for injury during a trespass.[362]

There are instances where persons are legally allowed to enter another's land without permission. For example, since a landowner has a duty to provide support to adjacent land, someone doing an excavation may have a legal right to enter the neighboring land, if doing so is necessary to protect the land. Also some states have statutes allowing entry on private land to persons such as surveyors.

Chapter 47 Verbal Abuse

There is not much which can be done legally about verbal abuse from neighbors. In a conversation between two parties there has rarely in history been any liability except in cases of extremely outrageous behavior which "shocks the conscience" and causes some physical injury to the other person.

Where a third party is present and defamatory remarks are made about one person in the presence of the other, then there may be liability for slander.

War stories: When a woman asked the price of a product in one of the stores owned by Food Fair Stores of Florida, the clerk said to her, "If you want to know the price you'll have to find out the best way you can...you stink to me." Some time later the woman had a heart attack and she sued the store. Florida's Supreme Court ruled that there was no ground for suing for an insult.[363]

When Burtie Self got into a conversation with a clerk while shopping in a store owned by Republic Iron & Steel Co. in Birmingham, Alabama, he said to her, "You are a liar and a dirty liar; I never took anything from you; no lady would have said that, and I consider you no lady." When she apologized for her comments he continued, "I never took anything from you; I don't consider no lady would have said that, and I consider you no lady. Get out of the store." She sued the company, claiming that she was greatly humiliated, suffered great mental and physical pain and anguish. The jury awarded her damages, but the company appealed and the Supreme Court of Alabama reversed.[364]

Profanity and Obscenity

War stories: Sarah Halliday was sitting on her back porch with a friend and the friend's two children when her neighbor, Dominic Cienkowski drove into his yard with his wife and two children. As Mrs. Halliday recalled it, he then called her a "Scotch bitch," a "bastard" and a "bum." She sued him, claiming nervous shock and headaches which required her to visit her mother in Ireland for ten months and loss of money when she had to sell her property at a low price to move from the neighborhood. The case was dismissed and

Mrs. Halliday appealed to the Supreme Court of Pennsylvania which held that as long as she did not have physical injuries she could not recover.[365]

Mrs. Marcia G. Samms filed suit against David Eccles in Salt Lake County, Utah, claiming that she was a respectable married woman, that she never encouraged Mr. Eccles' attentions, that from May to December 1957 he repeatedly called her soliciting her to have illicit sexual relations with him and that he made an indecent exposure of his person. Because the actions were found to be outrageous and intolerable to the Supreme Court of Utah, it made an exception to the rule that one cannot sue for solicitation to sexual intercourse.[366]

George F. Barnard filed a complaint stating that he ran a theater building in Dutchess County, New York, and that his performances were disturbed by Philip Finkbeiner and another who had "indulged in loud and profane swearing and vile obscene talk." The court held that this may render the building "unfit for comfortable or respectable occupation" and that it could be enjoined.[367]

Peter Vogler was charged with repeatedly using profane and obscene language on a CB radio. The complaining party had requested Vogler to stop using the profanity on the channel normally used for emergencies, and Vogler then directed his remarks at the complaining party. The court dismissed the charges stating that New York's aggravated harassment statute did not include CB radio transmissions, and that the regulation of CB transmission was the domain of the federal government under 18 USC 1464 and 47 CFR 95.83.[368]

Slander

Slander is when a person makes a verbal false and defamatory statement about a person to a third party. If the statement is written, then it is legally known as **libel**.

Truth is a defense to slander and libel. If someone calls you a crook and you have been convicted on a theft, then you cannot sue for slander. If the statement is false, it does not matter if the person making the statement *thought* it was true. The issue is whether the statement was

actually true or false. One exception to this is if the statement was made
in the form of an opinion. If a person states that in their opinion an act
is crooked, this can be considered as privileged opinion.

The statement must be made to a third person. If someone calls you
a crook and no one else hears it, it is not slander. The rationale behind
this is that if no one else heard it then your reputation could not have
been injured.

The statement must be defamatory. This means that it must injure
a person's reputation with a segment of the population. One court put
it this way: "Reputation is said to be injured by words which tend to
expose one to public hatred, shame, obloquy, contumely, odium,
contempt, ridicule, aversion, ostracism, degradation, or disgrace, or to
induce an evil opinion of one in the minds of right-thinking persons,
and to deprive one of their confidence and friendly intercourse in
society." [369]

The statement must also be clearly about a specific person and the
person defamed must be alive. A corporation can be defamed, but a
dead person cannot.

Some interesting examples of slander follow:

War stories: John Gardiner, with the intent of preventing Anne Davies'
marriage to Anthony Elcock, stated that she had had a child
by a London grocer. Anne Davies lost her marriage and
sued for slander. The court held for Anne saying that
Gardiner had caused her to lose her chance for advance-
ment by marriage, her livelihood, and was otherwise greatly
prejudiced.[370]

Mr. Crass allegedly caused Mr. Matthew to lose his marriage by saying the following: "Thou art an whore-master,
for thou hast lain with Brown's wife, and hadst to do with
her against a chair." Mr. Crass claimed this case was
dealing with a man losing his marriage and therefore the
Davies case (above) could be distinguished. The court held
there was not any real difference as to the hindrance of
marriage either of a man or woman. They held that Mr.
Matthew had sufficient grounds to sue (the aptly-named)
Mr. Crass.[371]

When Turner stated: "There goes Ogden, who is one of
those that stole my Lord S.'s deer," Ogden sued. The court
held that word must either endanger the party's life, or
subject him to infamous punishment to be actionable. That

one might be fined and imprisoned is not enough, the allegation must be scandalous. The court held there was no cause of action here because a deer is an animal of nature, and to say someone stole such an animal is not scandalous.[372]

Eliza Kelly sued for slander when Partington spoke of her in the following manner: "She secreted 1 shilling, 6 pence under the till; stating these are not the times to be robbed." The court held that these words were not slanderous because they were not injurious in their nature. The words imported great caution with money on Eliza Kelly's part, and were not injurious to her. Regardless of the consequences of the words, since they were not injurious in their nature Partington was not liable.[373]

After Eldon left the employment of Lincoln Laboratories, Inc. in Decatur, Illinois, to start his own business, the president of the company made the statement that Eldon was "queer" on another man and made other attacks on his honesty and integrity. In a suit against the company and its president, Savage was awarded $85,000 in damages. On appeal the award was reduced to $50,000.[374]

When a minister was called a "rotten egg" a federal court in Illinois ruled that this was libelous.[375]

In the 1880s in Indiana, when a Mr. Crocker called a John C. Hadley a "hoary-headed filcher" who "sold himself, Judas-like, for a few pieces of silver to sell his neighbors out," the latter was awarded $250.[376]

In the 1890s in Cumberland, Maryland, when The Daily News Co. of Cumberland said of David J. Lewis that he "would be an anarchist if he thought it would pay," the courts ruled that he was entitled to damages.[377]

J. S. Fry & Sons, Ltd. were chocolate manufacturers, and they published an advertisement depicting a Mr. Tolley, a prominent amateur golfer, as eating their chocolate while playing golf. They also depicted his caddy as eating the chocolate and claiming the chocolate tasted as good as Tolley could drive a ball. Tolley sued for libel claiming the advertisement had cast an imputation on his amateur status and might prevent his playing for the amateur championship. The lower court judge sent the question to the jury and the jury awarded plaintiff Tolley £1,000. The Appeals Court reversed and held for chocolate company. They felt the damages were excessive, and that the ad itself was not capable of a defamatory meaning since the words of the ad would not lead a reader to conclude there was implied in the ad a statement either that Tolley's consent had been obtained, or that he was paid for the ad.[378]

When the New York American published an article about evolution in 1929 it included a picture of wrestler Stanislaus Zbyszko next to that of a hideous gorilla with the caption, "Stanislaus Zbyszko, the Wrestler, Not Fundamentally Different from the Gorilla in Physique." this was held to be libelous in holding him up to ridicule.[379]

There are some exceptions to the law of slander and libel. In these situations the communication of a defamatory remark is privileged and does not subject the person making the statement to liability. The exceptions are:

- Judicial proceedings. Statements made in judicial or quasi-judicial proceedings are privileged because it is in the interest of the judicial body to have everyone speak freely without fear of liability.

- Legislative proceedings. Statements made by legislators in their legislative functions are privileged under the same rationale as for judicial proceedings.

- Government officials. Where a defamatory statement is made by a governmental official in the course of his or her job, it is privileged for all federal officials and many state officials.

- Husbands and wives. Communications between spouses are privileged because under the law they are considered one person.

- Consent. If a person consents to have statements made, he or she cannot sue over them.

Chapter 48 Vibrations

There have been numerous cases of neighbors who have been bothered by vibrations. These have usually come from industrial plants or quarries, but have also been produced by work being done at a neighbor's house.

In certain cases, vibrations which have been bad enough have been held to be a nuisance. Where people complained that the vibrations were trespassing on their property, they usually lost, because merely vibrating a piece of property has not been considered to be a legal trespass where nothing enters onto the property.

War stories: After an accidental nitroglycerin explosion at a chemical plant owned by Hercules, Inc. in Jefferson County, Alabama, Albert D. and Bonnie A. Lipscomb sued, claiming their home one mile away from the plant was damaged. A jury ruled against them and they appealed. The appeals court held that mere vibrations could not amount to a trespass and that to be liable Hercules would have to be proven to have been negligent in its operation of the plant.[380]

When Lillie Schlesinger needed some pile driving done on her lot in Louisiana she hired Globe Construction Co., Inc. as contractor. Globe hired Tassin Pile Driving Co., Inc. which did the work. Unfortunately, the vibrations from the pile driving caused damage to Joseph Burrell's property next door. Joseph sued Lillie and won. Lillie sued the contractor and subcontractor, claiming that they had caused the damage. The court ruled that since the pile driver didn't do anything negligent, he couldn't be held liable. Since the landowner paid to have the pile driving done, and it was done properly, the property owner was liable to the damages next door. Lillie appealed to the Louisiana Supreme Court, but they declined to take the case.[381]

Helen Boyd Dull and others had operated a limestone quarry for several years on William Penn Highway near Harrisburg, Pennsylvania, when the home of Charles E. Beecher and his wife was erected across the road. On December 29, 1926, 1,900 pounds of dynamite was used to bring down the breast of the quarry, and smaller amounts of dynamite were used to break down the stone further.

The blasts did damage to the Beechers' home and threw rocks onto their property. They sued and won a court order against the blasting. The court said that the quarry operator had not proved that she could not profitably operate without the large use of dynamite. (Poor preparation by her lawyer?)[382]

In the 1930s many people established homes in South Orange, New Jersey, near a quarry operated by Kern-O-Mix, Inc. In operating the quarry, the company did blasting and used a rock crusher, steam engine and other equipment. The vibrations and noise from this equipment was disturbing to the nearby residents and 48 of them filed suit against the company. The case went through many hearings and appeals, the file of the case became gigantic and the final hearing lasted several days. (A lawyer's dream come true!) In balancing the rights of the parties the judge ruled that the homeowners rights were more important than that of the quarry owners and were entitled to an injunction. But the quarry owners appealed and the New Jersey Court of Errors and Appeals limited the injunction. It said that the homeowners were entitled to be free from vibrations which damaged their homes, but not from vibrations which merely jarred, vibrated or shook their homes.[383]

Andrew Dittman and Henry Repp occupied adjoining premises on Bond Street in Baltimore. Dittman was a brewer who had recently changed the way he brewed beer. He added a steam machine along a wall of Repp's building. Repp alleged this new machinery caused continual loud and deafening noise when it was operating, and made it impossible for his family to live there. In addition to the noise, the machinery caused the walls to shake and vibrate. The court affirmed the lower court holding and granted an injunction from using the new machine because the noise along with the vibrations made the Repp's home unsafe and unfit for habitation and constituted a nuisance.[384]

Chapter 49 Water

The right to water and to protection from water have caused problems between neighbors for thousands of years. And while some distinct rules have been developed, the different states in this country have not agreed as to which are the right rules for dealing with these sorts of problems.

The problems regarding water fall into three main categories, drainage problems with surface waters, rights to water in watercourses and rights to underground water.

Drainage Problems

Water which falls as rain or washes across property in undefined streams is called "diffuse surface water." There are three different legal doctrines recognized by different states regarding diffuse surface water. Some of the states consider this water as a "common enemy" and give the property owner the right to dam it or deflect it in any way onto other properties. Other states hold that a property owner does not have the right to obstruct the "natural flow" of the water. A more modern approach has been to allow a landowner to make "reasonable use" of diffused surface water.

Common enemy rule:

War stories: Gerald and Patsey Boyd had a drainage problem on their property in Greene County, Arkansas, so they constructed a levee to ward off the drainage. This caused a road to flood and the county sued. The court ordered the Boyds to remove the levee but they appealed. The appeals court ruled that since the water was not in a water course such as a river, the Boyds had the right to deflect it in any way as long as they did not unnecessarily inflict damage on others.[385]

In 1969 Raymond and Helene Tucker bought a brand new home in *Marsh*field [emphasis added], Massachusetts on Winslow Cemetery Road near Daniel Webster Cemetery. Prior to closing, a nearby property owner placed fill material on his land and graded it. A week after moving into the house the Tuckers noticed water leaking into the basement which smelled like raw sewage. Up to three feet of water filled the back yard. As it turned out, the water table was higher than the level of the basement and cause the septic waste to enter the basement. It appeared that the grading had helped raise the water table. The Tuckers sued the builder, the neighboring property owner and others. The Supreme Court of Massachusetts reviewed the history of water law and held that the neighbor was not liable since "a landowner may with impunity grade and improve his land for a lawful purpose even though he thereby diverts surface water onto his neighbor's land." However, the court further ruled that in the future it would abandon this rule and adopt the reasonable use rule. It did not apply the reasonable use rule to this case because the attorneys didn't ask it to change existing law![386]

Natural flow rule:

War story: Franklyn and Muriel Lawrence acquired a home in Miami Springs, Florida, in 1951. Shortly thereafter, Eastern Air Lines, which owned land directly East of them filled in their land and had it paved. According to the Lawrences, this changes the natural flow of water and caused their land to flood with several inches of water for several days at a time. In addition to the actions of Eastern Air Lines, the City of Miami Springs had raised the elevation of a street which further obstructed the natural flow of water. The flooding caused severe damage to their home and they filed suit against Eastern and the city. The local trial court threw out their suit but the Florida Supreme Court said that they did have a right to pursue their claim for damages based upon diverting of surface waters.[387]

Reasonable use rule:

War story: After R. C. Aiken had some fill placed on his land in the Skyland area of Buncombe County, North Carolina, the basement of his neighbor J. W. Pendergrast began to flood. After an especially heavy rain he had over five feet of water in his basement. He sued Aiken and the jury ruled that the fill was a nuisance but that there were no damages. He appealed and the appeals court upheld the judgment. He appealed again to the North Carolina Supreme Court which used the case to examine the history and development of water law. It concluded that the state should follow the doctrine of reasonable use as follows; "Each possessor is legally privileged to make a reasonable use of his land, even though the flow of surface water is altered thereby and causes some harm to others, but liability is incurred when his harmful interference with the flow of surface waters is unreasonable and causes substantial damage." The court ordered that a new trial be held under this ruling.[388]

Watercourses and bodies of water

For rights regarding watercourses and bodies of water (commonly known as rivers, lakes, ponds) the states are divided into two camps. Most of the states subscribe to the doctrine of riparian rights, but seventeen western states have evolved a theory of "prior appropriation." The riparian rights states are further divided into those which prefer natural flow and those which allow reasonable use.

Basically, the riparian rights doctrine holds that persons who own land on which there is water have the right to use the water for domestic and commercial purposes as well as for boating, swimming and fishing. They have the rights in the quality, quantity and the velocity of the water.

The natural flow doctrine was developed in England and holds that a riparian owner may use water, but must return it to the stream or lake in substantially the same quality and quantity. In America most courts follow the reasonable use doctrine which allows a person to make use of the water as long as his use does not interfere with the needs of the other riparian owners.

The prior appropriation doctrine was developed in the western states of America. This doctrine holds that whoever begins making use of the water first has a right to continue that use. The rationale for this is that it encourages the development of water uses. It began with the needs of miners and farmers to divert water for long distances. Without this doctrine people might not make the investment necessary in such arid regions.

The states which subscribe solely to the prior appropriation doctrine are Arizona, Colorado, Idaho, Montana, Nevada, New Mexico, Utah and Wyoming. California, Texas and several other western states have combined the prior appropriation doctrine with the reasonable use doctrine.

War stories: Baker and Ore-Ida used wells to pump water from a ground water aquifer under their separate lands. Baker

filed suit to enjoin Ore-Ida from pumping from the wells
until his wells resumed normal production once adequate
rain fell. The lower court found that both parties had
withdrawn water from the aquifer far in excess of the
annual recharge rate, causing a 20-ft. per year drop in the
aquifer's water level. They granted the injunction. The
Supreme Court of Idaho held that where Ore-Ida had
continued pumping which had resulted in withdrawals
from the aquifer in excess of the annual recharge rate, they
were forbidden by the Ground Water Act to continue
doing so and could only withdraw amounts which would
not exceed the annual recharge rate. The court held there
was no basis for apportioning the water among all the
farmers in the area, and affirmed the lower decision.[389]

Mono Lake is the second largest in California, and sits at
the base of the Sierra Nevada escarpment near the Yosemite
National Park entrance. The lake was home to vast numbers of nesting and migratory birds who lived on islands in
the lake. Mono Lake received most of its water supply
from five streams carrying the snowmelt of the Sierra
Nevada to its shores. The Water Department of Los Angeles appropriated virtually the entire flow of four of the five
streams into aqueducts for the use of the citizens of L.A.
This caused the level of the lake to drop, and one of the
islands in the lake to become a peninsula, exposing the
birds there to coyotes and other predators. The birds
abandoned the island. Some felt the scenic beauty and
ecological value of Mono Lake were imperiled, and the
Audubon Society sued to enjoin the Water Department
from diverting the flow of the streams. They claimed the
waters and shores of the lake were protected by public
trust. The lower court held for the Water Department. The
California Supreme Court held that the public trust doctrine preserved the sovereign power of the state to protect
public trust uses, which included preventing the harm to a
public trust like the lake. The Court also held that the
human and environmental uses of the lake, uses protected
by public trust, deserved to be considered in this action.[390]

Underground water

There are three legal doctrines for rights to underground water.
Most states have adopted the principle that one must make reasonable

use of underground water. Some states have adopted the English rule that one may make unlimited use of such water. And a few western states give greater rights to those who have made previous use of the water.

Notice that the English rule allowing unlimited use of underground water compliments the English rule that water in streams and lakes cannot be interfered with. This is followed in many eastern states where water is plentiful.

In California landowners over a common underground water basin are allowed a proportionate quantity of the water but may not lower the water table.

War story: When the city of Pontiac, Illinois, authorized the alteration of a drainage ditch, a well on the property of J. B. Lee went dry. He sued and the courts held that Illinois follows the English rule that a landowner may intercept or impede groundwater even to the detriment of his neighbors.[391]

Rain

A relatively recent area of dispute between neighbors is when one steals the rain from another, or causes him to get too much rain. This can be done by seeding the clouds. The general rule in this area is that there is not a right to fly over another person's land to change the weather; landowners have a right to natural weather without modification. there is a difference, however, where the flight does not go over the landowner's property.

War stories: Southwest Water Research was hired by a number of farmers near Fort Stockton, Texas, to participate in a hail suppression program. Southwest Water would seed the clouds in an attempt to suppress hail. The cloud seeding also destroyed potential rain clouds over the land of Joe Rounsaville and some others. They sought and got an injunction which would keep Southwest Water from seeding any clouds. Southwest appealed and the court upheld the injunction as to the lands of Rounsaville and the others who were involved, but stated the injunction was too broad in restraining cloud seeding over the other lands.[392]

When a drought hit Fulton County, Pennsylvania, in 1964-1965, some of the property owners formed a nonprofit corporation to fight the Blue Ridge Weather Modification

Assn. which had been trying to stop hail storms in the area. The company had used cloud seeding and 110 ground-based generators of silver iodide to suppress hail in thunderstorms passing the area. The first judge assigned to the case died before he could issue an opinion, but the parties waived their right to a new trial. In the meantime the Pennsylvania legislature passed a law making weather modification illegal in some areas, then repealed the law and passed another providing that weather modification should be encouraged and licensed. The court ruled that while citizens have a property right in the clouds and moisture, the case was moot since the new law provided for damages to those injured by weather modification.[393]

Artificially sprayed water

Water which is sprayed from one property to another is a trespass and can also be a nuisance. Courts can order a stop to such activity.

War story: The B & R Luncheonette in Bronx County, New York intended to set up a summer garden in the rear yard of the property it was renting, but water spraying from the Fairmont Theatre next door made that impossible. B & R sued and was awarded $50 per month for lost value of the property for the 16 months it could not use the yard.[394]

Part III How to Solve a Neighbor Problem
Without Going to Court

Chapter 50 Avoidance

The easiest way to solve a problem with a neighbor is to avoid it. Depending upon the nature of the problem, you can stay out of the neighbor's path or you can move from the neighborhood entirely. This may not give you the satisfaction of making him squirm, and you may hate to see him get away with his mayhem, but it is probably the best solution as far as your nerves and your wallet are concerned.

Many of the cases in this book were in court for years. Every one of them was appealed at least once, some three times. They involved depositions, hearings, summonsing witnesses, and at least one full trial.

At $100 or $200 an hour, a lawyer can use up your entire life savings in no time. As one court pointed out (though not in a neighbor case) "[I]f this litigation continues at its present pace, not only their entire ... estate, whatever that may be, but perhaps their parents' estates as well, may be consumed by the cost of this litigation."[395]

If you are just not the kind of person who runs from a fight, or if practical considerations prevent you from avoiding the problem, you might be able to try the second way to solve the problem, talking it over.

Chapter 51 Talking It Over

Believe it or not, some neighbors would be glad to stop annoying you. They might not even know that their situation is annoying you. So before you take any drastic action you should at least bring up the problem.

Some people would be mortified to know that they were causing any offense in the neighborhood, and would be ever so glad to rectify it. Unfortunately, the one person in the world like this probably isn't the one that is bothering you.

If the problem is caused by a party who doesn't own the property but is a tenant, you might get some help from the landlord. Point out that the tenant's actions are *lowering the property values* in the neighborhood, and are likely to cause similar problems at neighboring properties.

If you are on a power trip, then you probably won't want to talk it over. Once you let them know that something they do annoys you, you have exposed a vulnerability, and they can use this to exert power over you. Every time they do they act in the future they will be exerting that power and pointing out to you that they are in control. Then it may be time to move on to the next methods for solving a neighbor problem.

Chapter 52 Abatement

One way to abate a nuisance is to go onto the offender's land and put a stop to it yourself. Sometimes this is allowed by law and sometimes it is not. Where the nuisance can be abated peacefully this is usually allowed, but occasionally the person abating the nuisance gets sued for trespass.

War stories: Williams lived next to Jones and was subjected to offensive and unwholesome smells, vapors, and stenches coming from Jones' property because he had allowed manure, filth and refuse to accumulate on his land. Williams finally went to Jones' land and removed the nuisance, causing some damage to a wall. Jones sued in trespass. The court held that because Jones had not been the one who originally caused the nuisance, notice or request to remove the nuisance must have been given to him before Williams abated the nuisance himself. [396]

In Rhode Island in the 1890s a Samuel Almy put a gate across a road blocking the access to the beach. Isaac White needed to go to the beach to get seaweed, which he had a legal right to do. So he got Emerson Ash to come with him and together they tried to crash the gate with an ox cart. An altercation ensued with Mr. Almy and Mr. Almy was injured. White and Ash were arrested for "assault with intent to kill and murder" (both?) and were found guilty. The court said that even if Mr. Almy was creating a public nuisance by blocking the road, the others did not have the right to stop him with violence. [397]

As with most rights, the right to abate a nuisance requires reasonableness. The person must act at a reasonable time of day and in a reasonable manner. What is reasonable depends upon the circumstances at the time. In an emergency it would be more reasonable to take drastic measures than if there were no emergency. A person causing damage to another's property while abating a nuisance can be held liable for the damage.

Trespass can often be stopped by putting up a fence, or some other sort of barricade. Sometimes this solves the problem. At other times it precipitates a shooting incident. Before taking such action you should have a survey done and be sure of your rights.

Chapter 53 Mediation or Arbitration

Mediation is where people present their dispute to a person who helps them come to a resolution. The mediator is usually trained in psychology and dispute resolution and his function is to help the parties understand each other's side and to guide them to a mutually agreeable resolution.

Arbitration is similar to a law suit. An arbitrator takes the place of the judge and decides the rights of the parties. If the parties agree ahead of time to be bound by the decision of the arbitrator, whatever it is, it is called binding arbitration. This means that the parties have no right to appeal the decision of the arbitrator.

The advantage of mediation and arbitration over a lawsuit is that it is faster and less expensive. Lawsuits involve elaborate rules covering pleadings and evidence and they must be fit into the schedules of the courts.

The decision of whether one or the other should be used in lieu of a law suit should be based upon the facts of the case and how much you wish to spend on it. As can be seen from this book, many people spent a lot of money over disputes which were only worth a few dollars. But for them the principle was important (or maybe they just loved a good fight).

If you may look like a "bad guy" compared to the other party, but the law is clearly on your side, court action using rules of law may be more appropriate for your case. But as explained later, courts do not always follow the law if the result would seem unfair to them.

Chapter 54 Criminal Action

Many of the problems mentioned in this book are violations of criminal laws or quasi-criminal regulations. You may have noticed in recent years the proliferation of laws in this country covering many of the minute aspects of our lives. In some areas of this free country it is illegal to water plants at certain hours, to cut down trees on one's own property, or to use a clothesline in one's yard. If your neighbor is doing something bothersome, there is a good chance it is against some law or rule.

Criminal action is much better than civil action because someone else goes to court for you and pays all the expenses. Government red tape can be a nightmare and a person may find it easier to stop being a nuisance than fighting the government.

The agencies of the various government bodies have been multiplying and having children. As each gets bigger it breaks into two or three. Then each of those breaks into smaller parts. It can sometimes be hard to find out which branch handles your type of problem.

Just try calling every department which sounds like it covers your problem. Once you find one that does, don't give up. Call a few more. Maybe you can get two or three agencies after the culprit.

In some areas filing a criminal complaint can start a war that may hurt you more than your neighbor. In some big cities the official building codes are horrendously strict, but in most cases they are not enforced. Enforcement is only used against those who "cause trouble." If you report your neighbor for something, he may note violations on your property and file a complaint against you.

Chapter 55 Civil Action

A civil court action is the most expensive and slowest way to stop a neighbor problem, but it is effective. Sometimes just the threat of a suit can convince your neighbor to solve the problem. With most lawyer's fees now in the $100 to $200 an hour range, a dispute which ends up in court can cost $10,000 easily.

Once a case is filed, the lawyer's meter starts running. If the other side sets a hearing your lawyer has to do research, prepare documents, and appear in court. That may be 10 hours work. If the other side sets a deposition of a dozen of the surrounding neighbors that may take two weeks of eight hour days.

If several neighbors are confronted with one problem neighbor, the costs may be greatly reduced by agreeing to share the costs of the suit. Meanwhile, the problem neighbor will have to pay his fees himself. Just be sure his son or daughter is not a lawyer.

In some cases you may be able to bring an action against a neighbor in small claims courts. Depending upon what state you live in, the maximum amount of your claim may be limited to $500, or as much as $10,000. In some states you may request "equitable relief," such as a court order that the neighbor stop doing something, but in many states small claims courts cannot give equitable relief.

Part IV How to Solve a Neighbor Problem in Court

Chapter 56 Who Can Sue

One basic aspect of nuisance and trespass law is that it involves the use of property. In its usual sense a nuisance is when one person uses his property in a way which affects another's use of his own property. This is based upon the old Latin maxim, "Sic utere ut alienum non lædas," which means, use your property so as not to injure another's property. A common example of this is someone diverting water on his own property which causes a flood on another's property. However, the definition has been expanded over the years to broadly define the term "use of property." Thus, a person who keeps a barking dog can be held to be using his property to cause a nuisance on another's property.

Since nuisance law regards interests in property, only persons who have some legal interest in property can take court action. Persons such as employees and guests cannot take legal action against those causing a nuisance.

War stories: When 20 employees in the yard of the Atlantic Coast Line Railroad Company in Jacksonville, Florida, were bothered by fumes, dust and gasses from the Niagara Chemical division of Food Machinery & Chemical Corp. they filed a suit for nuisance. However, their suit was dismissed because they were employees and not owners or renters of the land.[398]

Two employees of the W.P.A. were painting a school in Waterbury when the staging fell, injuring them. They sued the city saying that the staging was a nuisance, but they lost because the court noted that they did not own an interest in land.[399]

When S. C. Reber began living in a house provided by his employer in a factory district two miles north of Jackson, Mississippi, he discovered that a nearby roundhouse operated by the Illinois Central and Yazoo & Mississippi Railroad Companies emitted so much smoke that it caused him damage. He sued to abate the nuisance. He lost in the trial court and appealed to the Mississippi Supreme Court, but had no luck there either. The court held that as an occupant of an employer's house, he did not have the required

interest in the property to file a nuisance action. It also
noted that the cost of moving the roundhouse would be
hundreds of thousands of dollars and that the cost for him
to move would be relatively slight.[400]

Clarence A. Elliott was travelling with his team of horses
from a private piece of property onto a roadway when he
was thrown to the ground after hitting a ditch dug by the
Town of Mason, New Hampshire. He sued the town
claiming that the open ditch along the road was a nuisance.
He lost his case because he was just a guest of the property
owner and did not own any interest in property which
could be harmed by the alleged nuisance.[401]

However, the complainant need not actually own the land, he can
be a renter or own merely an easement on the land or have another claim
against the land.

War stories: In 1863 a Mr. Jones in England leased some houses on
Effingham Street from the owner and then rented them by
the week to tenants. Mr. Chappell, a neighbor, erected a
steam engine and a stone saw mill on his property. The
noise made the houses difficult to rent. Mr. Jones brought
suit against the neighbor, but it was dismissed because it
was held that only the tenant who was in possession of the
property could file a suit.[402]

Samuel C. Bowden was leasing the building at 121 East
Twelfth Avenue in New York City and renting it out to
tenants when the Edison Electric Illuminating Company,
in 1895, erected a power house next door. The noise and
vibrations caused a disturbance to Bowden and his tenants. He was awarded $250 in damages.[403]

When John L. Lloyd was living at 418 Conway Street,
Baltimore, Maryland, Charles C. Lurssen was operating a
steam engine next door at 414 and 416 Conway Street
which he used to manufacture cigar boxes and other light
wooden boxes. Mr. Lloyd sued saying that the noise and
vibrations were a nuisance. Mr. Lurssen contended that
Mr. Lloyd could not sue since the property had been sold
to the mortgage holder of the property. The court did not
accept this defense, holding that as long as the mortgagor
was still in possession he could maintain the suit.[404]

Regarding whether members of the family who do not own the property can sue, the courts have gone both ways.

War stories: In the 1870s the city of Auburn, New York, constructed a dry stone sewer for drainage of storm water. Later it was used to drain sewage and waste from homes and stables. Because it was not sufficient to carry the waste it often discharged into the basement of Margaret Hughes. Mrs. Hughes' daughter, who lived in the house, became ill with pneumonia and in 1892 died at the age of 22. In a suit against the city, her doctor testified that her illness had been caused by her unsanitary surroundings. However, the court found that since she was not an owner of the property, she could not sue for trespass.[405]

Beginning about the year 1930 the town of Drew, Mississippi, allegedly let its septic tank fall into disrepair. The overflow ran over a considerable amount of land and into Blue Lake. Seventy residents petitioned the town to repair it but no action was taken. Finally, T. J. Hodges and his wife filed suit against the town. Because the land was owned by Mrs. Hodges and worked by her husband the city tried to argue that she was not a proper party to the suit and that he could not sue for land he didn't own. The court didn't buy this, ruling that a person in possession of land has the right to sue.[406]

Chapter 57 Who You Can Sue

There is a lawyers' rule that when there is an incident you should sue everyone in sight. The logic is that you never know what a jury will decide, and some parties may make some payment to settle the case just because it is cheaper than paying an attorney to fight it.

But this rule is changing. In some states and in all federal courts there are rules that say if you file a frivolous lawsuit you may have to pay the other side's attorney fees. You may also have to pay a penalty called "sanctions."

To file a lawsuit against someone you should have at least an arguable case. There should be some legal argument for holding the person liable.

You should sue everyone against whom you have an arguable case. Your case can also be dismissed if you leave out a party who is a **necessary party** to a suit. A necessary party is one whose actions are so much a part of the case that it cannot be fairly decided without him or her present.

War story: On April 5, 1941, James C. Hartline was walking near 12th Street and Avenue A in Birmingham, Alabama, when "a piece of rock or other foreign substance was blown, blasted, thrown or caused to fall upon or against" him, causing his shoulder, collar bone, ribs and various other bones to be broken, and causing him to be "mashed, bruised, strained, sprained and otherwise injured in various parts of his person." He sued several parties involved in the nearby blasting operations including the Tennessee Coal, Iron & Railroad Co., the owner of the land on which the blasting was taking place, for $20,000 in damages. After reviewing the facts of the case, the court held that the owner of the land on which the blasting took place was not liable, since it had leased the land to the other parties which had control over the blasting operations.[407]

Chapter 58 What You Can Sue Over

In the colloquial sense, the word nuisance can describe anything annoying. But when an activity is so annoying that it warrants court action it is called an **actionable** nuisance. For a nuisance to be actionable, three elements must be present, a legal right, an invasion of that right and an injury.

The legal right in most cases is the right to quiet enjoyment of one's property. However, American courts have recognized that people are not entitled to absolute silence. The level of annoyance before a nuisance becomes actionable depends upon the time and the place. One court has said that it is important to note "the ordinary comfort of human existence as understood by the American people in their present state of enlightenment." A comment to the Restatement of Torts states, "Each individual in a community must put up with a certain amount of annoyance, inconvenience and interference, and must take a certain amount of risk in order that all may get on together."[408]

War story: In Bridgewater, Massachusetts in 1905 a person had a hen house near enough to another dwelling that the owner claimed it made it difficult to rent. However, the court held that poultry odors were not offensive to an ordinary citizen.[409]

The fact that a person is sensitive to the activity which is complained of does not matter. The law in America is that if people are more sensitive than others they should move to a suitable location, not expect others to change their lifestyle. As one commentator wrote, "Exceptionally nervous persons, or those whose refinement exceeds the standards of the 'American people in their present state of enlightenment,' as the Washington court put it, must seek refuge in sound proof rooms, if they can afford them, or take their chances of the padded cell."[410]

War stories: A Mr. Rogers was suffering from sunstroke and congestion of the brain and was living across from St. Peter's Roman Catholic Church in Provincetown, Massachusetts. Whenever the bell would be rung Mr. Rogers would go into convulsions which could cause his death. The bell ringer at the church, Mr. Elliott, was asked to stop but he just wanted to ring the bell even more. He said that he would not stop for any reason, "much less Mr. Rogers." He added that if it would kill Mr. Rogers he would still keep it up. It seems Mr. Rogers had previously had Mr. Elliott arrested for battery. The court decided that since Mr. Rogers was a sensitive person and that an ordinary person would not be disturbed by the bell, it was not a nuisance.[411]

A person with a weak heart sued someone who was blasting with dynamite, but because he was extra-sensitive the blasting was not considered a legal nuisance.[412]

Vibrations caused a house to fall down but the person causing the vibrations was not liable since the house was in poor condition.[413]

A race track was built across from a drive-in movie theater in Portland Oregon. The lights for night races made it difficult to see the films. In a law suit against the race track the court noted that the movie screen was especially sensitive to light and that it had to be specially recessed from the moon and star light and had to have other special barriers to make it useful. Therefore, the court found it to be unusually sensitive and ruled that the lights at the race track were not a nuisance.[414]

It also does not matter if the person is hardened and insensitive. An insensitive person may stop a nuisance even if it does not bother him, based upon the standard of what would bother a normal person.

The invasion of the right to quiet enjoyment of one's property can include many types of things. Noises, smells, vibrations, heat, smoke, flooding, keeping explosives or even running a brothel have been held to be nuisances. But it is required that the harm caused by an action must be *substantial* for it to be deemed a nuisance. One of the author's favorite Latin maxims (and one of the few he remembers) is "De minimis non curat lex," the law will not concern itself with trifles.

War story: In England in 1836 one person put rubbish into another person's well. The court noted that the well was not filled up but only temporarily muddied. This was found to be too trifling to be in court.[415]

Courts have not been sympathetic in cases in which the only damage claimed was the loss of property value. As the Court of Appeals of Kentucky once explained it:

It is fundamental that a buyer of property assumes the risk of changing community conditions. Sometimes the value of his property is enhanced, and he does not have to pay for the enhancement. Sometimes it declines and he has no recourse. These facts of life are not subject to an exception simply because the source of the transition can be identified and is suable.[416]

Chapter 59 What You Can Win in Court

There are two types of relief which a court can usually grant in a neighbor dispute, monetary damages or an injunction, which is a court order requiring the other party to take some action or to refrain from taking some action.

In most cases the monetary damages awarded for a nuisance are actual damages. Those are the actual amounts necessary to compensate you for the loss caused by the nuisance or trespass. This may be the loss of rental value of the property if the nuisance is temporary, or the loss of market value of the property if the nuisance is permanent. If there has been some physical damage to another piece of property the damages nay be the cost of restoring it.

In some cases where there are no actual damages, such as someone trespassing in your yard, you could get nominal damages, such as a dollar. In other cases, where actual or nominal damages are inadequate, a court might award special damages. An example of this would be where a nuisance makes a farm useless for farming but does not lower its value. The question in this type of situation is what would be fair compensation for the trouble, annoyance and anxiety of having to move from one's lifelong home.

Where the person acted deliberately and maliciously, you might be able to get punitive damages. This remedy is usually only available where the party did something especially shocking to the court. Punitive damages are only available in a case where the complaining party has been held to be entitled, first, to actual or nominal damages.

In some states there are statutes which specifically allow for punitive damages in certain cases. For example, Louisiana allows triple damages for cutting down another's trees without permission.

Courts are usually reluctant to issue injunctions. They are not usually issued unless the alternative monetary judgment would not be adequate compensation. However in neighbor cases there is usually a better than usual chance of obtaining an injunction because the case usually involves land and each piece of land is considered unique.

The injunction can tell the other party to stop the activity completely, or it can tell him to conduct it in a different manner. For example, courts have ordered the installation of noise suppression equipment and have ordered activities to be conducted only during certain hours of the day.

In nuisance and trespass law suits, attorney's fees are rarely awarded to the winner. This means that any amounts won will be reduced by the amounts owed to your attorney. Considering the thousands of dollars a suit would cost, going to court is not worth it for small sums. And the cost of an injunction, even if you win, will be substantial.

In some cases, such as where is some kind of written agreement between the parties, attorney's fees may be awarded. In some instances they have gotten seriously out of hand.

War story: In 1979 Royal Saxon, Inc., a cooperative apartment association, filed suit against Mildred R. Jaye to force her to obey the rules of the building, such as to "dress appropriately" in the lobby and use the right door to the pool and also to require her to supply them with an access key to her apartment. In 1982, while the 1979 case was still pending, Royal Saxon, Inc. filed a suit to evict Ms. Jaye over an assessment of $191.33 which she claimed was improper. In 1984, after a twelve-day trial, Ms. Jaye was declared to be the prevailing party and was entitled to have Royal Saxon pay her $87,375.00 attorney's fee.[417]

Chapter 60 What Considerations Will Be Weighed

When a court is faced with a case involving an alleged nuisance it must weigh the rights of the two sides and come to a decision which is as equitable as possible. A person awakened by a neighbor who must practice the trumpet may feel his rights are being violated, but the trumpet player also feels he has rights to use his property as he wishes. In striking a balance between the competing interests the courts will look at several factors.

With nuisance, as with many areas of the law, the court will look to what is **reasonable**. There has long been a "reasonable man" standard (more recently renamed the "reasonable person" standard) to decide whether conduct is allowable. In nuisance cases there is also an examination of the gravity of the harm versus the utility of the enterprise. In other words, the court will see if the person alleged to be creating a nuisance is doing more harm than good.

In examining the gravity of the harm and the utility of the enterprise, the court will look at the type of harm being caused to the person complaining, at the social value of what the person is doing, at the suitability of what he is doing in the location and at the burden on him to avoid the problem.

More recently courts have looked at whether it would be possible to compensate neighbors for the harm and loss of value of their property.

War story: A cement company had a factory which cost $45 million, paid substantial taxes and employed 300 people. It had done everything feasible to keep its operation clean and quiet but was still causing problems for its neighbors. The court held that it would not be reasonable to stop the operation completely so it ordered that the company pay $185,000 to the people who were bothered by the operation to compensate them for the problems. This payment would be considered a payment for the lost value of their property and would be a one-time payment. A future purchaser of the property could not sue for damages since he should have, theoretically, paid a reduced price for the land.[418]

Chapter 61 What Defenses Are Available

When a person is sued for nuisance, the burden will be upon the person filing the suit to prove that there was an actionable nuisance and that the person being sued caused it. If this is not proven, then the case should be dismissed. Even if it is proven, the person sued may have some defenses which justify the action.

Statutes of Limitations. These laws are specific limits of the time period in which you can file a suit for a certain type of action. For example, the time limit may be one year to file a suit for encroachments on your property if they are under six inches. One should check state statutes thoroughly for limitations. For example, the limitation for something such as simple trespass may be one time period, such as five years, but another statute may apply to certain types of trespass and be two years.

Consent. If a person consents to your action they cannot sue you for it unless they withdrew their consent prior to your action. For example, if your neighbor says you can walk through his yard, he cannot sue you for trespass if you do. If you are bitten by his dog he cannot use trespass as a defense to your suit over the dog bite. Sometimes consent can be presumed. For example, a person ordering a pizza can be assumed to have granted the delivery person permission to enter his property for the purpose of delivering the pizza.

Self defense. If you must take some action to protect yourself or your property, then in many cases this is a defense to a suit. For example, if your neighbor' sprinkler is spraying water onto your porch and ruining your furniture you could go on his land and redirect it without risk of being guilty of trespass (unless in moving the sprinkler you cause damage to the neighbor's property).

Defense of others. Similarly, defending someone else from injury can be a defense to a law suit.

Contributory negligence. Ordinarily nuisance does not involve negligence, so contributory negligence cannot be a factor considered. But occasionally nuisance and negligence overlap and the distinction between the two is not clear. Courts will sometimes confuse the two and call something negligent a nuisance or vice versa.

War story: While stepping from a driveway to a sidewalk in Niagara

Falls, New York, in the 1920s, Frances McFarlane caught her heel and stumbled. She sued the city for negligence, saying that the condition of the area was a nuisance. The court held that the condition could be a nuisance, but that the jury could consider if Ms. McFarlane had also been negligent when she fell.[419]

Assumption of the risk. In some cases a person's actions indicate that he consciously decided to assume the risk, waiving the right to sue. For example, a veterinarian can rarely sue for being bitten for an animal in his care.

Legislative authority. Just as the legislature can make an activity illegal, it can make it lawful. When a city zones a certain area for heavy industry, the city gives authority to occupiers of that land to engage in industrial activities. Activities which might be a nuisance in another area would be legal in an industrial area.

Variance. If some activity is against a zoning law it may be possible to be granted a variance or a special exception to the law.

Nonconforming use. If a property is being used a certain way when a zoning law is passed, in most cases the use will be allowed to continue. The is called "grandfathered in." If the use is not allowed to continue then the law will probably be held unconstitutional as a taking of property without compensation. However, some courts have allowed a use to be phased out through amortization.

Legalized nuisance. Even if a court finds some activity to be a nuisance, a legislative body may later make it legal.

War story: Henry Sawyer was a bell manufacturer in Plymouth, Mass. In a suit by Clarence Davis, he had been restrained by a court from ringing a bell on his mill before the hour of 6:30 a.m. Several years later, the legislature passed an act which allowed manufacturers and employers to ring bells, gongs and whistles in order to give notice to employees at times the towns could designate. Plymouth allowed the bell ringing to begin at 5 a.m., and Sawyer asked the court to lift the injunction from ringing before 6:30 a.m. Davis claimed the statute was unconstitutional. The court held the statute constitutional, and that since Sawyer had taken the proper procedures he was entitled to relief from the injunction.[420]

Right to farm laws. In some states there are "right to farm" laws which protect farmers from nuisance suits. These are useful when subdivisions are built closer and closer to farms and the residents are annoyed by the smells or noises from the farms.

Moving to the nuisance. If a person has been engaging in an activity for a number of years and another person moves nearby and objects to the activity, the first person may have the greater right. As discussed previously, many factors will be taken into account, such as the character of the locale and the amount of disturbance being created. If the activity is unreasonable, however, the person creating the nuisance will not be able to keep it up just because he got there first.

War stories: In the 1930s and '40s, Lanamark Road on the southern slope of Red Mountain in Birmingham, Alabama, was a high class residential area. The nearby railroad tracks of the Louisville & Nashville Railroad Co. had not been in use for some time. But during the war the railroad was needed for nearby coal mines and other operations. These operations caused dust and smoke, loud noises from the beating of the rail cars to empty them, and odors and fumes. In 1946 Martha Dick McClung and J. D. Gainey filed suit against the railroad and others in an attempt to abate the nuisance. By 1951 the case reached the Alabama Supreme Court which held that while some of the noise and fumes were unnecessary and must be reduced, the residents could not stop the lawful operation of the railroad which had been there first. (Moral: before you buy a house, check the neighborhood for railroad tracks.)[421]

When Autry Livestock Exchange opened its riding academy in the south half of block 1 of the Mesa Park addition to Albuquerque, New Mexico, there were no residences in the area. However, as the city grew it became surrounded with homes. Fourteen of the residents sued the academy because of annoyances from the manure and urine smells emanating from the stables, as well as blowing hay, mud, flies, disease hazards and braying of burros. The Supreme Court of New Mexico was not impressed by the fact that the stables had been in the neighborhood first. It gave the stable owner two and a half months to abate the nuisance.[422]

When Spur Industries, Inc. began its cattle feeding operations in Maricopa County, Arizona, it was far from the edge
of any city. However, Del E. Webb Development Co.
decided this was a good area for its Sun City retirement
community and purchased land nearby on which to create
its community. Because the odors, flies and other annoyances of the cattle feeding lot would make the community
less attractive to potential residents, the developer sued to
have the operations stopped. The Arizona Supreme Court,
in balancing the rights of the parties, decided that it would
order the cattle feed lot to stop operations, but that the
developer would have to pay all costs of moving or shut-
ting down the operation.[423]

Acts of others. The fact that others are also creating a nuisance is not a
defense to one charged with nuisance. But if an area is predominantly
industrial or commercial then others in the area will have less right to
complain about noise, smoke or smells than if it was a residential area.

Prescriptive right. A prescriptive right is a right which is acquired
through continued use. Although it has been held that one may not
acquire a prescriptive right to maintain a *public* nuisance, there have
been cases which have found a prescriptive right to take action which
might otherwise constitute a *private* nuisance.

War story: A plant located on a stream had emptied refuse into the
            stream for twenty years. When an owner further down the
            stream complained, the court held that the plant had
            acquired the right through constant use.[424]

Laches. Laches means that a person has not enforced his right for a
considerable length of time. In some cases failing to object may
constitute acquiescence and a person may lose his right to object in the
future. However, failing to object when a nuisance is slight does not
preclude one from objecting when it becomes greater.

War stories: Joseph Harris, Sr. and others started building greenhouses
            on their land in Coal township, Northumberland County,
            Pennsylvania, in 1897 near the land eventually owned by
            Susquehanna Collieries Co. In the operation of its coal
            business, the company washed and sifted rock and coal
            and piled it on their land. When it dried the dust blew onto
            the greenhouses, spotting the plants, pitting the glass and
            causing other problems. Beginning in 1918 Mr. Harris and

his partners complained a couple times about the problem but it wasn't until 1926 that they filed suit. The court held that under the doctrine of laches they had waited too long to seek an injunction but that they might be able to sue for monetary damages.[425]

In 1919, after becoming blind, Patrick Quinn purchased a home with his wife at 5621 Butler Street, Pittsburgh, Pennsylvania, in a mixed residential and manufacturing district. Later his wife died and he owned the home himself. American Spiral Spring & Manufacturing Company purchased the lot behind Mr. Quinn's home to build a manufacturing plant. They contacted him and told him the plant would be noisy and offered to buy his property. He refused to sell. They then opened their plant and placed the noisiest equipment closest to his home. He complained but they only offered to purchase his property at the value of the land with no payment for the building. Fourteen months later he sued. At trial it was shown that the vibrations were so bad that pictures and plaster shook from the walls and articles bounced off tables. The company contended that because he waited 14 months, Mr. Quinn was precluded from complaining about the noise. The court disagreed and said that the heavy machinery would have to be moved away from Mr. Quinn's house even though moving it would cost more than the house was worth.[426]

When an undertaking establishment opened for business the neighbors filed suit. The owners said that the neighbors had waited too long to object since he had already done all the remodelling. However, since the owner camouflaged what he was doing in the remodelling, the delay by the neighbors was justified.[427]

Emergency. In an emergency situation such as a war, a nuisance may be allowed to continue when the court weighs the equities.

War stories: In New Jersey the Atlantic City Electric Co. was using the best equipment available at the time, but it still caused fly ash, dirt, soot, dust and cinders in the neighborhood. The neighbors sued and the court held that during the war nothing would be done, but the neighbors could refile their suit after the war.[428]

Mt. Vernon Die Casting Corp. on 242nd Street in Bronx, N. Y. was causing a nuisance for a neighbor who owned rental property. In a lawsuit the court held that during the war the company would have to pay to the owner of the property the amount by which his property was lowered in rental value and after the war it would have to stop the nuisance.[429]

Prevention of disease. In some cases an effort to prevent the spread of a disease can constitute an emergency grave enough to be a defense to a court action.

War story: To prevent the further spread of a smallpox epidemic, the city of Knoxville had the hospital beds, sheets and clothing of infected patients burned once the patient left the hospital. The state brought suit claiming that the burning of the infected material infected and poisoned the atmosphere around the highways and homes of citizens near the hospital. The state claimed the air was so corrupt and unhealthy it was a nuisance. The court held the act was done by public authority for public safety to prevent the spread of disease. The court held the burnings were done with reasonable care and with a regard for safety. It said this was a temporary inconvenience which was justified under the circumstances and the state could not enforce criminal liability.[430]

Chapter 62 What Defenses Will Not Work

In both civil and criminal cases people often come into court with perfectly good excuses why they did or didn't do something in the matter being litigated. But often the excuse is not a legal defense, that is their excuse is not relevant to the issue. Each area of law considers some issues relevant and others irrelevant. If you do not address the relevant issues you cannot win your case, no matter how right you are on the irrelevant issues.

The following are examples of some defenses which didn't work. Keep in mind that the law is different in every jurisdiction and these cases might not be followed precisely in your area.

Benefit. It is irrelevant that the activity complained of increases the value of the property owned by the persons complaining.

War story: In the 1930s Angie Laurance and others filed suit against Jennie B. Tucker to stop them from maintaining a drain over their premises in Prairie City, Oregon, to carry away water from a septic tank. Ms. Tucker argued that having the drain on her property was a benefit to Ms. Laurence. However, the Supreme Court of Oregon ruled that a person can never justify a trespass by showing a benefit to the owner of the land.[431]

Unable to afford. The inability to afford a remedy to a nuisance is not a legal defense to a nuisance action.

War story: The Baltimore & Yorktown Turnpike Rd. was indicted for maintaining a public nuisance when it allowed its road to fall into such a ruinous and defective condition that it constituted a nuisance. The road authority contended that it did not have the money to pay for repairs. The court held that this was not a defense to the criminal charge.[432]

No other place to do it. A person's claim that he has no other place to conduct the activity is not a legal defense.

War story: In Portland, Maine, the Harts were in the business of pulling wool and sheep skins. This activity caused noxious odors, filth and noises which disturbed the neighbors. The state brought an action for nuisance. The Harts argued that they had no place else in which to do the work. The court ruled that this was not a legal defense. [433]

Chartered by state board of health under state approved plan. A license by the state to do an activity is not a defense to do it in a way that constitutes a nuisance.

War stories: When Collingswood Sewerage Co. of Camden, New Jersey was indicted for a criminal nuisance because of unpleasant odors from its plant, it defended on the ground that it was chartered by the state and under direction of the Board of health, using plans of the State Sewerage Commission. The courts said that was not a defense because the Board of health could not authorize a nuisance.[434]

When the Pennsylvania Railroad Co. was indicted for permitting a nuisance in Jersey City, New Jersey, by operating a roundhouse during unseasonable hours and allowing to be emitted noisome, unwholesome, and dense smoke and noxious, penetrating, and discoloring vapors and offensive odors. The company argued, among other things, that it could not be indicted since it was engaged in interstate commerce. The courts didn't buy it.[435]

Benefit to the public. The fact that an activity benefits the public is not a defense if it is done in such a way as to constitute a nuisance.

War story: When Wilkins Seacord was charged with criminal nuisance for operating a rendering plant in Warren County, Illinois, in close proximity to several residences in 1885, he argued that his business was a benefit to the public. However, the Supreme Court of Illinois held that this was not a defense to a charge of nuisance.[436]

Plaintiff failed to abate. Persons injured by a nuisance do not have a legal duty to lessen their damages by moving away or avoiding the area.

War story: A gas plant in the city of Reton, Washington, was annoying the neighbors by allegedly emitting noisome odors and discharging bothersome chemicals which injured the neighbors and damaged their house and some trees. A jury awarded $2,500 to the neighbors, but the verdict was set aside. In a second trial the jury awarded $500 but this was reversed by the appellate court because the trial judge erroneously told the jury that the neighbors had the duty to lessen their damages by moving from the premises. The court ruled that in nuisance cases a person does not have to minimize his own damages. Therefore the neighbors were allowed to conduct a third trial.[437]

Chapter 63 What the Law Is

When students go to law school they do not get books that tell them what the law is. They get books filled with cases like the ones in this book, and after reading these they are supposed to figure out what the law is. However, after three years and thousands of cases they come to the realization that no one knows what the law is.

Two cases look identical, the facts seem to be the same, but the results are completely the opposite. For a hundred years the results always went one way, but now in this case the court says there is an exception because of some minor detail. Could it be because the defendant was a minister? Did it matter that the plaintiff was a widow? A Nazi? Facts like these aren't always discussed in the case opinions.

Some people say that the law is what the judge assigned to your case says it is. If the law is completely on your side and you have carefully covered your position in every way, but the judge gets the impression that you are dishonest and are taking advantage of an innocent person you may still lose your case. There are exceptions to every rule and many of these exceptions were created so that a judge could reach the "right" decision at the time.

The purpose of appeals courts is to review the holdings of the trial judges and to be sure that the law was properly interpreted. Appeals courts do not see the parties or take any testimony. They just look at the written record of the case, listen to the lawyers' argument as to what law applies and see if the law was properly applied by the trial judge. Supposedly, this insulates them from getting involved with the emotional or personal aspects of the parties.

But appeals courts also use flexibility in interpreting the law and they even reverse the law when necessary to reach a result which is "right."

Chapter 64 How a Case is Decided

Most cases involve two types of questions, **questions of fact** and **questions of law.** Questions of fact may be decided by a jury, or if a jury is waived, by a judge. These involve issues of what actually happened. Questions of fact are decided upon the evidence presented to the court such as the testimony of the witnesses. Questions of fact cannot be appealed since litigants are usually allowed only one chance to present their evidence. Usually, the only way a litigant can get a second chance to present evidence is if there is some fundamental error in the trial and a new trial must be held.

Questions of law involve how the law applies to the facts that have been established. Questions of law are always decided by the judge and these may be appealed if the judge makes a legal error.

To make things even more complicated, sometimes a question can be either one of law or of fact.

Examples: A simple example explaining the difference between law and fact would be a theft. You charge your neighbor with taking your hose and he is charged with theft. The questions of fact for the jury would be whether it was your hose and whether your neighbor took it. If the jury agreed that it was your hose and that your neighbor did take it, it would then be a question of law for the judge as to whether the taking constituted a theft under the theft statute.

With things like nuisances it is a bit more complicated. Suppose you are kept up every night by a loud noise which rattles your house and you sue the factory next door. The questions of fact to be decided by the jury are: Were you kept up every night? Was your house actually rattled? Was this caused by the factory? Assuming the jury decides that all these things are true, the next question would be whether these facts constitute a nuisance. Some courts have ruled that such question is a question of fact for the jury,[438] but others have said it is a question of law.[439] Once it is decided that there is a nuisance and that you are entitled to an injunction halting the noise plus monetary compensation for damage to your house, the amount of monetary damage would then be a question of fact for the jury.

Chapter 65 What Your Chances Are

Out of all the cases brought to lawyers only a small percentage actually go to trial. Many are settled after negotiations, some are settled after a suit is filed and a large number are settled just before or during the trial. The reason for this is that there is no way to predict the outcome of a trial.

No matter how strong the law is, no matter how ideal your witnesses are, you can lose your case. Juries of six or twelve different individuals do not always act on logic. They do not always understand the instructions of the judge and they do not always believe the witnesses.

Waiving a jury and leaving all the questions to the judge may result in a more logical decision, but it may not always be a better decision.

Everyone taking a matter to court has a 50% chance of winning, and of losing. Lawyers know there is no such thing as a sure case. Anything can happen in a law suit. Even if you have all the facts and law on your side you can still lose. How can this happen? The judge may not believe you, he or she may misinterpret the law, or you may just end up looking like the "bad guy" after the other side tells their side of the case.

This is why so many cases are settled out of court. For every case that goes to trial, numerous more are settled before trial, especially in the 24 hours just before trial.

Keep this in mind when deciding how to handle your nuisance claim. If you can get the other side to make a reasonable offer, take it! Don't be greedy. Don't try to show him a lesson. Don't do everything you can to get even. You might end up losing.

Many judges like to do a little for each side, even if that means cutting the baby in half.

Part V   How to Research Your Case Further

Chapter 66 Using a Law Library

Because of the wide scope of material covered in this book, only general principles can be explained and only a few cases can be given as examples. Many of the subjects in this book are thoroughly researched and explained in thousands of pages of articles and cases.

If you have a specific problem which you would like to research further, you can easily find the information in a local law library or a larger public library. Many county courthouses have law libraries and many law libraries at law schools are open to the public.

The best place to find information about the current state of the law in your state on any subject is a state legal encyclopedia. Unfortunately, such encyclopedias are not available for every state. They have only been published for California, Florida, Illinois, Maryland, Michigan, New York, Ohio, Pennsylvania and Texas.

The best place to find information about a specific problem is in the American Law Reports. These are abbreviated "A.L.R." and there are four series of these. These books contain lengthy articles explaining in detail the state of the law on very specific topics such as crowds as nuisances or alienation of a child's affections.

If there is no legal encyclopedia for your state and no article in any of the A.L.R.s then you should check a national legal encyclopedia called Corpus Juris Secundum, or "C.J.S." This is a set of over 100 three-inch thick blue books on every conceivable subject. Each subject is thoroughly analyzed and the cases from around the country noted by state in the footnotes. Sometimes a page may have one line of text and the rest footnotes.

When using any of these books you should be sure to check inside the back cover to the "pocket part" This is a supplement of recent laws and cases which should bring the book up to date. Check the date of the pocket part to see how current it is.

From any of these sources you should be able to find at least a few cases related to your problem. Once you have these you should look them up in the national series of case reporters published by West Publishing. This is a series of books containing all of the published cases in this country divided by region. The Regions are as follows:

Atlantic (A.)	Pacific (P.)
California (Cal.Rptr.)	Southern (So.)
New York State (N.Y.S.)	Southeast (S.E.)
Northeast (N.E.)	Southwest (S.W.)
Northwest (N.W.)	

Your state might not be in the reporter you expect. For example, Kansas is in the Pacific Reporter, Michigan is in the Northwest Reporter and Vermont is in the Atlantic Reporter. As you may have surmised, the reporters were originally designed a long time ago.

A case citation has three parts, the volume, the series and the page. Thus, 394 N.Y.S.2d 777 would be found in Volume 394 of the New York Supplement Second Series Reporters at page 777.

Once you have found a case similar to yours in one of these reporters you should look at the beginning of the case for the "headnotes." These are the summaries of the different holdings of the case. A case may have one or dozens of holdings. Some of the holdings may be directly related to the issue you are researching and others may have nothing to do with it.

You should look for the holdings most closely related to your case, and write down the "key numbers." This is a system of categorizing cases by subject created and owned by the West Publishing Co. which publishes the reporters. By using these key numbers you can locate other cases which have ruled on the same issues.

After you have the West key numbers of the issues you are researching you should locate your state "Digest." This is a collection of all the head notes from all the cases in your state. There are digests for every state except Delaware, Nevada and Utah. By using the key numbers you can find all of the other cases in your state on the subject.

If you are in Delaware, Nevada or Utah, or if you want to check decisions from other states you can use the "Decennial Digest." which is a digest of all the cases in America published every ten years.

If your problem is similar to one in this book, you can look up the citation in the footnotes and find that case. Then take the headnotes in that case which cover your situation and use them to find other cases. This is done by using the Key numbers and going to your state digest.

There are several good books on the market which explain in detail how to do legal research. These are available at many larger bookstores or at law school book stores. If you cannot locate one locally you can get one through Sphinx Self Help Law Book Shop at 1725 Clearwater/Largo Rd. S., Clearwater, FL 34617. Tel. (813) 587-0999 or (800) 226-5291.

Chapter 67 Postscript

The law changes constantly and cases like the ones in this book are filed in courthouses across the country every day. If you know of an interesting neighbor case which has gone to court or appeared in the press, we'd like to hear about it.

Also, if you live near any of the buildings or properties mentioned in this book, we would like to see a photo of them. We might use the photos in a future edition of the book. If we use your photo, you'll get a free copy of the next edition.

Send photos, articles and letters to:

Mark Warda
Sphinx Publishing
Post Office Box 25
Clearwater, FL 34617

Footnotes

[1] Nissan Motor Corp. in U.S.A. v. Maryland Shipbuilding and Drydock Co., 544 FSupp 1104, affirmed 742 F2d 1449 (DCMd 1982)

[2] Shelley v. Kraemer, 334 US 1, 68 SCt 836, 92 LEd1161 (1948)

[3] Prosser, Torts, 4th Ed., 1971, p. 571

[4] 4 Blackstone's Commentaries 216

[5] Town of Green River v. Bunger, 58 P2d 456, 50 Wyo 52

[6] Hall v. Putney, 10 NE2d 204, 291 IllApp 508

[7] Village of Euclid v. Ambler Realty Co., 272 US 365, 388, 47 SCt 114, 118, 71 LEd 303, 311 (1926)

[8] Prosser, Torts, 4th Ed., 1971, p. 594

[9] Y.B. 27 Henry VIII, Mich. pl. 10.

[10] Florida statutes §60.05

[11] Michigan Statutes§14.528

[12] Wisconsin Statutes1958, §280.02

[13] Lord Coke, Liber 1, section 1, page 4. The origin of the maxim is believed to be Accursius a commentator on the Code who lived in Bologna around the year 1200.

[14] 49 U.S.C. 1304

[15] 49 U.S.C. 1301 (29)

[16] Swetland v. Curtiss Airports Corp., 41 F2d 929 (DC Ohio 1930)

[17] Oechsle v. Ruhl, 140 NJ Eq 355, 54 A2d 462 (1947)

[18] Gruber v. Dodge 45 MichApp 33, 205 NW2d 869 (1973)

[19] Rhoads v. Piacitelli, 64 PaD&C 565, 2 Av 14658 (1948)

[20] Hanover v. Morristown, 108 NJSuper 536, 261 A2d 692 (1969), supp. op. 118 NJ Super 136, 286 A2d 728, Aff'd. 121 NJ Super 536, 298 A2d 89 (1972)

[21] Ferguson v. Keene, 111 NH 222, 279 A2d 605 (1971)

[22] Morris v. Ciborowski 113 NH 563, 311 A2d 296, 79 ALR3d 248 (1973)

[23] Cunliffe v. County of Monroe, 63 Misc2d 62, 312 NYS2d 879 (1970)

[24] Chronister v. City of Atlanta 99 GAApp 447, 108 SE2d 731 (1959)

[25] Loma Portal Civic Club v. American Airlines, Inc., 61 Cal2d 582, 39 CalRptr 708, 394 P.2d 548 (1964)

[26] Coxsey v. Hallaby, 231 F.Supp. 978 (DC Okla 1964)

[27] Luedtke v. County of Milwaukee, 371 F.Supp. 1040 (DC Wis. 1974) Aff'd in part, vacated on other grounds, 521 F2d 387 (CA7 1974)

[28] United States v. Causby, 328 U.S. 256 66 S.Ct. 1062, 90 L.Ed. 1206 (1946)

[29] Thornburg v. Port of Portland, 233 Or 178, 376 P2d 100 (1962)

[30] Batten v. United States, 306 F2d 580 (1962)

[31] Nestle v. Santa Monica, 6 Cal3d 920, 101 CalRptr 568, 496 P2d 480 (1972)

[32] Baker v. Burbank-Glendale-Pasadena Airport Authority, 39 Cal3d 862, 218 CalRptr 293, 705 P2d 866, cert. den. 475 US 1017, 106 SCt 1200, 89 LEd2d 314 (1985)

[33] Greater Westchester Homeowners Assoc. v. Los Angeles, 26 Cal3d 86, 160 CalRptr 733, 603 P2d 1329 (1979)

[34] Wells v. Simpson, 52 So2d 682 (Fla 1951)

[35] Liles v. Jarnigan, US Av 90 (TennChCt 1950)

[36] Treisman v. Kamen, 126 NH 372, 493 A2d 466 (1985)

[37] Cannon v. Miller, 327 SE2d 888 (N.C. 1985)

[38] Vacek v. Ames, 377 NW2d 86, 221 Neb. 333 (1985)

[39] Nabors v. Keaton, 393 SW2d 382 (Tenn. 1965)

[40] Zarrella v. Robinson, 460 A 2d 415 (RI 1983)

[41] Nelson v. Jacobsen, 669 P2d 1207 (Utah 1983)

[42] Greenway v. Greenway, 693 SW2d 600 (1985)

[43] Lund v. Caple, 675 P2d 226 (Wash. 1984)

[44] Nash v. Baker, 522 P2d 1335 (OklA 1974)

[45] Warren Co. v. Dickson, 195 SE 568, 185 Ga 481 (1938)

[46] Carter v. Lake City Baseball Club, 62 SE2d 470, 218 SC 255 (1950)

[47] Neiman v. Common School District No. 95, 232 P2d 422 (Kan 1951)

[48] State ex rel. Trampe v. Multerer, 289 N.W. 600, 234 Wisc 50 (1940)

[49] State v. Canty, 105 S.W. 1078, 207 Mo 439, 123 AmSR 393, 15 LRA,NS, 747, 13 Ann Cas 787 (1907)

[50] Jaime Ganzales A. v. Ghingher, 145 A2d 769, 218 Md 132 (1958)

[51] Monterey Club v. Superior Court of Los Angeles, 119 P2d 349, 48 CalApp2d 131 (1941)

[52] Congregation Emunath Israel v. New York City Off-Track Betting Corp., 330 NYS2d 895, 69 Misc2d 781 (1972)

[53] Gleason v. Hillcrest Golf Course, 265 NYS 886, 148 Misc 246 (1933)

[54] Town of Davis v. Davis, 21 SE 906, 40 WVa 464 (1895)

[55] City of Chicago v. Shaynin, 101 NE 224, 258 Ill 69, 45 LRA,NS 23 (1913)

[56] City of Louisville v. Munro, 475 SW2d 479 (1972)

[57] Boudinot v. State, 340 P2d 268, 73 ALR2d 1027 (1959)

[58] Smith v. Steineauf, 36 P2d 995 (1934)

[59] City of Columbus v. Belcher, 180 NE2d 836, 173 Ohio St 197 (1962)

[60] Farrell v. Cook, 20 N.W. 720, 16 Neb 483 (1884)

[61] Biggerstaff v. State, 435 N.E.2d 621 (1982)

[62] State v. Tweedie, 444 A2d 855 (RI 1982)

[63] Duval v. Rowell, 269 P. 2d 249 (1954)

[64] Wyoming Game and Fish Commission v. Latham, 347 P2d 560, 54 Wyo 346 (1960)

[65] Leipskev. Guenther, 95 NW 2d 744 (Wisc 1959)

[66] Young v. Estep, 35 P2d 80 (Wash. 1934)

[67] Slack v. Villari, 476 A2d 227, 59 MdApp 462 (1984)

[68] Rickrode v. Wistinghausen, 340 NW2d 83(1983)

[69] Moore v. Lindeman, 488 So2d 1300 (LaApp 1986)

[70] McDonald v. Jodrey, 8 PaCo 142 (1890)

[71] Doerfler v. Redding, 205 A.2d 502 (1964)

[72] Bessent v. Matthews, 543 So2d 438 (Fla1 DCA 1989)

[73] Vasques v. Lopez, 509 So2d 1241 (Fla4 DCA 1987)

[74] Noble v. Yorke, 490 So2d 29 (Fla 1986)

[75] Olmsted v. Rich, 6 NYS 826(1889)

[76] H.E. Butt Grocery Co. v. Perez, 408 SW2d 576 (1966)

[77] Doornbos v. Ihde, 228 P2d 235 (Mont 1951)

[78] Helsel v. Fletcher, 235 P 514, 98 Okl 285, 33 ALR 792 (1924)

[79] Thomas v. State, 148 So 225, 165 Miss 897 (1933)

[80] Mitzel v. Zachman, 16 NW2d 472, 219 Minn 253 (1945)

[81] Cadenhead v. Goodman, 114 So 124, 148 Miss 88 (1927)

[82] Quave v. Bardwell, 449 So2d 81 (1984)

[83] Mendenhall v. Struck, 224 NW 95, 207 Iowa 1094 (1929)

[84] Georgia Code §44-9-2 (1982)

[85] Mohr v. Midas Realty Corp., 431 NW2d 380 (Iowa 1988)

[86] Collinson v. John L. Scott, Inc., 778 P2d 534, 55 WashApp 481 (1989)

[87] Tenn v. 889 Associated, Ltd., 500 A2d 366 (NH 1985)

[88] Flaherty v. Moran, 45 NW 381, 81 Mich 52 (1890)

[89] Hullinger v. Prahl, 233 NW2d 584 (SD 1975)

[90] Fountainebleu Hotel Corp. v. Forty-Five Twenty-Five, Inc., 114 So2d 357 (Fla 3 DCA 1959)

[91] Campbell v. Hammock, 90 SE2d 415, 212 Ga 90 (1955)

[92] Prah v. Maretti, 321 N.W. 2d 182, 108 Wis. 2d 223 (1982)

[93] Gevurtz, Comment, Obstruction of Sunlight as a Private Nuisance, 65 Cal. Law Rev. 94 (1977)

[94] Sher v. Leiderman, 181 CalApp3d 867, 226 CalRep.698 (1986)

[95] New Mexico Statutes §47-3-4 (1978)

[96] Hall v. Eaton 29 NE 660 (Mass 1885)

[97] Pilgrim v. Kuipers, 679 P2d 787 (Mont 1984)

[98] Sowerwine v. Nielson, 671 P2d 295 (Wyo 1983)

[99] Sanders v. Williams, 434 So.2d 172, writ denied 440 So2d 759 (LaApp.3 cir. 1983)

[100] U.S. v. Citko, 517 FSupp 233 (DCWis 1981)

[101] Town v. Castleton v. Fucci, 431 A2d 486, 139 Vt 598 (1981)

[102] Island County v. Dillingham Development Co., 662 P2d 32, 99 Wash.2d 215 (1983)

[103] Lethin v. U.S., 583 FSupp 863 (DCOr 1984)

[104] Albrecht v. U.S., 529 FSupp 135 (DCWyo 1981)

[105] Weber v. Johannes, 673 SW2d 454 (MoApp 1984)

[106] Walkup v. Evinger, 653 SW2d 383 (MoApp 1983)

[107] Alaska Nat'l Bank v. Linck, 559 P.2d 1049 (1977)

[108] Marengo Cave Co. v. Ross, 10 NE2d 917 (Ind 1937)

[109] Bushnell v. Martin, 553 So2d 92 (Ala 1989)

[110] Howard v. Kunto, 477 P2d 210 (CtAppWash 1970)

[111] Mercer v. Wayman, 137 NE2d 815, 9 Ill2d 441 (1956)

[112] People v. Oliver, 195 P2d 926, 86 CalApp2d 885 (1948)

[113] Worm v. Wood, 223 SW 1016 (TxCivApp 1920)

[114] Slaird v. Klewers, 271 A.2d 345 (1970)

[115] Sea Pines Plantation Co. v. Wells, 363 SE2d 891 (SC 1987)

[116] Rose v. Chaikin, 453 A2d 1387, 187 NJSuper 210, 36 ALR4th 1160 (1982)

[117] Dreher v. Yates, 43 NJLaw 473 (1881)

[118] Rowley v. Marrcrest Homeowners' Ass'n., 656 P2d 414 (Utah 1982)

[119] Blair v. 305-313 East 47th Street Associates, 474 NYS.d 353, 123 Misc2d 612 (NYSup 1983)

[120] Moss v. Burke & Trotti, 3 So2d 281, 198 LA 76 (1941)

[121] Winget v. Winn-Dixie Stores, Inc., 130 SE2d 363 (SC 1963)

[122] Sarraillon v. Stevenson Packing Co., 43 NW2d 509, 153 Neb 182 (1950)

[123] Palfrey v. Killian, 27 SW2d 462, 224 MoApp 325 (1930)

[124] Knowles v. Central Allapattae properties, 198 So 819, 145 Fla 123 (1940)

[125] Board of Health of Buncombe County v. Lewis, 146 SE 592, 196 NC 641 (1929)

[126] Young v. Brown, 46 SE2d 673, 212 SC 156 (1948)

[127] McCaw v. Harrison, 259 SW2d 457 (1953)

[128] Children's Playground as Nuisance, 32 ALR3d 1127

[129] Kasala v. Kalispell Pee Wee Baseball League, 439 P2d 65, 151 Mont 109, 32 ALR3d (1968)

[130] Hennessy v. Boston, 164 NE 470, 263 Mass 559 (1929)

[131] City of White Plains v. Ferraioli, 313 NE2d 756 34 NY2d 300 (NY 1974)

[132] 42 UCS §§3601-3619

[133] People v. Siegal and People v. Spitzer, 309 NYS.d 991, 62 Misc 921 (1970)

[134] Grau v. John McNulty & Sons Holding Co., 9 NYS2d 444, 170 Misc 1 (1939)

[135] Murphy v. Cupp, 31 SW2d 396, 182 Ark 334 (1930)

[136] Dorsett v. Nunis, 13 SE2d 371, 191 Ga 559 (1941)

[137] Spencer Chapel M. E. Church v. Brogan, 231 P 1074, 104 Okl 123 (1924)

[138] Rex v. Betterton, Skinner 625, 90 EngRep 281 (1695)

[139] Rex v. Carlisle, 6 C. & P. 636, 172 EngRep 1397 (1834)

[140] Elias v. Sutherland, 18 Abb. NC 126 (NY 1886)

[141] Tushbant v. Greenfield's Inc., 308 Mich. 626, 14 NW2d 520 (1944)

[142] Shamhart v. Morrison Cafeteria Co., 32 So2d 727 (Fla 1947) Second appeal, 35 So.2d 842 (Fla1948)

[143] Ember v. B.F.D., Inc., 490 NE2d 764 (IndApp 2Dist. 1986)

[144] Dwyer v. Mansfield, KB 437, 2 All Eng. 247 (1946)

[145] Smilie v. Taft Stadium Board of Control, 201 Okla 303, 205 P2d 301 (1949)

[146] Pontardawe Rural District Council v. Moore-Gwyn, 1 Ch. 656 (Eng. 1929)

[147] Smith v. Central Power Co., 137 NE 159, 103 Ohio St. 681 (1921)

[148] Petition of Grand River Dam Authority, 484 P2d 505 (1971)

[149] Koos v. Roth, 652 P2d 1255, 293 Or 670 (Or 1982)
[150] Anderson v. Emigrant Industrial Savings Bank, 49 NYS2d 204, 268 AppDiv 129 (1944)
[151] Campbell County v. Ridenour, 120 SW2d 1000, 22 TennApp 250 (1938)
[152] McGuffey v. Pierce-Fordyce Oil. Assn., 211 SW 335 (1919)
[153] Brownsey v. General Printing Ink Corp., 193 A 824, 118 NJLaw 505 (1937)
[154] Kilts v. Kent County, 127 NW 82, 162 Mich. 646 (1910)
[155] Oxenrider v. Gvoic, 66 NW2d 80, 340 Mich. 591 (1954)
[156] Anderson v. Mitchell, 253 IllApp 509 (1929)
[157] Androwski v. Ole McDonald's Farms, Inc., App., 407 So2d 455 (LaApp. 1982)
[158] St. Joseph Ice Co., v. Bertch, 71 NE 56, 33 IndApp 491 (1904)
[159] Kalipi v. Hawaiian Trust Co., Ltd., 656 P2d 745, 66 Haw 1 (1982)
[160] Baldwin v. Boston & M. R. R., 63 NE 428, 181 Mass 166 (1902)
[161] Brown v. Voss, 715 P2d 514, 105 Wash2d 367 (Wash. 1986)
[162] Bang v. Forman, 222 NW 96 , 244 Mich 571 (1928)
[163] Cameron v. Barton, 272 SW2d 40 (Ky.1954)
[164] Pasadena v. California-Michigan Land & Water Co., 110 P2d 983 (Cal 1941)
[165] Kelly v. Schmelz, 439 SW2d 211 (Mo 1969)
[166] Ward v. McGlory, 265 NE2d 78 (Mass 1970)
[167] Herman v. Roberts, 23 NE 442, 119 NY 37 (1890)
[168] Crimmins v. Gould, 308 P2d 786 (DistCtAppCal. 1957)
[169] People ex rel. Hoogasian v. Sears Roebuck & Co., 287 NE2d 677, 52 Ill2d 301 (1972)
[170] Page County Appliance Center v. Honeywell, Inc., 347 NW2d 171, 45 ALR4th 1191 (Iowa 1984)
[171] Weis v. Cox, 185 NE631, 205 Ind 43 (1933)
[172] Wells Amusement Co. v. Eros, 85 So 692, 204 Ala 239 (1920)
[173] Leffingwell v. Glendenning, 238 SW2d 942, 218 Ark 767 (1951)
[174] Christensen v. Badger Improvement Co., 204 NW 510, 187 Wis 598 (1925)
[175] Lapp v. Gutenkunst, 44 SW 964, 19 KyL 1950 (1898)
[176] Marcus v. Brody, 149 NE 673, 254 Mass 152 (1925)
[177] Schwartz v. Atlantic Building Co., 41 AppDC 108
[178] Wells v. Parks, 268 P 889, 148 Wash 328 (1928)
[179] Gerring v. Gerber, 219 NYS2d 558, 28 Misc2d 271 (1961)
[180] Phillips v. Isham, 244 P2d 716, 111 CA2d 537 (1952)
[181] Zerr v. Heceta Lodge No. 111, Independent Order of Odd Fellows, 523 P2d 1018, 269 Or 174 (1974)
[182] Wahl v. Kelly, 217 NW 307, 194 Wis 559 (1928)
[183] Fung v. Chang, 384 P2d 303, 47 Haw 149 (1963)
[184] Noone v. Price, 298 SE2d 218, (WVa 1982)
[185] Charles F. Harper Co. v. De Witt Mortgage and Realty Co., 300 P 839, 115 CalApp 15 (1931)
[186] McCabe v. City of Parkersburg, 79 SE2d 87, 138 WVa 830 (1953)
[187] Kelley v. Falangus, 388 P2d 223, 63 Wash2d 581 (1964)
[188] Turnstall v. Christian, 80 Va 1, 56 AmR 581 (1885)
[189] Jones v. Hacker, 178 P 424, 104 Kan 187 (1919)
[190] Sime v. Jensen, 7 NW2d 325, 213 Minn 476 (1942)
[191] Tortolano v. DiFilippo, 349 A2d 48, 115 RI 496 (1975)
[192] Maye v. Yappen, 23 Cal 306 (1863)
[193] North Jellico Coal Co. v. Helton, 219 SW 185, 187 Ky 394 (1920)
[194] Edwards v. Lee, 19 SW2d 992, 230 Ky 375 (1929); Edwards v. Sims, 24 SW2d 619, 232 Ky 791 (1929); Edwards v. Lee, 61 SW2d 1049, 250 Ky 166 (1933); Edwards v. Lee's Adm'r., 96 SW2d 1028, 265 Ky 418 (1936)
[195] Boehringer v. Montalto, 254 NYS 276, 142 Misc 560 (1931)
[196] Railroad Commission of Texas v. Manziel, 361 SW2d 560 (Tex 1962)
[197] Friendswood Development Co. v. Smith-Southwest Ind., 576 SW2d 21 (Tex 1978)
[198] Friendswood Development Co. v. Smith-Southwest Ind., 576 S.W. 2d 21 (Texas 1978)

[199] Consolidated Rock Products v. Los Angeles, 370 P2d 342, 57 Cal2d 515, 20 CalRptr 638 (1962)

[200] Exton Quarries, Inc. v. Zoning Board of Adjustment, 228 A2d 168, 425 (1967)

[201] Lyon Sand & Gravel v. Township of Oakland, 190 NW2d 354, 33 MichApp 614 (1971)

[202] 30 USC §§1201-1328

[203] Shelton v. Byrom, 177 SW2d 421, 206 Ark 665 (1944)

[204] Butman v. Fence Viewers of Chelsea, 99 NE2d 44, 327 Mass 386 (1951)

[205] Bryson v. Carroll, 41 A2d 240, 93 NH 287 (1945)

[206] Rose v. Linderman, 110 NW 939, 147 Mich 372 (1907)

[207] K & E Land and Cattle, Inc. v. Mayer, 330 NW2d 529 (SD 1983)

[208] Rotolante v. Dasilva, 460 So2d 560 (Fla 3 DCA 1984)

[209] Adair v. Stallings, 165 SW 140 (CCA.Tex1914)

[210] Loveland v. Gardner, 21 P 766, 79 Cal 317 (1889)

[211] Abilene Cotton Oil Co. v. Briscoe, 66 SW 315, 27 TexCivApp 157 (1901), rehearing denied, writ denied by Texas Supreme Court

[212] Herdt v. Koenig, 119 SW 56, 137 MoApp 589 (1909)

[213] Skalling v. Sheedy, 126 A 721, 101 Conn 545, 36 ALR 540 (1924)

[214] Jones v. Hernandez, 263 NE2d 759 (1970)

[215] Blodgett v. Olympic Sav. and Loan Ass'n., 646 P2d 139, 32 WashApp 116 (1982)

[216] Bridges v. Hawkesworth, 21 LJNS 75 (Q.B. 1851)

[217] McAvoy v. Medina, 11 Allen 548 (Mass 1866)

[218] South Staffordshire Water Co. v. Sherman, 2 QB 44 (Eng. 1896)

[219] Pierson v. Post, 3 Cai R 175 (SupCtNY 1805)

[220] Hatcher v. Hitchcock, 281 P2d 869, 129 Kan 88 (1929)

[221] Jordan et al. v. Nesmith et al, 269 P 1096 (1928)

[222] Dawson v. Laufersweiler, 43 NW2d 726, 241 Iowa 850 (1950)

[223] Grubbs v. Wooten, 5 SE2d 874, 189 Ga 390 (1939)

[224] Santa Fe v. Gamble-Skogmo, 389 P2d 13, 73 NM 410 (1964)

[225] Maher v. City of New Orleans, 516 F2d 1051 (5th Cir 1975)

[226] Penn Central Transportation Co. v. New York, 366 NE2d 1271 (NY 1977)

[227] Penn Central Transportation Co. v. New York, 438 US 104, 98 SCt 2646, 57LEd2d 631 (1978)

[228] Magel v. Gruelti Benev. Soc., 218 SW 704, 203 MoApp 335 (1920)

[229] State ex rel. Carroll v. Gatter, 260 P2d 360, 43 Wash2d 153 (1953)

[230] York v. Sidne Enterprises Inc., 394 NYS2d 777, 90 Misc2d 386 (1977)

[231] City of Chicago v. Geraci, 332 NE2d 487, 30 IllApp3d 699, 80 ALR3d 1013 (1975)

[232] Weis v. San Diego County Super. Ct., 159 P. 464, 30 CalApp 730 (1916)

[233] State v. Toole, 11 SE 168, 106 NC 736 (1890)

[234] State v. Turner, 18 SE2d 372, 198 SC 487 (1942)

[235] Williams v. Hathaway, 400 FSupp 122 (DMass 1975)

[236] Tuberville v. Savage, 1 Mod. 3 (Ct. of K.B. 1669)

[237] Beach v. Hancock, 27 NH 223, 59 AmDec 373 (1853)

[238] Gibbons v. Pepper, 1 Ld.Raym. 38, 91 EngRep 922 (1695)

[239] Cleghorn v. Thompson, 64 P2d 605, 62 Kan 727 (1901)

[240] Kreis v. Owens, 38 NJSuper 148, 118 A2d 420 (1955)

[241] Palsgraf v. Long Island R. Co., 162 NE 99, 248 NY 339 (1928)

[242] Pillars v. R. J. Reynolds Tobacco Co., 78 So 365, 117 Miss 490 (1918)

[243] Lubitz v. Wells, 113 A2d 147 19 Conn 322 (1955)

[244] Guthrie v. Powell, 290 P2d 834, 178 Kan 587 (1955)

[245] Weaver v. Ward, Hob. 134, 80 EngRep 284 (1616)

[246] Luthringer v. Moore, 190 P2d 1 (Cal 1948)

[247] Siegler v. Kuhlman, 502 P2d 1181 (Wash 1973)

[248] Pritchett v. Knox County, 85 NE 32, 42 IndApp3 (1908)

[249] Moore v. Baldwin County, 74 SE2d449, 209 Ga 541 (1953)

[250] Pharr v. Garibaldi, 115 SE2d 18, 252 NC 803 (1960)

251 Amphithretres, Inc. v. Portland Meadows, 198 P2d 847, 184 Or 336 (1948)

252 Hansen v. Independent School Dist., 98 P2d 959, 61 Idaho 109 (1939)

253 Board of Education of Louisville v. Klein, 197 SW2d 427, 303 Ky 234 (1946)

254 Rodrigue v. Copeland, 465 So2d 67, writ granted 466 So2d 1294, reversed 475 So2d 1071, motion for contempt granted 479 So2d 356, issued Klein v. Copeland, 479 So2d 911, stayed 479 So2d 912 (LaApp 5 Cir. 1985)

255 Weber v. Mann, 42 SW2d 492 (TexCivApp 1931)

256 Shepler v. Kansas Mill. Co., 278 P 757, 128 Kan 554 (1929)

257 McKinney v. High Point, 79 SE2d 730, 239 NC 232 (1954)

258 Shelbourne, Inc. v. Crossan Corp., 122 A 749, 95 NJ Eq 188 (1923)

259 Born v. Exxon Corp., 388 So2d 933 (Ala 1980)

260 153 So. 629; 31 A2d 99; 50 NW2d 132

261 Abend v. Royal Laundry Service, 192 A 239, 122 NJEq 77, affirmed 192 A 241, 122 NJEq 77 (1937)

262 De Longpre et al v. Carroll et al, 50 NW2d 132, 331 Mich 474 (1951)

263 Meadowbrook Swimming Club v. Albert, 197 A 146 (1938)

264 Collier v. Ernst, 46 PaDist & Co. 1, 31 DelCo 49 (1942)

265 Myer v. Minard, 21 So2d 72 (1945)

266 Wilson v. Interlake Steel Co, 649 P2d 922, 32 Cal3d 229, 185 CalRptr 280 (1982)

267 Wilson v. Wilkins, 25 SW2d 428 (1930)

268 Burnett et al v. Rushton et ux, 52 So2d 645 (1951)

269 Medford v. Levy, 8 SE 302, 31 WVa 649 (1888)

270 Melvin v. Burling, 490 NE2d 1011, 141 IllApp3d 786, 95 IllDec 919 (Ill.App.3 Dist. 1986)

271 Bennett v. City of Hope, 161 SW2d 186, 204 Ark 147 (1942)

272 Coty v. Ramsey Associates, Inc., 546 A.2d 196 (Vt. 1988)

273 William Aldred's Case, 9 Co.Rep. 57, 77 EngRep 816 (KB 1611)

274 Wade v. Miller, 73 NE 849, 188 Mass 6 (1905)

275 Hundley v. Harrison, 26 So 294, 123 Ala 292 (1899)

276 De Longpre v. Carroll, 50 NW2d 132, 331 Mich 474 (1951)

277 Hedrick v. Tubbs, 92 N.E.2d 561 (App.Ind. 1950)

278 Cain v. Roggero, 38 A.2d 735 (1944)

279 Cropsey v. Murphy, 1 Hilt 126 (NY1856)

280 Ruckman v. Green, 9 Hun 225 (NY 1876)

281 Grand Rapids Board of Health v. Vink, 151 NW 672, 184 Mich 688 (1915)

282 State ex rel Pansing v. Lightner, 32 Ohio NPNS, 376 (1934)

283 Cappelletti et al v. Auerbach et al, 87 FSupp 355 (1949)

284 Lancaster v. Connecticut Mut. Life Ins. Co., ** SW 23 (1887)

285 Yeakel v. Driscoll, 467 A2d 1342, 321 PaSuper 238 (1983)

286 Blackmer v. Montcalm County Board of Commissioners, 407 NW2d 646 (MichApp1987)

287 Lederer & Strauss v. Colonial Inv. Co. et al, 106 NW 357, 130 Iowa 157 (1906)

288 City of LaCrosse v. Jiracek Cos. Inc., 324 NW2d 440, 108 Wis2d 684 (Wis.App. 1982)

289 Shelley v. Kraemer, 334 US 1, 68 SCt 836, 92 LEd 1161 (1948)

290 Barrows v. Jackson, 346 US 249, 73 SCt 1031, 94 LEd 1586(1953)

291 Lauderbach v. Williams, 186 A2d 39, 409 Pa 351 (1962)

292 Penthouse Properties, Inc. v. 1158 Fifth Avenue, Inc. 11 NYS2d 417 (1939)

293 Gale v. York Center Community Cooperative, Inc., 171 NE2d 30 21 Ill2d 86 (1960)

294 Village of Belle Terre v. Boraas, 416 US 1, 94 SCt 1536 39 LEd 2d 797(1974)

295 Moore v. City of East Cleveland, 431 US 494, 97 SCt 1932 52 LEd2d 531(1977)

296 Crane Neck Association, Inc. v. New York City/Long Island County Services Group, 460 NE2d 1336, 61 NY2d 154 (1984)

297 Southern Burlington County NAACP, et al v. Township of Mt. Laurel, 336 A2d 713, 67 NJ 151 (1975) and 456 A2d 390, 92 NJ 158 (1983)

298 Village of Arlington Heights v. Metropolitan Housing Development Corp., 429 US 252, 97 SCt 555, 50 LEd2d 450(1977)

[299] City of Cleburne, Texas v. Cleburne Living Center, 473 US 432, 105 SCt 3249, 87 LEd 313 (1985)

[300] Moore v. Mayor, etc. of Statesboro, 187 SE2d 531, 228 Ga 619 (1972)

[301] Robie v. Lillis, 299 A2d 155, 112 NH 492 (1972)

[302] Arkansas Release Guidance Foundation v. Needler, 477 SW2d 821, 251 Ark 194 (1972)

[303] Brooker v. Silverthorne, 99 SE 350, 111 S.C. 553 (1919)

[304] Housh v. Peth, 133 N.E.2d 340, 165 Ohio St 35, (1956) affirming 135 NE2d 440, 99 Ohio App 485 (1955)

[305] Wiggins v. Moskins Credit Clothing Store, 137 FSupp 764 (E.D.S.C. 1956)

[306] Moore v. Savage, 359 SW2d 95, (TexCivApp 1962) writ or error refused, N.R.E., 362 SW2d 298

[307] Carey v. Statewide Finance Co., 223 A2d 405, 3 ConnCC 716 (1966)

[308] Wilkinson v. Downton, 2 QBD 57 (1897)

[309] Nickerson v. Hodges, 84 So 37, 146 La 735 (1920)

[310] Savage v. Boies, 272 P2d 349, 77 Ariz 355 (1954)

[311] Halio v. Lurie, 222 NYS2d 759, 15 AppDiv2d 62 (1961)

[312] Kahalley v. State, 48 So2d 794 (Ala. 1950)

[313] Souder v. Pendleton Detectives, Inc., 88 So2d 716 (LaApp 1956)

[314] State ex rel. Warner v. Hayes Inv. Corp., 125 P2d 262, 13 Wash2d 306 (1942)

[315] DeMay v. Roberts, 46 Mich 160, 9 NW 146 (1881)

[316] Berthiaune's Estate v. Pratt, 365 A2d 792, 86 ALR3d 365 (Me 1976)

[317] Novel v. Beacon Operating Corp., 446 NYS2d 118, 86 AD2d 602 (N.YAD 1982)

[318] Merz v. Professional Health Control of Augusta, Inc. 332 SE2d 333, 175 GaApp. 110 (1985), rehearing denied, certiorari denied.

[319] Marshall v. Consumers Power Co., 237 NW2d 266, 65 MichApp 237 (1975)

[320] State, Dept. of Environmantal Protection v. Jersey Cent. Power & Light Co., 351 A2d 337, 69 NJ 102 (1976)

[321] Good Fund, Ltd.-1972 v. Church, 540 FSupp 519 (1982)

[322] McKay v. United States, 703 F2d 464 (1983)

[323] Village of Euclid v. Ambler Realty Co., 272 US 365 (1926)

[324] Baltimore v. Mano Swartz, Inc., 299 A2d 828, 268 Md 79 (1973)

[325] National Advertising Co. v. County of Monterey, 464 P2d 33, 1 Cal3d 875, 83 CalRptr 577 (1970)

[326] Metromedia, Inc. v. City of San Diego, 453 US 490, 101 SCt 2882, 69 LEd 2d 800 (1981)

[327] People v. Stover, 191 NE2d 272, 12 NY2d 462 (1963)

[328] Mahlstadt v. City of Indianola, 100 NW2d 189 (1959)

[329] Rodenhausen v. Craven, 21 A 774, 141 Pa 546, 23 AmSR 306 (1891)

[330] Hannum et al v. Gruber, 31 A2d 99, 36 Pa 417 (1943)

[331] Smith v. City of Ann Arbor, 6 NW2d 752, 303 Mich 476 (1942)

[332] State ex rel Heck v. Grillot, 128 NE2d 552 (Ohio 1955)

[333] Wideman v. Faivre, 163 P 619, 100 Kan 102 (1917)

[334] Hoffman v. Armstrong, 48 NY 201, 8 AmR 537 (1871)

[335] Mease v. Dinius & Bingaman, 98 PaSuper 554 (1929)

[336] Musch v. Burkhart, 48 NW 1025, 83 Iowa 301, 12 LRA 484 (1891)

[337] Lemon v. Curington, 306 P2d 1091, 78 Idaho 522, 64 ALR2d 665 (1957)

[338] Cooke v. McShane, 142 A 460, 108 Conn 97 (1928)

[339] Grandona v. Lovdal, 11 P 623, 70 Ca 161 (1886)

[340] Loggia v. Grobe, 491 NYS2d 973, 128 Misc2d 973 (NYDC 1985)

[341] Taylor v. Olsen, 578 P2d 779 282 Or 343 (1978)

[342] Ivancic v. Olmstead, 490 NYS2d 914, 112 A2d 508 (NYAD, 3D. 1985), affirmed 497 NYS2d 326, 66 NY2d 349, 488 NE2d 72, reargument denied 500 NYS2d 103, 67 NY2d 754, 490 NE2d 1229, cert. denied 106 SCt 1975, 90 LEd 658

[343] Star v. Rookesby, 1 Salk 336, 91 EngRep 295, 3 Bl. Comm. 309 (1711)

[344] Dougherty v. Stepp, 18 NC 371 (1835) In this case a surveyor and his chain carriers entered a person's land and surveyed it. They did not mark the trees but they did

upset a few shrubs.
[345] Kenney v. Barna, 341 NW2d 901, 215 Neb 863 (Neb 1983)
[346] Cobai v. Young, 679 P2d 121 (ColoApp 1984)
[347] Herro v. Board of County Road Commissioners, 118 NW2d 271, 368 Mich 263 (1962)
[348] Herrin v. Sutherlin, 241 P 328 (Mont 1925)
[349] Miller v. McClelland, 173 NW 910 (1919)
[350] Mawson v. Vess Beverage Co., 173 S.W.2d 606 (MoApp 1943)
[351] Sally v. Whitney Co., 154 P 1089, 89 Wash 674, LRA 1916D 764 (1916)
[352] Perry v. Jefferies, 39 SE 515, 61 SC 292 (1901)
[353] Evans v. Watkins, 83 A. 915, 76 NH 433, 41 LRA,NS, 404 (1912)
[354] Bass v. African M.E. Church, 104 SE 437, 150 Ga 452 (1920)
[355] Walden v. Conn, 1 SW 537, 84 Ky 312 (1886)
[356] The Six Carpenters' Case, 8 Coke Rep. 146a, 77 Reprint 695 (1610)
[357] Melchior v. Jago, 723 F2d 486, cert. denied 104 SCt 2156, 466 U.S. 952, 80 LEd 542
       (CAOhio 1983)
[358] Rogers v. Board of Road Commissioners, 30 NW2d 358, 319 Mich 661 (1948)
[359] Hamm v. City of Rock Hill, 379 US 306, 85 SCt 384, 13 LEd2d 300 (1964)
[360] Navratil v. Smart, 400 So2d 268, writ denied 405 So2d 320 (La.App. 1981)
[361] Granchelli v. Walter S. Johnson Bldg. Co., Inc., 446 NYS2d 755, 85 AD2d 891 (1981)
[362] Longenecker v. Zimmerman, 267 P2d 543, 175 Kan 719 (1954)
[363] Slocum v. Food Fair Stores of Florida, 100 So2d 396 (Fla 1958)
[364] Republic Iron & Steel Co. v. Self, 68 So 328, 192 Ala 403 (1915)
[365] Halliday v. Cienkowski, 3 A2d 372, 333 Pa 123 (1939)
[366] Samms v. Eccles, 358 P2d 344, 11 Utah 2d 289 (1961)
[367] Barnard v. Finkbeiner, 147 NYS 514, 162 AppDiv 319 (1914)
[368] People v. Vogler, 395 NYS2d 881, 90 Misc2d 709 (1977)
[369] Kimmerle v. New York Eveing Journal, 186 NE 217, 262 NY 99 (1933)
[370] Davies v. Gardiner, Popham 36, 79 EngRep 1155 (1593)
[371] Matthew v. Crass, Cro.Jac. 323, 79 EngRep 276 (1614)
[372] Ogden v. Turner, 5 Mod. Rep. 104, 87 EngRep 862 (1703)
[373] Kelly v. Partington, 5 B. & Ad. 645, 110 EngRep 929 (1833)
[374] Buck v. Savage, 323 SW2d 363, (TexCivApp 1959)
[375] Pfitzinger v. Dubs, 64 F 696 (7 Cir. 1894)
[376] Cocker v. Hadley, 1 NE 734, 102 Ind 416 (1885)
[377] Lewis v. Daily News Co., 32 A 246, 81 Md 466 (1895)
[378] Tolley v. J. S. Fry & Sons, Ltd., 1 KB 467 (1930) AC 333 (1931)
[379] Zbyszko v. New York American, 239 NYS 411, 228 AppDiv 277 (1930)
[380] Lipscomb v. Hercules, Inc., 414 So2d 82, quashed exparte Lipscomb, 414 So2d 86
       (AlaCivApp. 1981)
[381] Burrell v. Schlesinger, 459 So2d 1195 (LaApp4Cir 1984), writ denied, 463 So2d
       1320 (1985)
[382] Beecher v. Dull, 143 A 498, 294 Pa 17 (1928)
[383] Benton v. Kernan, 13 A2d 825, 127 NJEq 434 (1940), modified 21 A2d 755, 130
       NJEq 193 (1941)
[384] Dittman v. Repp, 50 Md 516, 33 AmR 325 (1878)
[385] Boyd v. Greene County, 644 SW2d 615, 7 ArkApp 110 (1983)
[386] Tucker v. Badoian, 384 NE2d 1195 (Mass 1978)
[387] Lawrence v. Eastern Air Lines, 81 So2d 632 (Fla 1955)
[388] Pendergrast v. Aiken, 236 SE2d 787, 293 NC 201 (1977)
[389] Baker v. Ore-Ida Foods, Inc., 513 P2d 627 (Idaho 1973)
[390] National Audubon Soc. v. Superior Court, 658 P2d 709, 33 Cal3d 419, 189 CalRptr
       346 (1983)
[391] Lee v. City of Pontiac, 426 NE2d 300, 55 IllDec 325, 99 IllApp3d 982 (1981)
[392] Southwest Weather research, Inc. v. Rounsaville, 320 SW2d 211 (Tex 1959)

[393] Pennsylvania Natural Weather Assn. v. Blue Ridge Weather Modification Assn., 44 PaD&C2d 749 (1968)

[394] B & R Luncheonette v. Fairmont Theatre Corp., 103 NYS2d 747, 278 AppDiv 133, rearg. denied 104 NYS2d 799, 278 AppDiv 808, motion dismissed 100 NE2d 194, 302 NY 944 (1951)

[395] Kass v. Kass, 560 So2d 293 (Fla4DCA 1990)

[396] Jones v. Williams, 11 Mees. & W. 176 (Ct. of Exchequer 1843)

[397] State v. White, 28 A 968,18 RI 473 (1894)

[398] Page v. Niagra Chemical division of Food Machinery & Chemical Corp., 68 So2d 382 (Fla 1953)

[399] Broderick v. City of Waterbury, McKeeman v. Same, 36 A2d 585, 130 Conn 601 (1944)

[400] Reber v. Illinois Central R. Co., 138 So 574, 161 Miss 885 (1932)

[401] Elliott v. Town of Mason, 81 A 701, 76 NH 229 (1911)

[402] Jones v. Chappell, LR 20 Eq 539 (1875)

[403] Bowden v. Edison Electric Illuminating Co., 60 NYS 835, 29 MiscRep 171 (1899)

[404] Lurssen v. Lloyd, 25 A 294, 76 Md 360 (1892)

[405] Hughes v. City of Austin, 55 NE 389, 161 NY 96 (1899)

[406] Hodges et ux. v. Town of Drew, 159 So 298, 172 Miss 668 (1935)

[407] Tennessee Coal, Iron and R. Co. v. Hartline, 11 So2d 833, 244 Ala 116 (1943)

[408] Restatement of Torts, §822, Comment f.

[409] Wade v. Miller, 73 NE 849, 188 Mass 6 (1905)

[410] Lloyd, Noise as a Nuisance, 1934, 82 U.Pa.L.Rev. 567, 582.

[411] Rogers v. Elliott, 15 NE 768, 146 Mass 349 (1888)

[412] Lord v. Dewitt, 116 F 713 (CCNY 1902)

[413] Cremidas v. Fenton, 111 NE 855, 223 Mass 249 (1916)

[414] Amphithretres, Inc. v. Portland Meadows, 198 P2d 847, 184 Or 336 (1948)

[415] Taylor v. Bennett, 7 C. & P. 329, 173 EngRep 146 (1836).

[416] Louisville and Jefferson County Air Board v. Porter, Ky, 397 SW2d 146 (19**)

[417] Royal Saxon, Inc. v. Jaye, 536 So2d 1046 (Fla 4DCA1988)

[418] Boomer v. Atlantic Cement Co., 55 Misc2d 1023, 287 NYS2d 112, (Sup.Ct. 1967) aff'd. 30 AD2d 480, 294 NYS2d 452 (1968) aff'd. 26 NY2d 219, 309 NYS2d 312, 257 NE2d 870 (1970).

[419] McFarlane v. City of Niagra Falls, 160 NE 391 (NY 1928)

[420] Sawyer v. Davis, 136 Mass 239, 49 AmRep 27 (SCt Mass 1884)

[421] McClung v. Louisville & N. R. Co., 51 So2d 371, 255 Ala 302 (1951)

[422] Mahone v. Autry, 227 P2d 623, 55 NM 111 (1951)

[423] Spur Industries, Inc. v. Del E. Webb Development Co., 494 P2d 700 (Ariz 1972)

[424] Anneberg v. Kurtz, 28 SE2d 769, 197 Ga 188, 152 ALR 338 (1944)

[425] Harris v. Susquehanna Collieries Co., 156 A 159, 304 Pa 550 (1931)

[426] Quinn v. American Spiral Spring & Mfg. Co., 141 A 855, 293 Pa 152, 61 ALR 918 (1928)

[427] Fink v. Smith, 36 P2d 976, 140 Kan 345

[428] Stubbins v. Atlantic City Electric Co., 41 A2d 794, 136 NJEq 327 (1945)

[429] Frederick w. Horne v. Mt. Vernon Die Casting Corp., 44 NYS 2d 520, 181 Misc 758 (1945)

[430] State v. Knoxville, 12 LeaTenn 146, 47 A R 331 (1883)

[431] Laurance, et al v. Tucker, 85 P2d374, 160 Or 474 (1938)

[432] Baltimore & Yorktown Turnpike. Rd. v. State, 1 A 285, 63 Md 573 (1885)

[433] State v. Hart, 34 Me.36 (1852)

[434] State v. Collingswood Sewerage Co., 89 A 525, 85 NJLaw 567, aff'd. 92 A 1087, 86 NJLaw 703 (1914)

[435] State v. Pennsylvania Railroad Co. 87 A 86, 84 NJLaw 550 (1913)

[436] Seacord v. People, 13 NE 194, 121 Ill 623 (1887)

[437] Champa v. Washington Compressed Gas Co., 262 P 228, 146 Wash 190 (1927)

[438] Landwer v. Fuller, 187 SW2d 670 (1945)

[439] Davoust v. Mitchell, 257 NE2d 332, 146 IndApp 536 (1970)

Index

State and City Index (by footnote)